Studies in Natural Language Processing

Computational linguistics
An introduction

Studies in Natural Language Processing
Executive Editor: Aravind K. Joshi
Sponsored by the Association for Computational Linguistics

This series publishes monographs, texts, and edited volumes within the interdisciplinary field of computational linguistics. Sponsored by the Association for Computational Linguistics, the series will represent the range of topics of concern to the scholars working in this increasingly important field, whether their background is in formal linguistics, psycholinguistics, cognitive psychology or artificial intelligence.

Also in this series:
Natural language parsing, edited by David R. Dowty, Lauri Karttunen and
   Arnold Zwicky
Text generation by Kathleen R. McKeown
Planning English sentences by Douglas E. Appelt

Computational linguistics
An introduction

RALPH GRISHMAN
*Courant Institute of Mathematical Sciences,
New York University*

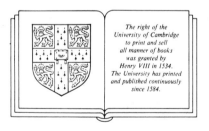

The right of the
University of Cambridge
to print and sell
all manner of books
was granted by
Henry VIII in 1534.
The University has printed
and published continuously
since 1584.

CAMBRIDGE UNIVERSITY PRESS

CAMBRIDGE

LONDON   NEW YORK   NEW ROCHELLE

MELBOURNE   SYDNEY

Published by the Press Syndicate of the University of Cambridge
The Pitt Building, Trumpington Street, Cambridge CB2 1RP
32 East 57th Street, New York, NY 10022, USA
10 Stamford Road, Oakleigh, Melbourne 3166, Australia

First published 1986

Printed in Great Britain by Billing & Sons Ltd, Worcester

British Library cataloguing in publication data
Grishman, Ralph
Computational linguistics: an introduction.
– (Studies in natural language processing)
1. English language – Data processing
I. Title II. Series
420′.28′54   PE1074.5

Library of Congress cataloguing in publication data
Grishman, Ralph.
Computational linguistics.
(Studies in natural language processing)
Bibliography.
Includes index.
1. Linguistics – Data processing.   I. Title.
II. Series.
P98.G75 1986   410′.28′5   86-4236

ISBN 0 521 32502 1 hard covers
ISBN 0 521 31038 5 paperback

SE

Contents

Acknowledgements

I would like to acknowledge first of all the influence of Naomi Sager, who introduced me to computational linguistics and taught me much about the way in which computational linguistics should be done. The example she has set of careful analysis and fidelity to the linguistic data has often served to put me straight when my pet theories have led me astray.

I would like to thank the many members of the Linguistic String Project down the years, who provided me with such a pleasant environment for my initiation into computational linguistics.

I wish to thank all those who have offered their suggestions during the preparation of this volume: the classes at New York University who have worked their way through succeeding versions of this text; Tomasz Ksiezyk, Dan Gordon, Asher Meth, Lynette Hirschman, and others who have provided detailed comments; and my wife Eileen for many discussions linguistic.

Finally, I want to acknowledge the support of the National Science Foundation and the Office of Naval Research for my research, and in particular the continued early support of Marv Denicoff of ONR.

Introduction

Natural language is an integral part of our lives. Language serves as the primary vehicle by which people communicate and record information. It has the potential for expressing an enormous range of ideas, and for conveying complex thoughts succinctly. Because it is so integral to our lives, however, we usually take its powers and influence for granted.

The aim of computational linguistics is, in a sense, to capture this power. By understanding language processes in procedural terms, we can give computer systems the ability to generate and interpret natural language. This would make it possible for computers to perform linguistic tasks (such as translation), process textual data (books, journals, newspapers), and make it much easier for people to access computer-stored data. A well-developed ability to handle language would have a profound impact on how computers are used.

The potential for natural language processing was recognized quite early in the development of computers, and work in computational linguistics – primarily for machine translation – began in the 1950s at a number of research centers. The rapid growth in the field, however, has taken place mostly since the late 1970s. A 1983 survey by the Association for Computational Linguistics (Evens and Karttunen 1983) listed 85 universities granting degrees in computational linguistics. A 1982 survey by the ACM (Association for Computing Machinery) Special Interest Group on Artificial Intelligence (Kaplan 1982) listed 59 university and research centers with projects in computational linguistics, and the number continues to grow. This growth has spawned a large literature, in journals, conference proceedings, and anthologies. There have, however, been few books which try to survey this field in a unified fashion. The volume before you is an attempt to fill this gap. It was initially prepared as lecture notes for a course entitled Advanced Topics in Artificial Intelligence which I taught at New York University in the Spring of 1980, and was subsequently revised for courses in 1982 and 1984.

To attempt a unified survey of a field where there is sharp disagreement even about basic approaches may seem foolhardy. I freely admit that some points of view have received short shrift, and that the organization reflects the biases of my own research efforts. I hope that, despite these inadequacies, this survey will be helpful to some of those starting off in computational linguistics.

People come to computational linguistics with a wide range of backgrounds and interests; I have tried to organize this survey to accommodate this variety. I assume that readers have some background in computer science, so that they can grasp the descriptions of algorithms and visualize how they might be implemented. At the least, readers should have a knowledge of programming and data structures – how lists and trees are represented. More advanced material, in programming languages, compilers, or the basics of artificial intelligence, is not essential but will aid in appreciating some of the material. In addition, readers should have some familiarity with finite mathematics – trees, sets, formal languages, and formal logic. For those with only a passing acquaintance with formal languages and logic, I have provided brief background sections on these topics, along with references for further study.

I have also included some historical (or pseudo-historical) material in the narrative. I felt that some idea of how computational linguistics has developed would be worthwhile to the novice researcher. Also, in view of the many different approaches which are still being considered, I thought that a presentation of approaches which were tried and found wanting in the past would be useful. More than once, I have heard at conference 'novel' approaches which, in different guise, had been considered and rejected a decade ago. A review of past efforts will allow readers to direct their energies toward genuinely novel investigations.

Lack of time, energy, and knowledge have led me to omit a number of topics which others might consider central to computational linguistics. Among these are

* processing of languages other than English, including in particular the problems of morphology (the structure of individual words) and the analysis of 'free word order' languages
* speech analysis and generation
* applications of computational linguistics to areas such as machine translation and information retrieval

I would hope to remedy some of these omissions in future editions.

Earlier classes with which I used this text commented on the need for a detailed presentation of one or more specific systems, in order to tie together and provide concrete examples of the various algorithms presented in the text. To satisfy this need we have prepared a number of teaching materials centered about the computational linguistics tools developed at New York University. Among these is a small question-answering system which illustrates issues in parsing, transformational analysis, semantic constraints, quantifier analysis, and the use of formal logic. Information on these teaching materials can be obtained by writing to the author.

Since I began work on this text, a number of books have appeared in computational linguistics, each with a somewhat different approach from the current text. Let me mention two: *Language as a Cognitive Process: Volume I –*

Syntax by Terry Winograd (1983) offers a detailed and thorough survey of the grammatical theories and parsing algorithms used in computational linguistics, far more comprehensively than I do here. It will be a standard reference work in the field for years to come. *Natural Language Processing* by Harry Tennant (1981) is a small volume whose greatest strength is its large number of 'case studies' – descriptions of specific systems to illustrate particular aspects of natural language processing.

Computational linguistics is a rapidly developing field, so it has not been possible to include many of the most recent research themes in this volume. To keep abreast of the field, readers should consult the journal *Computational Linguistics* (before 1984 entitled the *American Journal of Computational Linguistics*) and the proceedings of the annual meeting of the Association for Computational Linguistics, the biennial International Conference on Computational Linguistics (COLING), the biennial International Joint Conference on Artificial Intelligence (IJCAI), and the annual meeting of the American Association for Artificial Intelligence.

Ralph Grishman

Courant Institute of Mathematical Sciences
New York University
251 Mercer Street
New York, NY 10012

1   What is computational linguistics?

1.1   The objectives of computational linguistics

Computational linguistics is the study of computer systems for understanding and generating natural language. In this volume we shall be particularly interested in the structure of such systems, and the design of algorithms for the various components of such systems.

Why should we be interested in such systems? Although the objectives of research in computational linguistics are widely varied, a primary motivation has always been the development of specific practical systems which involve natural language. Three classes of applications which have been central in the development of computational linguistics are

> *Machine translation.* Work on machine translation began in the late 1950s with high hopes and little realization of the difficulties involved. Problems in machine translation stimulated work in both linguistics and computational linguistics, including some of the earliest parsers. Extensive work was done in the early 1960s, but a lack of success, and in particular a realization that fully-automatic high-quality translation would not be possible without fundamental work on text 'understanding', led to a cutback in funding. Only a few of the current projects in computational linguistics in the United States are addressed toward machine translation, although there are substantial projects in Europe and Japan (Slocum 1984, 1985; Tucker 1984).

> *Information retrieval.* Because so much of the information we use appears in natural language form – books, journals, reports – another application in which interest developed was automatic information retrieval from natural language texts. In response to a query, the system was to extract the relevant text from a corpus and either display the text or use the text to answer the query directly. Because the texts in most domains of interest (particularly technical and scientific reports) are quite complex, there was little immediate success in this area, but it led to research in knowledge representation. Automatic information retrieval is now being pursued by a few research groups (Sager 1978; Hirschman and Sager 1982; Montgomery 1983).

Man–machine interfaces. Natural language seems the most convenient mode for communication with interactive systems (such as data base retrieval and command language applications), particularly for people other than computer specialists. It has several advantages over the first two application areas as a test for natural language interfaces. First, the input to such systems is typically simpler (both syntactically and semantically) than the texts to be processed for machine translation or information retrieval. Second, the interactive nature of the application allows the system to be useable even if it occasionally rejects an input ('please rephrase', 'what does . . . mean?'). As a result, a greater measure of success has been obtained here than in other applications. We are reaching the point where such systems are being used for real (albeit simple) applications, and not just for demonstrations. Most computational linguistics work since the early 1970s has involved interactive interfaces.

In addition to these 'engineering', applications-oriented motives for work in computational linguistics, most investigators have some 'scientific' research objectives which are independent of any particular application. One natural function for computational linguistics would be the testing of grammars proposed by theoretical linguists. Because of the complex interactions possible in transformational grammars, it would be desirable to use the computer to verify that a proposed set of rules actually works. At least one such system has been described – Friedman's Transformational Grammar Tester (Friedman 1971). This system generated sentences in accordance with a proposed transformational grammar, so that linguists could verify that their grammars did in fact generate only grammatical sentences. However, much of the formal framework of linguistic theory (the nature of movement rules, the constraints on transformations, the form of semantic interpretation rules) is being questioned, and the emphasis in theoretical linguistics is not on the building of substantial grammars for which computerized testing would be suitable. As a result, there has been little use of computers as a test vehicle for linguistic theories.

On the other hand, the need to develop complete 'understanding' systems has forced computational linguists to develop areas of research which had been inadequately explored by the traditional sciences. Two of these areas are

Procedural models of the psychological processes of language understanding. While traditional linguists have sought to focus on particular aspects of language, such as grammaticality, some computational linguists have tried to look on the understanding process as a whole. They have tried to model these processes, as yet very crudely, and tried to mimic some aspects of human performance. An example of this is Marcus's parser (Marcus 1980), which was designed to mimic human performance on 'garden path' sentences (a 'garden path' sentence is one where people get stuck and have to retrace their steps in analyzing a sentence, such as 'The horse raced past the barn fell.'). These efforts, together with those of psychologists and other researchers, have led to the creation of a new subfield, *cognitive science*.

Representation of knowledge. The recognition that language processors must make reference to large amounts of 'real-world knowledge' and the need to translate natural language into some formal representation to facilitate such operations as search and inferencing have led computational linguists to study the problems of knowledge representation. Many general suggestions for structuring information – frames, scripts, information formats – have developed since the early 1970s; some of these will be discussed in the chapter on discourse analysis.

Engineering and scientific objectives, of course, usually go hand in hand. The needs of practical systems may lead to research in and better understanding of linguistic processes, which in turn produces better natural language systems. In some areas, such as syntactic analysis, a distinction can be made between systems oriented towards psychological modeling and those designed for a particular application. In other areas, however, which have been less intensively studied, there is as yet no clear division between psychologically-motivated and applications-oriented approaches. To the extent that a division can be made, we shall emphasize applications-oriented approaches.

1.2 Computational and theoretical linguistics

Although both are ultimately concerned with understanding linguistic processes, computational and theoretical linguists have rather different approaches and outlooks. Computational linguists have been concerned with developing procedures for handling a useful range of natural language input. They are (in general) willing to accept approximate solutions which cover most sentences of interest, and put up with a system which fails on a few peculiar inputs. The requirement of constructing complete, working systems has led them to seek an understanding of the entire process of natural language comprehension and generation.

Theoretical linguists, in contrast, have focused primarily on one aspect of language performance, grammatical competence – how people come to accept some sentences as grammatical and reject others as ungrammatical. They are concerned with language universals – principles of grammar which apply to all natural languages – and are interested in finding the simplest, computationally most restricted theory of grammar which can account for natural language. They hope thereby to gain some insight into the innate language mechanisms which enable people to learn and use languages so readily. In their efforts to evaluate alternative theories, they are often led to study peculiar sentences which some computational linguists would regard as pathological.

Despite these differences in outlook, theoretical linguistics can provide valuable input to computational linguists, an input which is too often ignored. Questions of grammaticality *are* important, because experience has shown that a grammatical constraint which in one case determines whether a sentence is or is not acceptable will in other cases be needed to choose between correct and incorrect analyses of a sentence. The relations between sets of sentences, which are a prime focus of transformational grammar, particularly in the Harrisian framework, are essential to language analysis procedures, since they enable a large variety of sentences to be reduced to a relatively small number of structures. Formal rules of semantic interpretation, studied by Montague and his disciples and increasingly by other linguists, are also beginning to make a significant contribution to computational linguistics.

On the other hand, one should not assume that a 'solution' in an area of theoretical linguistics (e.g., a formal, concise grammar of English) is *per se* a solution to the corresponding problem of computational linguistics. As we shall see in our discussion of early transformational parsers, direct implementations of simple theories do not always lead to effective analysis procedures. As in many areas of science, considerable effort may be required to translate an elegant formal theory into a computable one.

1.3 Computational linguistics as engineering

Constructing a fluent, robust natural language interface is a difficult and complex task. Perhaps as our understanding of the language faculty improves, we will be able to construct simpler natural language systems. For the present, however, much of the challenge of building such a system lies in integrating many different types of knowledge – syntactic knowledge, semantic knowledge, knowledge of the domain of discourse – and using them effectively in language processing. In this respect, the building of natural language systems – like other large computer systems – is a major task of engineering.

As with other system building tasks, there are certain general techniques we can use to make our job easier. One of these is *modularity*: dividing our system's knowledge into relatively independent components. Dividing the problem allows us to attack the subproblems independently (or nearly so), so that we are not overwhelmed by the task before us. If the modules are carefully designed, we may find that the division reduces not just the size of the individual components but also the size of the total system (Grishman 1980).

Another technique for simplifying complex systems is the use of *formal models*. Large programs are difficult to design, modify, or understand. Our odds of developing a successful program are much increased if we can create a relatively simple abstract model and then develop our system as an implementation of that model. The use of a simple model will also increase the chances that our work will be understood by our colleagues, so that we can contribute to the development of the field as a whole.

As our exposition of computational linguistics proceeds, we shall return to these issues from time to time, considering how alternative approaches impact the task of system design.

1.4 The structure of this survey – a tree diagram

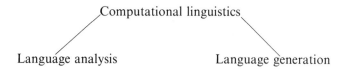

Analysis and generation

Most natural language systems require the ability to both analyze and generate language. Analysis has been regarded as the more crucial component for practical systems. If a natural language system is to be successful, it must be able to recognize many paraphrases for the same command or information; on the other hand, it is sufficient if it is able to generate any one of these forms. We shall therefore devote most of our time to language analysis. However, as we shall see, there may be substantial symmetry between the analysis and generation procedures.

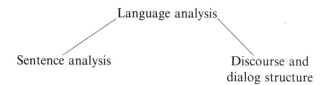

Sentence and discourse analysis

Much more is known about the processing of individual sentences than about the determination of discourse structure, and presumably any analysis of discourse structure presupposes an analysis of the meaning of individual sentences. Furthermore, for many simple applications an analysis of discourse or dialog structure is not essential (even when references are made to earlier sentences in the discourse, they can often be understood without a thorough analysis of the discourse structure). As a result, we shall concentrate first on the processing of individual sentences, and follow this with a less detailed study of discourse and dialog.

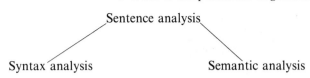

Sentence analysis

Syntax analysis   Semantic analysis

Syntax and semantic analysis

The overall objective of sentence analysis is to determine what a sentence 'means'. In practice, this involves translating the natural language input into a language with a simple semantics (e.g., a formal logic) or into a language which can be interpreted by an existing computer system (e.g., a data base retrieval command language). In most systems, the first stage of this translation is syntax analysis – the determination (and possible regularization) of the sentence structure. This stage was also historically the first to be developed by computational linguists. We will therefore begin our survey with an examination of syntax analysis.

2 Syntax analysis

2.1 The role of syntax analysis

Syntax analysis performs two main functions in analyzing natural language input:

> *Determining the structure of the input.* In particular, syntax analysis should identify the subject and objects of each verb and determine what each modifying word or phrase modifies. This is most often done by assigning a tree structure to the input, in a process referred to as *parsing*.
>
> *Regularizing the syntactic structure.* Subsequent processing (i.e., semantic analysis) can be simplified if we map the large number of possible input structures into a smaller number of structures. For example, some material in sentences (enclosed in brackets in the examples below) can be omitted or 'zeroed':

> > John ate cake and Mary [ate] cookies.
> > . . . five or more [than five] radishes . . .
> > He talks faster than John [talks].

> Sentence structure can be regularized by restoring such zeroed information. Other transformations can relate sentences with normal word order ('I crushed those grapes. That I like wine is evident.') to passive ('Those grapes were crushed by me.') and cleft ('It is evident that I like wine.') constructions, and can relate nominal ('the barbarians' destruction of Rome') and verbal ('the barbarians destroyed Rome') constructions. Such transformations will permit subsequent processing to concern itself with a much smaller number of structures. In addition, if the structures are appropriately chosen, operator–operand (e.g., verb-subject, verb-object) relations should be clearly evident in the output of the syntactic stage.

There is no agreement as to the amount of regularization which should be done as part of the syntactic component. The trend in theoretical linguistics has been to restrict the types of relations which are accounted for by the syntactic component; in particular lexical processes (such as nominalization) are no longer generally accounted for by syntactic rules. Some computational linguists have chosen to omit syntactic regularization altogether, and have the semantic component operate directly on the full variety of sentence structures. In such systems, syntactic regularization is in effect subsumed within the semantic analysis process. This does require, however, more complex semantic rules, so the inclusion of a syntactic regularization component remains the norm in natural language processing systems.

2.2   Is syntax analysis necessary?

From time to time, developers of systems have suggested that natural language processing can be done without syntax analysis. It seems to us that such claims are exaggerated, but they do arise out of some observations that are not without validity:

> (1) The very limited semantics of some on-line 'natural language' systems effectively restricts the user to relatively simple sentences for which sophisticated syntactic processing is unnecessary.

This was certainly true of some early question-answering systems, whose syntax was limited to a few fixed imperative structures, into which adjective and prepositional phrase modifiers could be inserted. It is doubtful that this is true of the most syntactically sophisticated of today's systems. In any case, it is hard to imagine how sentences of the complexity typical in technical writing could be understood without utilizing syntactic (as well as semantic) restrictions to select the correct analysis.

> (2) Syntactic analysis may appear in guises other than the traditional parsing procedures; it can be interwoven with other components of the system and can be embedded into the analysis programs themselves.

The early machine translation systems were characterized by a 'grammar in program' approach which blended the rules of grammar and the analysis procedure. Although such an approach might have some advantage in terms of efficiency, the advantage is minimal when compared with currently existing systems which are able to compile formal grammar rules into executable code. More important as research goals should be the ability to manage grammatical complexity and to communicate successful methods to others. In both these regards, a syntactic analyzer using a separate, semiformal set of rules is bound to be more effective.

> (3) Syntax analysis can be driven by semantic analysis (instead of being a separate, earlier stage), and, in particular, can be done by looking for semantic patterns in the sentence.

A primary rationale for making syntax analysis a separate stage of processing is the existence of rules of sentence formation and transformation which can be stated in terms of the relatively broad syntactic categories (tensed verb, count noun, etc.). If the semantic classes are subcategorizations of the syntactic ones, then clearly the transformations could be stated in terms of sequences of semantic classes. For those transformations which are properly syntactic, however, we would find that several transformations at the semantic stage would be required in place of one at the syntactic stage; certain useful generalizations would be lost.

The strongest argument of those advocating a semantics-driven syntax analysis is the ability of people to interpret sentences from semantic clues in the face of syntactic errors or missing information (e.g., 'He go movies yesterday.'). A prime example of an approach which minimizes syntactic analysis is the work of Schank and his co-workers. Their analyzers build a semantic analysis (a 'conceptual dependency network') directly from the input sentence. For example, an early analyzer developed by Schank and Riesbeck (Schank 1973) began by identifying the 'main noun' and 'main verb' of the sentence and building an incomplete semantic structure. The sentence was then searched for words of the proper class to complete this structure. A strict left-to-right analysis of the sentence is not required. This approach should therefore be able to handle some ungrammatical sentences which would cause a syntax analyzer difficulty.

An analogous argument, however, can be made in the other direction – people can also use syntactic rules when semantics is lacking; for example, to understand the function of a word in a sentence without knowing its meaning ('Isn't that man wearing a very frimple coat?'). More generally, we expect that in complex sentences, particularly those involving conjunctions and comparatives, a semantic analyzer will not be successful without some syntactic guidance. Ultimately, we want an analyzer which can work from partial information of either kind, and research in this direction is to be welcomed (we shall discuss later in this chapter some work done by speech-understanding groups on parsing in the face of uncertainty). Success in this direction will require a solid understanding both of semantic analysis and of the syntactic analysis techniques described in this chapter.

2.3   Phrase-structure languages

Before we delve into the problem of natural language syntax analysis, we shall briefly review the basic concepts of formal language theory and phrase-structure grammar. For a more detailed and rigorous exposition, the reader can refer to any text covering formal language theory, such as Hopcroft and Ullman (1979) or Davis and Weyuker (1983).

Formally, a *language* is a set of *sentences*, where each *sentence* is a string of one or more symbols (words) from the vocabulary of the language. A *grammar* is a finite, formal specification of this set. This grammar can take many forms. If the language has only a finite number of sentences, we can list them. Most interesting languages, though, have an infinite number of sentences. One way of specifying such a language is by writing a program which reads a series of words and then outputs.

THIS IS A SENTENCE

or

THIS IS NOT A SENTENCE

(Such a program is called a *recognizer* for the language.) Another way is to use a formalism based on *productions*. This approach, which has been widely adopted to characterize formal and natural languages, is called production grammar or *phrase-structure grammar*.

A phrase-structure grammar has four components:

T the *terminal vocabulary*: the words (or symbols) of the language being defined

N the *non-terminal vocabulary*: the symbols (distinct from the terminal vocabulary *T*) which are used in specifying the grammar (we define the vocabulary *V* to be the union of the terminal and non-terminal vocabularies:

$$V = T \cup N)$$

P a set of productions. Each production is of the form

$$a \rightarrow b$$

where *a* is a sequence of one or more symbols from *V* (i.e., $a \in V^+$) and *b* is a sequence of zero or more symbols from *V* (i.e., $b \in V^*$).

S the start symbol, a member of *N*

The basic operation in a phrase-structure grammar is that of rewriting one sequence of symbols as another. If $a \rightarrow b$ is a production, we can rewrite any string of symbols which contains the substring *a*, replacing *a* by *b*. We denote this operation on strings by the symbol '⇒'. Formally, if $u, v \in V^*$,

$$u\,a\,v \Rightarrow u\,b\,v$$

We say that $u\,a\,v$ *directly produces* $u\,b\,v$, or that $u\,b\,v$ is *directly derived* from $u\,a\,v$. For example, if we have a grammar where

$$N = \{S\}$$
$$T = \{a, b, c\}$$
$$P = \{S \rightarrow a\,S\,c,$$
$$\quad\;\; S \rightarrow b\}$$

then, starting with the string '*S*', we can apply the first production to obtain the string '$a\,S\,c$'. We can then apply the second production to obtain '$a\,b\,c$':

$$S \Rightarrow a\,S\,c \Rightarrow a\,b\,c$$

Alternatively, we could apply the first production twice, and then the second production:

$$S \Rightarrow a\,S\,c \Rightarrow a\,a\,S\,c\,c \Rightarrow a\,a\,b\,c\,c$$

If $S_1, S_2, \ldots, S_n$ are strings and

$$S_1 \Rightarrow S_2 \Rightarrow \ldots \Rightarrow S_{n-1} \Rightarrow S_n$$

we write

$$S_1 \overset{*}{\Rightarrow} S_n$$

and say that S_1 *produces* S_n or that S_n is *derived from* S_1. Thus with our simple grammar

$$S \overset{*}{\Rightarrow} a\,b\,c$$
$$S \overset{*}{\Rightarrow} a\,a\,S\,c\,c$$
  etc.

By applying the productions in different sequences, we can produce many different strings from the same symbol. The *language* defined by a phrase-structure grammar is the set of terminal strings (sequences composed entirely of terminal symbols) which can be derived from the start symbol S. The language defined by our tiny grammar is

$$b, \quad a\,b\,c, \quad a\,a\,b\,c\,c, \quad a\,a\,a\,b\,c\,c\,c, \quad \ldots$$

A program which determines the derivation(s) of a sentence (according to a particular grammar) is called a *parser*.

2.3.1 *Recursive languages*

Phrase-structure grammar provides a simple yet very powerful formalism for characterizing languages. What do we mean by a 'powerful' formalism? A more powerful formalism can be used to define a wider variety of languages; a weaker formalism a more limited set of languages. For example, if formalism F can define 10 different languages, and formalism G can define 20 different languages, including all of those definable by F, we would say that G is more powerful than F. Any grammar formalism worth its salt can define an infinite number of languages, but the subset/superset notion still holds (G is more powerful than F if the set of languages definable by G is a superset of those definable by F).

In describing sets of sentences (languages), there are two notions to which theorists frequently refer: the notion of a *recursive language* and that of a *recursively enumerable* language. A language is recursively enumerable if we can write a program which will output ('enumerate') the sentences of the language one after another in some sequence; in other words, a program which would print

> THE FIRST SENTENCE OF THE LANGUAGE IS . . .
> THE SECOND SENTENCE OF THE LANGUAGE IS . . .
> THE THIRD SENTENCE OF THE LANGUAGE IS . . .

A language is recursive if we can write a program which will read a sequence of symbols and eventually print either the message

> THIS SEQUENCE OF SYMBOLS IS A SENTENCE OF THE LANGUAGE

or

> THIS SEQUENCE OF SYMBOLS IS NOT A SENTENCE OF THE LANGUAGE

Although it may seem at first that these are equivalent criteria, they are not. Just because a language is recursively enumerable does not mean that it is recursive (and there are in fact some languages which are recursively enumerable but not recursive). Suppose we were given a recursively enumerable language and some mechanism for enumerating the sentences of the language. If we are now given a sequence of symbols and are asked whether this sequence is a sentence in the language, we can turn on our enumerating mechanism and compare each sentence which is generated against the sequence we were given. If we find a match, we can produce the message

> THIS SEQUENCE OF SYMBOLS IS A SENTENCE OF THE LANGUAGE

If we don't find a match after a few years, though, we cannot say with confidence that THIS SEQUENCE OF SYMBOLS IS NOT A SENTENCE OF THE LANGUAGE; there's always that chance that the next sentence to be generated will match the input sequence. In this way, a language can be recursively enumerable but still not be recursive.

Now that we have defined these terms, we can be more specific about the power of phrase-structure grammars. Phrase-structure grammar can describe any recursively enumerable language. This means in particular that some of the languages we can define with phrase-structure grammars are not recursive: we can create grammars for which it will not be possible to write a program which can decide whether or not an input string is in the language defined by that grammar.

This suggests that the formalism is 'too powerful'. If we are going to process languages by computer, it seems natural to want to write a program which can take in a grammar and a sequence of symbols, and decide whether or not the sequence of symbols is a grammatical sentence. It is not possible to write a program which can do this for any arbitrary phrase-structure grammar.[1]

We are therefore led to consider the possibility of constrained phrase-

---

[1] None the less, some natural language analysis systems have been designed to accept unrestricted phrase-structure rules; these systems will be discussed in section 2.7.

structure grammars. By placing certain constraints on our formalism, we can be assured that the languages generated will be recursive and, further, that (depending on the constraints) it will be easy to write efficient programs for analyzing these languages.

The constrained phrase-structure formalisms which are most relevant to us are the members of the *Chomsky hierarchy* (Chomsky 1959). Chomsky identified four classes of grammars: unrestricted phrase-structure grammars, such as we considered above (which he called type 0 grammars); context-sensitive grammars (type 1); context-free grammars (type 2); and regular grammars (type 3). Higher numbered types are more constrained (weaker) than lower numbered types, and so can generate a smaller set of languages. We shall briefly consider each of these types in turn, beginning with type 3, the most constrained.

2.3.2   Regular grammars

Regular grammars come in two flavors: left-linear grammars and right-linear grammars. In a left-linear grammar, all rules must be of the form

$$A \rightarrow B \, t$$

or

$$A \rightarrow t$$

where A and B are non-terminal symbols, and t is a terminal symbol. In a right-linear grammar, the rules must be of the form

$$A \rightarrow t \, B$$

or

$$A \rightarrow t$$

For example, the following is a right-linear grammar:

$$S \rightarrow a \, A$$
$$A \rightarrow b \, B$$
$$B \rightarrow c \, A$$
$$B \rightarrow d$$

where S, A, and B are non-terminal symbols, S the start symbol, and a, b, c, and d are terminal symbols. This grammar generates sentences consisting of '$a \, b$' followed by zero or more instances of '$c \, b$' followed by a 'd'.

We can use a board game as a device for generating the sentences from a regular grammar. We construct a directed graph (or network) as follows: for each non-terminal symbol, we create a node labeled by that non-terminal symbol; in addition, we create a special node called the final node, marked by a diagonal line through the node. For each rule of the form

$$A \rightarrow t \, B$$

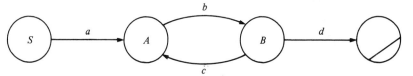

Figure 2.1

we draw an arc from node A to node B and label the arc 't'. For each rule of the form

$$A \to t$$

we draw an arc from node A to the final node and label the arc 't'. Thus, for the grammar above we would get the graph shown in figure 2.1.

The game is played as follows: we begin by placing our marker on the node corresponding to the start symbol. At each step, we move our marker along any arc from the current node to a new node, and write down the symbol labelling that arc. When we reach the final node, the sequence of symbols we have written down is a sentence. In other words, each path from start node to final node corresponds to one sentence of the language generated by this grammar.

Regular grammars are also called *finite-state* grammars. The 'finite states' refer to the finite set of nodes in the graph. When we are in the middle of generating a sentence, the only information we need to know in order to finish the sentence correctly is which of these states (nodes) we are currently in. We do not need to know anything else about the portion of the sentence we have already generated in order to decide what would be a correct continuation for the sentence.

Regular grammars are appealing because finite-state networks provide a simple mechanism for language generation and analysis. Unfortunately, many interesting languages cannot be generated by regular grammars. A simple example of such a language is the letter 'x' surrounded by an arbitrary number of pairs of balanced parentheses:

$$x, (x), ((x))(((x))), ((((x)))), \ldots$$

Why isn't this regular? Suppose we are generating a sentence from this language. When we get to the 'x' we have to know how many '(' we have generated so that we can generate the same number of ')'. The only information retained by our finite-stage 'board game', however, is the state it is in, so a graph with N states can remember at most N different values. Hence a finite-state network with N states could generate at most N different sentences of this language, and not the whole (infinite) language.

Perhaps that doesn't worry us: in a practical application we may be satisfied with a grammar which recognizes expressions with up to 25 pairs of balanced parentheses. Even so, a regular grammar is not very efficient: to handle sentences with up to 25 pairs of parentheses, we need at least 25 nodes (actually quite a few more, if you work out the grammar). Such a grammar fails to capture the regularity of the language. We shall see that a slightly more powerful grammatical formalism can describe this language very succinctly.

Similar 'nested' constructions arise in English (Chomsky 1957, section 3.2). Let S_1, S_2, . . . be English sentences. We can combine them to form larger sentences using such constructs as

> if S_1 then S_2
> either S_1 or S_2
> the man who said that S_1 is arriving tomorrow

These can be nested to form even larger sentences, such as

> if the man who said that either S_1 or S_2 is arriving tomorrow then S_3

A program for generating English sentences would have to remember, when it got past S_1, what constructs it had generated and in which order, so it would know to generate an 'or' matching the 'either' and a 'then' matching the 'if ' (it wouldn't do to generate 'either S_1 then S_2'). This is similar to the problem we faced in generating correct parenthesized expressions. Such constructs indicate that a finite-state network (regular grammar) is as unsuitable for describing English as it was for describing parenthesized expressions.

It is therefore time to turn to the next more powerful formalism in the Chomsky hierarchy, context-free (type 2) grammars.

2.3.3 Context-free grammars

In a context-free grammar, every rule is of the form

> $A \rightarrow x$

where A is a non-terminal symbol and x is a sequence of zero or more terminal and non-terminal symbols. Our first phrase-structure grammar, given above, with productions

> $S \rightarrow a\,S\,c$
> $S \rightarrow b$

is an example of a context-free grammar. If we change the symbols in this grammar, we can produce a grammar for the language

> $x, (x), ((x)), (((x))), ((((x)))), \dots$

which we struggled with before:

> $S \rightarrow (S)$
> $S \rightarrow x$

In this way, we can capture with context-free grammar the nested structures which are beyond the reach of regular grammars.

Context-free grammars are extensively used in describing both formal (e.g., programming) and natural languages. In presenting context-free grammars, you will often see (both in this text and elsewhere) a notation called BNF ('Backus–Naur Form') which is slightly different from the notation we have used until now for phrase-structure grammars. In BNF, we distinguish non-terminal symbols by enclosing them in the brackets '<' and '>' and we use the symbol '::=' in place of '→'. Furthermore, if there are two or more productions with the same left-hand side, they are grouped together as a single BNF *definition*, separated by the symbol '|'. Our grammar for parenthesized x's, therefore, would be written as a single BNF definition,

$$<S> ::= (<S>)|x$$

The sequences to the right of the '::=' which are separated by '|' are called the *alternatives* or *options* of the definition; thus, our definition of S has two options.

In addition to presenting context-free grammars, we shall frequently present *derivations* of sentences using a particular grammar. The derivation shows how a particular sentence can be generated by rules from the grammar. We could show the derivation as a linear sequence of applications of productions. For example, if we have the grammar

```
<SENTENCE>    ::= <SUBJECT> <VERBPHRASE>
<SUBJECT>     ::= John | Mary
<VERBPHRASE>  ::= <VERB> <OBJECT>
<VERB>        ::= eats | drinks
<OBJECT>      ::= wine | cheese
```

we could represent the derivation of the sentence 'Mary eats cheese' as follows:

```
<SENTENCE> ⇒ <SUBJECT> <VERBPHRASE>
           ⇒ Mary <VERBPHRASE>
           ⇒ Mary <VERB> <OBJECT>
           ⇒ Mary eats <OBJECT>
           ⇒ Mary eats cheese
```

However, it is probably clearer if we represent this derivation as a (parse) *tree* (figure 2.2).

The start symbol always appears as the root of the tree and the terminal symbols as the leaves of the tree. If 'x' was rewritten as 'y' followed by 'z' in the derivation, the tree will contain a node 'x' immediately above nodes 'y' and 'z'.

Strictly speaking, this tree diagram corresponds to a set of derivations, since the diagram does not indicate the order in which the symbols are rewritten. For example, the following derivation would also correspond to this tree:

$$\begin{aligned}
<\text{SENTENCE}> &\Rightarrow\ <\text{SUBJECT}>\ <\text{VERBPHRASE}>\\
&\Rightarrow\ <\text{SUBJECT}>\ <\text{VERB}>\ <\text{OBJECT}>\\
&\Rightarrow <\text{SUBJECT}>\ \text{eats}\ <\text{OBJECT}>\\
&\Rightarrow \text{Mary eats}\ <\text{OBJECT}>\\
&\Rightarrow \text{Mary eats cheese}
\end{aligned}$$

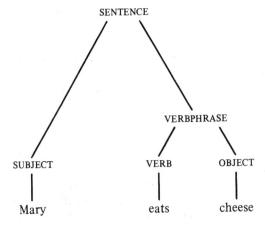

Figure 2.2

In determining the derivation of a sentence, we are normally not interested in these variations in order. We therefore define some standard ordering, and only generate derivations conforming to this ordering. One such ordering is the *leftmost derivation*, in which at each step the leftmost non-terminal symbol is rewritten. The first derivation we gave for 'Mary eats cheese' is an example of a leftmost derivation. Each parse tree corresponds to exactly one leftmost derivation.

These grammars are called 'context-free' because a production of the form

$A \rightarrow x$

means that 'A' can be replaced by 'x' anywhere it appears, regardless of context (of the symbols surrounding the A). Generally speaking, it is easier to deal with such grammars than with more powerful grammars. However, in some situations (we will give examples later on in this chapter) we do want to place constraints on the contexts in which a production can be applied. To do so, we turn to the next class of grammars in the Chomsky hierarchy, the context-sensitive (type 1) grammars.

2.3.4   Context-sensitive grammars

A context-sensitive grammar is a phrase-structure grammar which satisfies the following constraint: for every production of the form

$$x \to y$$

the length of y (i.e., the number of symbols in y) is greater than or equal to the length of x. Thus

$$A B \to C D E$$

would be a valid production in a context-sensitive grammar, but

$$A B C \to D E$$

would not. This constraint is sufficient to assure us that context-sensitive languages are recursive.

An alternative notation is sometimes used for context-sensitive grammars. In this notation, each production is of the form

$$A \to y \,/\, x\_\_z$$

where A is a non-terminal symbol, y is a sequence of one or more terminal and non-terminal symbols, and x and z are sequences of zero or more terminal and non-terminal symbols. The meaning of this production is that A can be rewritten as y if it appears in the context '$x\_\_z$', i.e., immediately preceded by the symbols x and immediately followed by the symbols z. This is equivalent to the production

$$x A z \to x y z$$

in our usual notation.

This alternative notation emphasizes the notion of rewriting a symbol depending on context. We shall use this notation in our few examples of context-sensitive grammar later in this chapter. You may note that this notation actually imposes a tighter constraint on allowed grammars than our first definition of context-sensitive grammar. For example, a production of the form '$A B \to B A$' could not be rewritten using this notation. However, it is possible to show that any *language* which can be defined by a grammar of the first form can also be defined by a grammar of the second form.

Most natural language grammars advanced in the 1950s and early 1960s were either context-free grammars or context-free grammars with added constraints which made them equivalent in power to context-sensitive grammars (Postal 1967). Context-sensitive grammars, however, have not proven to be a particularly suitable formalism for stating most grammatical constraints; context-free grammars with other types of restrictions have proven more effective. We shall therefore begin by focusing on context-free grammars and parsers; in section 2.6 we shall consider in detail the restrictions which can be added to context-free grammars.

2.4   Early systems: context-free parsers

The next four sections present our overview of the principal natural language parsing algorithms. In the first three of these sections we shall cover what we perceive to be, historically, the three most important classes of parsing algorithms: the context-free parsers, the early transformational parsers, and the augmented context-free parsers. These three classes correspond to a rough historical division: context-free parsers were dominant in the late 1950s and early 1960s; the early transformational parsers were developed in the mid 1960s; and augmented context-free parsers have dominated the scene since the early 1970s. Of course, not all the major parsing procedures fit within such a simple outline, so we have set aside a fourth section to cover some important systems which did not fit in the first three classes.

We shall begin, then, with an examination of natural language procedures based on context-free grammar. In the next subsection we will present a very simple context-free natural language grammar; we shall then examine some context-free analysis algorithms and some of the early natural language systems which used them.

2.4.1   *A small context-free natural language grammar*

To provide a concrete example of a natural language grammar, we will now present a small grammar based on a linguistic theory called *linguistic string theory* (Z. Harris 1962). This grammar will include only a few of the simplest English constructions; for a grammar of much broader coverage see Sager (1981).

Linguistic string theory sets forth, in terms of particular syntactic categories (*noun, tensed verb*, etc.), a set of elementary strings, and rules for combining the elementary strings to form sentence strings. The simplest sentences consist of just one elementary string, called a *center string*. Examples of center strings are *noun tensed-verb*, such as 'Tapes stretch.' and *noun tensed-verb noun*, such as 'Users cause problems.' Any sentence string may be made into a more complicated sentence string by inserting an *adjunct string* to the left or right of an element of some elementary string of the sentence. For example, 'Programmers at our installation write lengthy code.' is built up by adjoining 'at our installation' to the right of 'programmers' and 'lengthy' to the left of 'code' in the center string 'programmers write code.' Sentences may also be augmented by the insertion of a *conjunct string*, such as 'and debug' in 'Programmers at our installation write and debug lengthy code.' Finally, string theory allows an element of a string to be replaced by a *replacement string*. One example of this is the replacement of *noun* by *what noun tensed-verb* to form the sentence 'What linguists do is puzzling.'

Table 2.1

Category		Examples
N	*noun*	tapes, stretch, users, cause, problems
TV	*tensed verb*	is, are, tapes, stretch, code, write
V	*untensed (infinitive) verb*	be, tape, stretch, code, write
P	*preposition*	at, of
T	*article*	a, an, the
ADJ	*adjective*	lengthy, old
D	*adverb*	slowly, poorly

Each word of the language is assigned one or more word categories on the basis of its grammatical properties. The assignment is based on the word's use in the language as a whole, not its use in a particular sentence or text. For example, 'users' and 'problems' would each be classified as a *noun*, while 'cause' would be assigned the three categories *tensed verb*, *untensed verb*, and *noun*. Every sequence of words is thereby associated with one or more sequences of word categories. Linguistic string theory claims that each sentence of the language has at least one sequence of word categories which is a sentence string, i.e., which can be built up from a center string by adjunction, conjunction, and replacement.

However, not every combination of words drawn from the appropriate categories and inserted into a sentence string forms a valid sentence. Sometimes only words with related grammatical properties are acceptable in the same string, or in adjoined strings. For example, one of the sequences of word categories associated with 'Tape stretch.' is *noun tensed-verb*, which is a sentence string; this sentence is ungrammatical, however, because a singular *noun* has been combined with a plural *tensed-verb*. We shall mention several such grammatical constraints later in this section.

For our small string grammar we shall use the word categories given in table 2.1.

To conform to the formal language theory given above, we shall structure our grammar as a context-free phrase-structure grammar, using the standard BNF notation. We could write our word category definitions as a set of productions:

    <T> ::= a | an | the
    <V> ::= be | tape | stretch | code | write
    etc.

and make them part of the grammar. However, it is more convenient and conventional to place these definitions in a separate component, the *word dictionary*, and to list the categories for each word (as in a normal dictionary) rather than the words in each category. The word categories become then, in effect, the terminal symbols of the grammar. To distinguish these symbols in our BNF grammar, we shall write them with an asterisk to the left of their name, thus:

$<^{*}\text{ADJ}>$

We can begin our BNF grammar by defining a SENTENCE as a CENTER string followed by a period:

$<\text{SENTENCE}> ::= <\text{CENTER}> \, .$

The various center strings are normally classified as assertions (i.e., declarative sentences), questions, and imperatives. Although our tiny grammar will only cover assertions, we shall include the definition

$<\text{CENTER}> ::= <\text{ASSERTION}>$

as a reminder of the other types of center strings which are possible. We can then define ASSERTION as

$<\text{ASSERTION}> ::= <^{*}\text{N}> \; <^{*}\text{TV}> \; | \; <^{*}\text{N}> \; <^{*}\text{TV}> \; <^{*}\text{N}>$

To allow for adjunction in our grammar, we have to include a symbol for each position where an adjunct string can be inserted. Certain adjuncts are allowed to the left or right of words of category x; we will use the symbols Lx and Rx for these positions, and the symbol LxR

$<\text{L}x\text{R}> ::= <\text{L}x> \; <^{*}x> \; <\text{R}x>$

for a word category x and its adjuncts. For example,

$$
\begin{aligned}
<\text{LNR}> \;\; &::= \; <\text{LN}> \; <^{*}\text{N}> \; <\text{RN}> \\
<\text{LN}> \;\; &::= \; <\text{TPOS}> \; <\text{APOS}> \\
<\text{TPOS}> \;\; &::= \; <^{*}\text{T}> \; | \; null \\
<\text{APOS}> \;\; &::= \; <^{*}\text{ADJ}> \; | \; null \\
<\text{RN}> \;\; &::= \; <\text{PN}> \; | \; null \\
<\text{PN}> \;\; &::= \; <^{*}\text{P}> \; <^{*}\text{N}>
\end{aligned}
$$

indicates that a noun may be preceded by an article and/or adjective ('the men', 'young men', 'the young men') and may be followed by a prepositional phrase, PN ('men from Philadelphia'). The symbol *null* is the empty string; its presence indicates that all of these adjuncts are optional. We should then replace every occurrence of N in other strings (like ASSERTION and PN) by LNR.

Some adjuncts – so called *sentence adjuncts* – can occur at the beginning, at the end, or between any two elements of a center string. Among these are adverbs such as 'generally' and prepositional phrases such as 'on Wednesday' and 'in Rome'. For these adjuncts we define the symbol SA

$<\text{SA}> ::= <^{*}\text{D}> \; | \; <\text{PN}> \; | \; null$

and put it everywhere in the ASSERTION strings:

```
<ASSERTION> ::= <SA> <LNR> <SA> <LTVR> <SA> |
                <SA> <LNR> <SA> <LTVR> <SA>
                <LNR> <SA>
```

We can shorten this definition by introducing the symbol OBJECT for the things which can follow a verb:

```
<ASSERTION> ::= <SA> <LNR> <SA> <LTVR> <SA> <OBJECT>
                <SA>
<OBJECT>    ::= <LNR> | null
```

This done, we can enlarge the grammar slightly to include the object sequence *to* + v + OBJECT ('to eat fish', as in the sentence 'I like to eat fish.'):

```
<OBJECT> ::= <LNR> | <TOVO> | null
<TOVO>   ::= to <LVR> <SA> <OBJECT> <SA>
```

For uniformity, we shall also introduce familiar symbols for the other elements of ASSERTION, even though in our tiny grammar they will have only one value:

```
<ASSERTION> ::= <SA> <SUBJECT> <SA>
                <VERB> <SA> <OBJECT> <SA>
<SUBJECT>   ::= <LNR>
<VERB>      ::= <LTVR>
<OBJECT>    ::= <LNR> | <TOVO> | null
```

We will include one example of a replacement string, the noun replacer of the form *what* + N + TV ('what John likes'). We introduce the symbol NSTG (noun string) to designate a noun or its replacement string:

```
<NSTG> ::= <LNR> | <NREP>
<NREP> ::= what <SUBJECT> <SA> <VERB> <SA>
```

If we put all this together, we get the following grammar:

```
<SENTENCE>  ::= <CENTER> .
<CENTER>    ::= <ASSERTION>
<ASSERTION> ::= <SA> <SUBJECT> <SA> <VERB>
                <SA> <OBJECT> <SA>
<SA>        ::= <*D> | <PN> | null
<PN>        ::= <*P> <NSTG>
<SUBJECT>   ::= <NSTG>
<NSTG>      ::= <LNR> | <NREP>
<LNR>       ::= <LN> <*N> <RN>
<LN>        ::= <TPOS> <APOS>
<TPOS>      ::= <*T> | null
<APOS>      ::= <*ADJ> | null
<RN>        ::= <PN> | null
```

<NREP>	::= what <SUBJECT> <SA> <VERB> <SA>
<VERB>	::= <LTVR>
<LTVR>	::= <LV> <*TV> <RV>
<LV>	::= <*D> | *null*
<RV>	::= <*D> | <PN> | *null*
<LVR>	::= <LV> <*V> <RV>
<OBJECT>	::= <NSTG> | <TOVO> | *null*
<TOVO>	::= to <LVR> <SA> <OBJECT> <SA>

As we noted earlier, not all of the word sequences generated by this grammar are acceptable English sentences.[2] Among the basic grammatical constraints which have not been included are:

> *number agreement.* There must be number agreement between subject and verb ('Men eat.', *'Men eats.') and between a noun and its article or quantifier, if present (*'A men eat.').
>
> *count nouns.* Some nouns (roughly, those naming countable objects) require a preceding article when they appear in the singular ('The cat eats.', *'Cat eats.').
>
> *subcategorization.* Each verb can occur with only a subset of the possible values of OBJECT ('The cat wants to eat.', *'The cat sleeps to eat.').
>
> *selection.* In normal usage, some verbs require 'human' subjects (*'The cat argued.') and some require 'animate' subjects (*'The rock slept.'). In contrast to the previous constraints, which are grammatical, selection may be considered a semantic constraint; sentences violating selection may be acceptable in special contexts, such as metaphors or fairy tales.

In principle, any one of these constraints could be captured within the framework of context-free grammar (Salkoff and Sager 1967). However, the number of productions which must be added to do so can be quite large. Consider, for example, adding subject–verb number agreement to the grammar given above. Basically, this constraint requires that a singular subject take a singular verb and a plural subject a plural verb:

> <ASSERTION> ::= <SA> <SINGULAR-SUBJECT> <SA> <SINGULAR-VERB> <SA> <OBJECT> <SA> \|
> ::= <SA> <PLURAL-SUBJECT> <SA> <PLURAL-VERB> <SA> <OBJECT> <SA>

We must therefore define SINGULAR- and PLURAL-SUBJECT:

> <SINGULAR-SUBJECT> ::= <SINGULAR-NSTG>
> <PLURAL-SUBJECT>   ::= <PLURAL-NSTG>

---

[2] Following the usual linguistic convention, we shall use an asterisk before a word sequence to indicate that it is not an acceptable English sentence.

\<SINGULAR-NSTG\>	::= \<SINGULAR-LNR\> |\<NREP\>
\<PLURAL-NSTG\>	::= \<PLURAL-LNR\> | \<NREP\>
\<SINGULAR-LNR\>	::= \<LN\> \<*SINGULAR-N\> \<RN\>
\<PLURAL-LNR\>	::= \<LN\> \<*PLURAL-N\> \<RN\>

and SINGULAR- and PLURAL-VERB:

\<SINGULAR-VERB\>	::= \<SINGULAR-LTVR\>
\<PLURAL-VERB\>	::= \<PLURAL-LTVR\>
\<SINGULAR-LTVR\>	::= \<LV\> \<*SINGULAR-TV\> \<RV\>
\<PLURAL-LTVR\>	::= \<LV\> \<*PLURAL-TV\> \<RV\>

The other constraints can be captured in similar fashion. Note, however, that if two constraints involve the same construction the effect on the number of productions will be multiplicative; as a result, the grammar will rapidly become enormous. In sections 2.5 and 2.6 we shall consider better ways of incorporating these constraints in a grammar.

2.4.2 *Parsing algorithms for context-free grammars*

Parsing a sentence with a phrase-structure grammar means finding a derivation – a sequence of productions – leading from the start symbol to the sentence. The derivation is usually represented as a parse tree; if the sentence is ambiguous (has several derivations), there will be several parse trees.

For example, if our grammar were

> \<S\> ::= \<NP\> \<VP\>
> \<NP\> ::= \<*N\> \| \<*PRO\>
> \<VP\> ::= \<*TV\> \| \<*TV\> \<NP\>

the (leftmost) derivation of the sentence 'I like cheese' (where 'I' is a PRO, 'like' a TV, and 'cheese' an N) is

> $S \Rightarrow$ NP VP
> $\Rightarrow$ PRO VP
> $\Rightarrow$ PRO TV NP
> $\Rightarrow$ PRO TV N

which would be represented in a tree as in figure 2.3.

Parsers are classified as *top-down* or *bottom-up*. A top-down parser builds the parse tree starting from the top; in terms of derivation sequences, it works from the start symbol toward the sentence. Conversely, a bottom-up parser builds the tree from the bottom (from the words or word categories which are the leaves of the tree); in terms of derivation sequences, it works from the sentence, applying *reductions* (productions in reverse) until the start symbol is reached. Parsers can also be classified into *backtracking* algorithms, which try one derivation at a time and 'back up' to try an alternative derivation when one gets

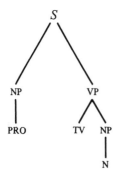

Figure 2.3

stuck, and *parallel* algorithms, which in effect pursue all derivation sequences concurrently.

Many different context-free parsers have been developed, and there are extensive descriptions and taxonomies of these algorithms (Aho and Ullman 1972). Only a few, however, have seen extensive use in computational linguistics. This is true in part because most real natural language analyzers have many special tests and operations added to the basic context-free parser, and these operations are more difficult to 'tack onto' some parsers than others.

The most common parser is a simple top-down backtracking algorithm. In effect, it enumerates derivations until it finds one which generates the input sentence. We can write this as a serial algorithm as follows.

This algorithm operates on a derivation of the form

$$S \Rightarrow z_1 \Rightarrow z_2 \Rightarrow \ldots \Rightarrow z_n$$

Initially the derivation contains just the start symbol S. We assume that productions with left-hand-side A are ordered: $P_{A,1}, P_{A,2}, \ldots$.

(1) Let B be the leftmost non-terminal symbol in z_n; expand B using $P_{B,1}$ (thus adding one element to the derivation: $n = n + 1$).

(2) Let the i be the position of the leftmost non-terminal symbol in z_n ($i =$ [length of z_n] $+ 1$ if z_n has no non-terminals). If the first $i - 1$ (terminal) symbols of z_n match the first $i - 1$ words of the sentence, go to (3), else go to (5).

(3) If z_n contains any non-terminals, go to (1).

(4) If z_n matches the sentence being parsed, record the current derivation as a derivation of the sentence.

(5) Let $P_{B,i}$ be the last production applied in the derivation; if their exists a production $P_{B,i+1}$ then replace the last step of the derivation by an application of $P_{B,i+1}$ and go to (2), else go to (6).

(6) Delete the last production from the derivation ($n = n - 1$); if no productions remain (the derivation contains only the start symbol), quit, else go to (5).

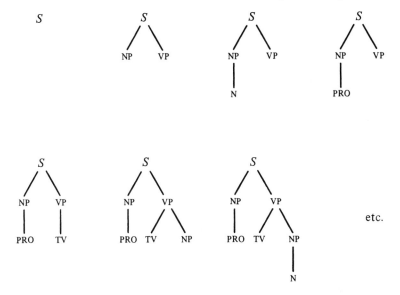

Figure 2.4

This algorithm can handle any grammar without left recursion.[3] For left recursive grammars, additional tests must be included to avoid infinite loops.

For example, for the three-rule grammar given at the beginning of this subsection and the sentence 'I like cheese' (PRO TV N), the derivation will grow and shrink as follows:

S
$S \Rightarrow$ NP VP
$S \Rightarrow$ NP VP $\Rightarrow$ N VP
$S \Rightarrow$ NP VP $\Rightarrow$ PRO VP
$S \Rightarrow$ NP VP $\Rightarrow$ PRO VP $\Rightarrow$ PRO TV
$S \Rightarrow$ NP VP $\Rightarrow$ PRO VP $\Rightarrow$ PRO TV NP
$S \Rightarrow$ NP VP $\Rightarrow$ PRO VP $\Rightarrow$ PRO TV NP $\Rightarrow$ PRO TV N
                  (record derivation as a parse)
$S \Rightarrow$ NP VP $\Rightarrow$ PRO VP $\Rightarrow$ PRO TV NP $\Rightarrow$ PRO TV PRO
$S \Rightarrow$ NP VP $\Rightarrow$ PRO VP $\Rightarrow$ PRO TV NP
$S \Rightarrow$ NP VP $\Rightarrow$ PRO VP
$S \Rightarrow$ NP VP
S

This process may also be represented by a series of trees, growing from the top down (figure 2.4).

[3] A grammar is left recursive if, for some non-terminal symbol A, there exists a sequence of productions which rewrite A as a string beginning with the symbol A.

The other commonly-used algorithm is a parallel, bottom-up parser. The parser builds partial parses, where each partial parse represents an analysis of a substring of the sentence as some symbol of the grammar. Formally, the partial parse with index i has four components, $root\,(i)$, $first\,(i)$, $last\,(i)$, and $constituents$ (i). Its significance is that sentence words numbered $first\,(i)$ through $last\,(i)$ can be derived from $root\,(i)$, and furthermore that, if $constituents\,(i)$ is the n-tuple[4] $\langle c_1, \ldots, c_n \rangle$, the derivation consists of the production

$$root\,(i) \rightarrow root\,(c_1) \ldots root\,(c_n),$$

followed by the derivations associated with the partial parses $c_1, \ldots, c_n$. The algorithm is as follows:

(1) If the sentence words are $s_1, \ldots, s_k$,
    then for $i = 1, \ldots, k$:
        create a partial parse with $root = s_i$,
            $first = last = i$,
            and $constituents =$ the empty n-tuple,
        and for each word category c assigned to s_i,
            create a partial parse with $root = c$,
                $first = last = i$,
                and $constituents =$ the empty n-tuple.

(2) Repeat indefinitely:
    if there exists a production $A \rightarrow r_1 r_2 \ldots r_n$
    and partial parses $i_1, \ldots i_n$
        such that for $j = 1, \ldots, n$, $root\,(i_j) = r_j$
            and for $j = 2, \ldots, n$, $last\,(i_{j-1}) = first\,(i_j) - 1$,
    then create a new partial parse with $root = A$,
                $first = first\,(i_1)$,
                $last = last\,(i_n)$,
                and $constituents = \langle i_1, \ldots, i_n \rangle$;
    else (if no such production exists), quit.

One complication in actually implementing this procedure is making sure you don't apply the same reduction twice. This is usually accomplished by replacing the unstructured *repeat* by a nested set of loops, with the outermost loop most often being over the last word of the partial parses being created (alternative nestings are discussed in chapter 6 of Hays (1967)).

If the right-hand-sides of productions only have one or two symbols, we can structure the bottom-up algorithm as follows:

(1) Repeat steps (2) through (7) for $i = 1, \ldots, k$
(2) Create a partial parse with $root = s_i$,
            $first = last = i$,
            and $constituents =$ the empty n-tuple,

---

[4] We use the notation $\langle e_1, \ldots, e_n \rangle$ for an n-tuple (vector) with elements $e_1, \ldots, e_n$.

and for each word category c assigned to s_i,

create a partial parse with $root = c$,

$$first = last = i,$$

and *constituents* = the empty n-tuple.

Place the indices of these partial parses in the set '*todo*'.

(3) Repeat steps (4) through (7) until *todo* is empty.

(4) Select an element (the index of a partial parse) from *todo* and call it r. Remove r from *todo*.

(5) Let P be the set of productions for which the last (and possibly only) symbol on the right side is $root\,(r)$.

(6) Repeat step (7) for each member p of P.

(7) If p is of the form $A \rightarrow y, y = root\,(r)$

then create a partial parse with $root = A$,

$$first = first\,(r),$$
$$last = last\,(r),$$

and *constituents* $= \langle r \rangle$

else p is of the form $A \rightarrow x\,y, y = root\,(r)$:

for each partial parse m such that $root\,(m) = x$

and $last\,(m) = first\,(r) - 1,$

create a partial parse with $root = A$,

$$first = first\,(m),$$
$$last = last\,(r),$$

and *constituents* $= \langle m, r \rangle.$

Add to *todo* the indices of all the partial parses just created.

This algorithm uses the set *todo* to keep track of partial parses which have been generated but not yet incorporated as the final constituent of other partial parses. With a suitable generalization of step (7), this algorithm can be extended to grammars with an arbitrary number of symbols on the right side of a production.

If this algorithm is applied to the three-definition grammar given above and the sentence 'I like cheese' (PRO TV N), it will produce partial parses in the sequence shown in table 2.2.

This algorithm will work for any grammar without null elements. Grammars with nulls can be handled by converting them to equivalent grammars without nulls (Aho and Ullman 1972, p. 148), or by marking those symbols from which the null string may be derived and then modifying the parser to freely assume the existence of partial parses involving these symbols whenever they are needed.

Once all the partial parses have been constructed, the sentence parses can be extracted: those partial parses with $root$ = the start symbol, $first$ = 1, and $last$ = the length of the sentence. The parse trees can be found by following the constituents pointers. Note that, for an ambiguous sentence, two or more parse trees can share a partial parse – the partial parses and constituent pointers form an acyclic graph, not a tree.

Table 2.2

Partial parse	root	first	last	constituents
1	'I'	1	1	⟨ ⟩
2	PRO	1	1	⟨ ⟩
3	NP	1	1	⟨2⟩
4	'like'	2	2	⟨ ⟩
5	TV	2	2	⟨ ⟩
6	VP	2	2	⟨5⟩
7	S	1	2	⟨3,6⟩
8	'cheese'	3	3	⟨ ⟩
9	N	3	3	⟨ ⟩
10	NP	3	3	⟨9⟩
11	VP	2	3	⟨5,10⟩
12	S	1	3	⟨3,11⟩

In comparing these two algorithms, we must weigh both their space and time requirements. The space requirements are clearly much greater for the parallel algorithm, which must store all partial parses; the backtracking algorithm, in contrast, requires little more space than that needed for a single parse tree. Because a long sentence, when analyzed by a rich grammar, may involve thousands of partial parses, in the past this has often been a decisive factor.

A parser's time requirements may be roughly gauged by the number of productions or reductions performed in the course of analyzing a sentence. The advantage of the top-down parser is that, in working on word $n+1$, it eliminates from consideration symbols which could not occur in any parse tree whose first n terminal symbols match the first n words of the sentence. The bottom-up parser has no such contextual constraints, so it will perform reductions (build partial parses) in many cases where the top-down parser would have avoided the corresponding productions. On the other hand, the top-down parser will try to expand symbols whose expansion always includes a particular word or word category, even if that word or category is not present in the sentence being analyzed; the bottom-up parser will avoid the corresponding reductions. The magnitude of these effects depends on the characteristics of the grammar being used. There is little hard quantitative data to weigh these countervailing advantages, although some experiments comparing different parsers have been conducted by Slocum (1981).

A clear advantage of the bottom-up approach is that a partial parse will be built just once, even if it is subsequently used as a constituent of many different partial parses. In contrast, the top-down algorithm may end up re-expanding a given symbol many times starting at the same word, if that symbol arises in many different contexts. This is a serious problem with some adjunct strings, as we will discuss later in this chapter.

It is possible to combine some of the advantages of the top-down and bottom-up approaches by taking one of these algorithms and incorporating some of the features of the other. For example, we can take the bottom-up parser and add a 'filter' which passes only partial parse trees which would be created by a top-down parser (this is called an 'oracle' by Pratt (1975)). The procedure makes use of a 'selectivity relation' S, where $S(A,B)$ holds if there exists some derivation starting from symbol A which generates a string beginning with symbol B. This matrix can also be used to convert the top-down parser to a selective top-down parser (Griffiths and Petrick 1965), which, when the next sentence word to be matched is w, will expand a symbol A only if $S(A,w)$ holds.

The top-down algorithm can also be combined with a mechanism for saving any subtrees it constructs which match portions of the sentence – in effect, partial parses. The next time the parser tries to expand the same symbol starting at the same sentence word, it can simply retrieve the partial parse, rather than having to repeat the process of expanding the symbol. We thus combine the virtue of the top-down algorithm in building partial parses selectively, based on left context, with the virtue of the bottom-up algorithm in building each partial parse only once. The table of partial parses is often called a 'well-formed substring table'. In *chart parsers* (Kaplan 1973; Thompson 1981; Thompson and Ritchie 1984) the well-formed substring table and the tree built by a top-down parser are unified in a single data structure – the chart.

2.4.3   Some early systems

The largest and probably most important of the early projects was the Harvard Predictive Analyzer (Kuno and Oettinger 1962). A predictive analyzer is a top-down parser for context-free grammars written in what later came to be known as Greibach normal form;[5] this formulation of the grammar was adopted from earlier work by Ida Rhodes for her Russian–English translation project. The size of the grammar was staggering: a 1963 report (Kuno 1963) quotes figures of 133 word classes and about 2100 productions. Despite its size, the grammar did not incorporate such elementary grammatical constraints as subject–verb number agreement. Since the program was designed to produce parses for sentences which were presumed to be grammatical (and not to differentiate between grammatical and ungrammatical sentences), it was at first hoped that it could operate without these restrictions. It was soon discovered, however, that these restrictions were required to eliminate invalid analyses of grammatical sentences. Because the direct inclusion of subject–verb number agreement would cause a large increase in an already very large grammar, the Harvard group chose instead to include a special mechanism in the parsing program to perform a rudimentary check on number agreement. Thus the Harvard

---

[5] In Greibach normal form, the first symbol on the right side of every production must be a terminal symbol.

Predictive Analyzer, though probably the most successful of the context-free analyzers, clearly indicated the inadequacy of a context-free formulation of natural language grammar.

The Harvard Predictive Analyzer parsing algorithm progressed through several stages. The first version of the predictive analyzer produced only one analysis of a sentence. The next version introduced an automatic backup mechanism in order to produce all analyses of a sentence. This was an exponential time algorithm, hence very slow for long sentences; a 1962 report gives typical times as 1 minute for an 18-word sentence and 12 minutes for a 35-word sentence. An improvement of more than an order of magnitude was obtained in the final version of the program by using a bit matrix for a path-elimination technique (Kuno 1965). When an attempt was made to match a non-terminal symbol to the sentence beginning at a particular word and no match was found, the corresponding bit was turned on; if the same symbol came up again later in the parsing at the same point in the sentence, the program would not have to try to match it again.

Another important early parser was the immediate constituent analyzer used at RAND. This system used a grammar in Chomsky normal form[6] and a parsing algorithm designed by John Cocke, which produced all analyses bottom-up in a single left-to-right scan of the sentence (Hays 1967). This was a fast algorithm but, because all parses were developed simultaneously, it needed a lot of space for long sentences; the RAND system appears therefore to have been limited to sentences of about 30 words.

The first linguistic string analysis program, developed at the University of Pennsylvania (Z. Harris 1962), was basically a bottom-up parser but – in contrast to the parsers described in the previous section – was specifically designed for string grammars. The string parser recognized two classes of strings: first order, not containing verb–object, and second order, containing verb–object; the reduction of the sentences was correspondingly done in two stages. In addition to these reductions, which correspond to context-free rules, the parsing program also included some syntactic restrictions which were checked when second order strings were reduced.

2.5   Transformational analyzers: first systems

The theories of immediate constituent and string analysis, which provided the basis for the parsers just discussed, were concerned with describing the structure of individual sentences. Harris introduced the notion of a linguistic *transformation* to relate pairs of sentences which have constituents in common (Z. Harris 1957). For example, the *passive* transformation would relate 'Mary

---

[6] In Chomsky normal form, every production is of the form $A \rightarrow B\,C$, where B and C are non-terminal symbols, or $A \rightarrow t$, where t is a terminal symbol.

ate the muffin.' to 'The muffin was eaten by Mary.'; the *cleft* transformation would relate 'Mary ate the muffin.' to 'It was Mary who ate the muffin.'; and the *question* transformation would relate 'Mary ate the muffin.' to 'Did Mary eat the muffin?'.

One important property which Harris pointed out is that many of these transformations are *paraphrastic*: the pairs of sentences which they relate are paraphrases of one another (i.e., they convey the same information, if perhaps with different emphasis). This property suggests an immediate practical value which transformations can offer. In computational linguistics, our objective is normally not just the parsing of a sentence, but figuring out what the sentence means. This task is complicated by the many different constructions which can be used to express a particular idea. We can use paraphrastic transformations to reduce this variety, taking a group of sentences related by paraphrastic transformations and mapping them all into a single sentence. For example, we could map passive sentences ('The muffin was eaten by Mary.') into active sentences ('Mary ate the muffin.'). In this way the subsequent stages of analysis have to handle a smaller range of constructions (Harris himself pointed out quite early the potential value of transformations for information retrieval (Z. Harris 1958)).

Transformations can also be of value in characterizing the set of English sentences. (Characterizing this set is not an exercise of interest to theoretical linguists alone; as we noted earlier, a constraint which is needed in one case to distinguish an acceptable English sentence from an unacceptable one may be needed in another case to distinguish correct and incorrect analyses for a valid sentence.) Instead of characterizing the set 'directly' (by a context-free grammar, for example), we can specify a smaller set of sentences (called kernel sentences by Harris) and a set of transformations. The set defined by this *transformational grammar* consists of the kernel sentences plus those sentences obtained by applying one or more transformations to a sentence in the kernel. For example, a simple active sentence such as 'Mary ate the muffin.' would be in the kernel set. By applying the passive transformation, we get 'The muffin was eaten by Mary.'; by applying the cleft transformation, we get 'It was Mary who ate the muffin.'; and by applying the passive *and then* the cleft transformation, we get 'It was the muffin which was eaten by Mary.'

This notion of transformational grammar was taken up and greatly developed by Chomsky, who was originally a student of Harris. Chomsky's work has been the starting point for the 'transformational generative school' which now dominates theoretical linguistics; two of his most seminal works have been *Syntactic Structures* (1957) and *Aspects of the Theory of Syntax* (1965). This school has had as a basic objective finding the simplest grammar which can account for all the complexities of grammatical judgement made by a speaker of a natural language. At first, it involved showing how transformations could readily account for phenomena which could only be awkwardly handled in non-transformational grammar. Now it involves weighing the relative simplicity of grammars using alternative types of transformational rules.

As Chomsky's theory developed, his formalism became very different from Harris's. In particular, his transformations operate on phrase-structure trees rather than sentence strings. Many aspects of Chomsky's theory have changed over the past 25 years, and have been substantially modified by other linguists, so the notion of a transformational grammar is not well defined. We present, in the next subsection, somewhat simplified, the formulation of transformational grammar of the early 1960s; this was the time when the first transformational parsers were written.

2.5.1   Transformational grammar

A transformational grammar consists of a *base component* and a *transformational component*. The base component is a context-free grammar which produces a set of *deep structure* trees. The transformational component is a set of tree-rewriting rules which, when applied to a deep structure tree, produces one or more *surface structure* trees. The frontiers (terminal node sequences) of the surface structure trees are the sentences of the language.

The root symbol of the base component is named s. The base component also contains a distinguished symbol COMP which appears on the left side of only one production:

$$\text{COMP} \rightarrow \# \text{ s } \#$$

\# is referred to as the sentence boundary marker. Without this production, the grammar is not recursive.

Each transformation consists primarily of a *structural index* and a *structural change*. The structural index is an n-tuple (vector), $\langle si_1, \ldots, si_n \rangle$, each of whose components is either a symbol (the name of a node) or 'x'. The structural change is a vector $\langle sc_1, \ldots, sc_n \rangle$, of the same length as the structural index. Each of its components is in turn a vector $sc_i = \langle sc_{i,1}, \ldots, sc_{i,n(i)} \rangle$, possibly empty ($n(i) = 0$). Each of the $sc_{i,j}$ is either a terminal symbol or an integer between 1 and n.

The application of transformational rules is based on the notion of a *proper analysis*, which is in turn based on the concept of a *cut* of a tree. Roughly speaking, a cut is defined by drawing a line from left to right through a tree, passing only through nodes (not through the lines connecting nodes); the nodes thus passed through form the cut. For example, for the tree in figure 2.5 the sequence of nodes NP, VERB, N forms a cut. More formally (Aho and Ullman 1972, p. 140), a cut is a subset C of the nodes D of the tree such that

(1) no node in C is on a successor path from some other node in C
(2) no other node of D can be added to C without violating rule (1)

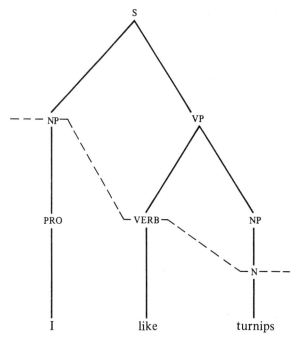

Figure 2.5

If the names of the nodes in the cut, arranged in sequence from left to right, match the structural index of the transformation, the cut is a proper analysis of the tree with respect to this transformation. A structural index matches the sequence of node names if there exists a substitution of sequences of symbols (possibly null and not including #) for the occurrences of 'x' in the structural index which will make the structural index identical to the sequence of names. For example, the cut

   NP VERB N

would be matched by any of the structural indices

     NP VERB   N
   X NP VERB   N X
     NP   X
        X

The proper analysis associates with each element of the structural index (except possibly 'x's) a node in the tree and hence a subtree, the tree dominated by that node. The structural change indicates how these subtrees are to be shuffled to effect the transformation. sc_i specifies what is to go into the position occupied by the node matching si_i. If sc_i is a 1-tuple, we simply have a case of

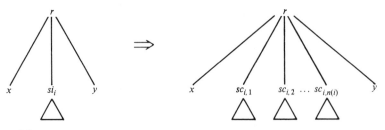

Figure 2.6

one node (and the subtree it dominates) replacing another; if sc_i is an n-tuple, $n > 1$, we first substitute $sc_{i,1}$ for the original node and then insert $sc_{i,2}, \ldots, sc_{i,n(i)}$ as right siblings of that node (figure 2.6). If $sc_{i,j}$ is an integer between 1 and n, the new node is the node matched to the $sc_{i,j}$-th element of the structural index; if $sc_{i,j}$ is a terminal symbol, the new node is a terminal node with that name. Following the usual linguistic notation, we shall write sc_i as $sc_{i,1} + sc_{i,2} + \ldots + sc_{i,n(i)}$, and shall use 0 to designate the null tuple.

Because the value of sc_i may be the null tuple, it is possible for a node in the tree to be left with no successors. We therefore 'clean up' the tree after applying the transformation by deleting any non-terminal node not dominating at least one terminal node.

The prescription just given is inadequate for components of the structural index equal to 'x', since these may match zero or more than one node. We shall constrain the transformations so that nodes in the cut which are matched by 'x's do not take part in the transformation. In terms of the structural change, if $si_k =$ 'x', then $sc_k = k$, and no other $sc_{i,j} = k$.

As an example (an adaptation of the example in Keyser and Petrick 1967, p. 9), consider the *passive* transformation. Its structural index is

NP   AUX   V   NP   by   pass

and its structural change is

4   2   be+en+3   0   5   1

Applied to the tree in figure 2.7, it produces the proper analysis indicated by the dashed line (————). Applying the transformation yields the tree in figure 2.8.

In addition to the structural index and structural change, some transformations may have an identity condition, requiring that the subtrees matched by two elements of the structural index be identical for the transformation to apply.

The rule COMP → # s #, which makes the base component recursive, also plays a special role in the transformations. If the structure shown in figure 2.9 appears in the parse tree, we call the tree dominated by that s a *constituent* (or

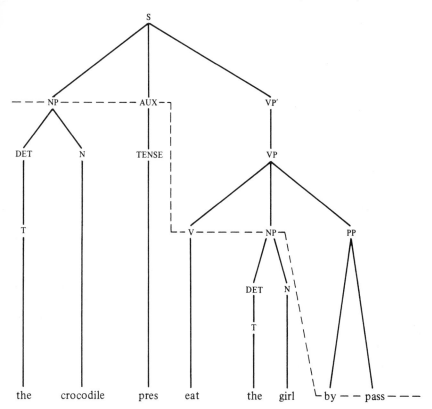

Figure 2.7

embedded) sentence, and the tree dominated by the next s above COMP the
matrix sentence parse tree.

The transformations are of two types, *singulary* and *binary* (or embedding).
In a singulary transformation, the structural index does not contain the
symbol ╪. In a binary transformation, the structural index is of the form
$a \mathbin{╪} b \mathbin{╪} c$, where a, b, and c are strings of symbols not containing ╪. The
binary transformation deletes these boundary markers (if the boundary
markers ╪ are the ith and jth components of the structural index then neither i
nor j will appear anywhere in the structural change), thus combining a
constituent sentence with its matrix sentence. For example, a binary transformation would combine the tree for 'I believe COMP' and the tree (under COMP) for
'Mary likes cheese' to form 'I believe Mary likes cheese'.

The transformations are also classed as *optional* or *obligatory*. Just like the
generation of sentences with a context-free grammar, the application of
transformations to a base structure may be viewed as a non-deterministic
process. Depending on the choices made, one of several possible surface

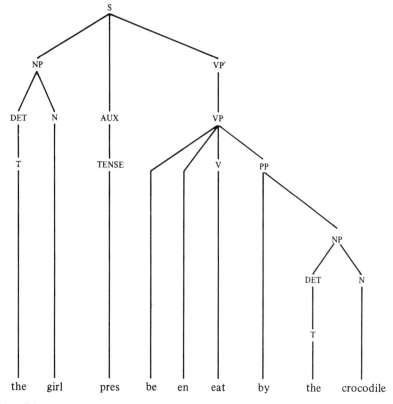

Figure 2.8

structures may be obtained from a single deep structure. The transformations are considered in a fixed order to be described momentarily. If there exists no proper analysis for a transformation, the transformation is skipped. If there exist several proper analyses, one is chosen. If the transformation is obligatory, it is then applied; if it is optional, a choice is made to apply it or not.

The singulary and binary transformations are separately ordered. The transformational process begins by selecting an embedded sentence tree not including any other embedded sentence. The singulary transformations are applied in sequence to this tree; structural indices are matched against the embedded tree, not the entire tree. The binary transformations are then applied to this tree and its matrix sentence tree; one of these should actually transform the tree, deleting the embedded sentence boundaries #...# (if none applied, we would eventually be left with a surface structure containing #'s, which would be rejected). Another deepest embedded sentence is selected and the process repeats until no embedded sentences remain. The singulary transformations are then applied to the entire tree, completing the generating

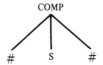

Figure 2.9

process (if the base structure contained no embedded sentences, this would be the only step).

2.5.2 *A small transformational grammar*

Just as we did for context-free grammars in the previous section, we shall present here a very small sample of an English transformational grammar. Its coverage will be extremely limited; our main purpose here is to show the reader how transformations can be used to create a natural language grammar and capture linguistic regularities. (There are many introductory texts available on transformational grammar, but relatively few develop an explicit formal grammar; one which does is Culicover's *Syntax* (1976). The grammar presented here borrows some rules from Culicover (1976) and some from Keyser and Petrick (1976).)

The base component. As we described in the previous subsection, a transformational grammar has two components: a base component and a transformational component. The base component for our grammar is as follows:

```
<S>      ::= [Q] <NP> <AUX> <VP>
<AUX>    ::= <TENSE> <*M>
<TENSE>  ::= past | pres
<VP>     ::= [have en][be ing] <VP'>
<VP'>    ::= <*V> [<NP>][<PP>] | be <*ADJ> | be <PP>
<NP>     ::= [<DET>] <*N> [<COMP>]
<PP>     ::= <*P> <NP> | by pass
<DET>    ::= [wh] <*T>
<COMP>   ::= # S #
```

First, a word of explanation is needed about some new notation. The square brackets, as in

```
<A> ::= <B> [<C>] <D>
```

indicate that the element *C* is an optional constituent.[7] In other words, this production may be viewed as an abbreviation for

```
<A> ::= <B> <C> <D> | <B> <D>
```

---

[7] Most linguists use parentheses for this purpose.

Most of the word categories have already appeared in our small string grammar: N for noun, V for verb, P for preposition, T for article, and ADJ for adjective. M represents the class of modal auxiliaries: 'do', 'can', 'may', etc. Some of the non-terminal symbols correspond closely to symbols in the string grammar: NP to NSTG, PP to PN, and S to ASSERTION. On the other hand, we do not have symbols corresponding to SUBJECT, VERB, or OBJECT. Recall that these symbols were introduced into the string grammar to group alternative subject and object strings; in a transformational grammar, the more complex strings are introduced transformationally, so this need does not arise. (In order to state some transformations, however, we have grouped the verb and its object under a symbol VP ('verb phrase').)

Some of the terminal symbols also deserve a word of comment. The base component only contains one verb form: the infinitive. Instead of including tensed verbs, present and past participles, the base component generates *markers*: *pres* for present tense, *past* for past tense, *ing* for present participle, and *en* for past participle. After all the transformations have been applied, the *morphological component* uses these markers to generate the correct inflected forms. *Pres* plus the immediately following verb is replaced by the present tense of the verb; *past*, *ing*, and *en* operate similarly. For example, the terminal sequence

John pres may have en eat the brownies.

would be reduced to

John   may   have eaten the brownies.

The arrangement of markers makes it quite easy to account for the various patterns of simple, perfect, and progressive forms in English. Depending on which of the optional elements of VP we choose to include, we can get

John pres may eat the brownies.
→ John may eat the brownies.
John pres may be ing eat the brownies.
→ John may be eating the brownies.
John pres may have en eat the brownies.
→ John may have eaten the brownies.
John pres may have en be ing eat the brownies.
→ John may have been eating the brownies.

The transformations. We shall begin our presentation of transformations with one we have cited several times before – the passive transformation. Essentially, the passive does three things:

(1) move the subject into the object of a 'by' phrase
(2) move the direct object to the subject position
(3) change the verb to 'be' + past participle

We can do all of this with a single transformation, as follows:

structural index: NP AUX V   NP by pass
structural change: 4   2   be + en + 3   0   5   1

Earlier in this section we showed a tree before and after the application of a passive transformation.[8]

One point which requires some explanation is the 'by pass' in the structural index. At first thought, one might try to write a transformation which *creates* a prepositional phrase with the word 'by' and then moves the subject into it. However, the transformational formalism we have described does not allow a transformation to create a new structure and theoretical linguists – who want to use the least powerful grammatical mechanisms which suffice to describe language – are reluctant to add such a capability. Instead, we assume that the deep structure for passive sentences contains a prepositional phrase with the 'place holder' *pass* in place of a noun.

To try something a bit more complicated, let us examine the transformation which changes an assertion into a yes–no question. We shall assume that the deep structure of a question has the special marker 'Q' as the first element of s, but is otherwise identical to the structure of the assertion. If we consider then a sample assertion–question pair,

John can chop wood.
Can John chop wood?

it seems that the AUX node (which subsumes the auxiliary 'can') has moved to the beginning of the sentence – to the position occupied by the Q marker. Thus our first attempt at a question transformation might be.

structural index: Q   NP AUX X
structural change: 3   2   0   4

Unfortunately, by itself this doesn't account for very many questions. Consider

Carolyn ate the cake.
Did Carolyn eat the cake?

In this case a 'did' suddenly appeared in the question form. We can account for this in two ways. First, we could write a transformation which inserts 'do' in such cases (when there is no auxiliary). Alternatively, we could postulate that the deep structure *always* has an auxiliary, and specifically that the deep structure for 'Carolyn ate the cake.' is

Carolyn past do eat the cake.

---

[8] In drawing these trees we omitted the M node under AUX; the role of this node will be discussed shortly.

The question transformation would then move the 'past' and 'do', so the question would come out correctly. To generate the assertion correctly, we would add a 'do deletion' transformation *after* the question transformation to delete the 'do' in the case when it hasn't moved:

structural index: x   do   v   x
structural change: 1   0   3   4

We still have a third case to consider: sentences with 'have' and/or 'be'. For example,

Elaine is drinking an egg cream.
Is Elaine drinking an egg cream?

Judy has brought the lunch.
Has Judy brought the lunch?

Chester has been feeding the bear.
Has Chester been feeding the bear?

In this case, the 'have' or 'be' is moved to the front, just like an auxiliary is. We could account for this by writing additional transformations similar to question formation and do deletion. However, it is simpler to write a 'do replacement' transformation, which specifies that, if the auxiliary is 'do' and a 'have' or 'be' immediately follows the 'do', the 'have' or 'be' should be moved into the AUX, replacing the 'do':

structural index: x   do   {have/be}   x
structural change: 1   3   0   4

The braces mean that the index matches either 'have' or 'be' (you can consider this an abbreviation for two separate transformations). This transformation must be ordered *before* question formation, so that the 'have' or 'be' will be in AUX at the time when the AUX is moved to the front of the sentence. You should try a number of combinations of auxiliaries, 'have', and 'be', to convince yourself that this triple of transformations (do replacement / question formation / do deletion) works in all cases.

The third group of transformations we shall consider involves noun modifiers. In keeping with the thinking of the early 1960s, we will transformationally derive all these modifiers (except for determiners) from full sentence structures (s's) in the COMP node of the NP. Let us begin by considering the relative clause, which is quite similar in structure to a full sentence. We propose to derive a sentence such as 'The crocodile which ate Peter got indigestion.' from the deep structure 'The crocodile # the crocodile ate Peter # got indigestion.' More generally, a relative clause will be derived by deleting from the s a noun phrase identical to the host (the word being modified) and inserting 'which'. This is a binary (or embedding) transformation:

```
s.i.:  X  DET  N  #  DET  N  AUX  VP  #  X
s.c.:  1   2   3  0  which 0  7   8   0  10
identity conditions:  2 = 5 and 3 = 6
```

This is the first transformation to include an identity condition, to insure that the DET and N of the constituent sentence are the same as those of the host. (This embedding transformation only handles deletion from the subject; other transformations would be required to handle deletion from other positions, as in 'The crocodile which Peter ate gave him indigestion.'.)

Other modifiers can be obtained by reduction from a relative clause. For example, 'the red house' can be considered a reduced form of 'the house which is red', and 'the house in the meadow' a reduced form of 'the house which is in the meadow'. We can achieve this reduction by a transformation such as

```
s.i.:  X  DET  N  wh  the  pres  be  {ADJ/PP}  X
s.c.:  1   2   3   0    0    0    0      8      9
```

Unfortunately, this leaves the adjective after the noun, so we need one more transformation for adjective reordering:

```
s.i.:  X  DET   N    ADJ  X
s.c.:  1   2   4 + 3   0   5
```

The reduction transformation is *optional* – we will get a satisfactory surface structure whether or not the transformation is applied. The reordering transformation, and all the transformations previously described, are obligatory – if the structural index matches, the transformation must be applied to obtain a well-formed surface structure.

More about the base. We have seen, through a few examples, how transformations can be used to characterize the grammatical word sequences of English more concisely than could a phrase-structure grammar. Transformational grammar also offers an advantage in stating some of the grammatical constraints mentioned at the end of section 2.4.1.

In considering such constraints, one may at first suppose that they can be concisely captured by context-sensitive phrase-structure rules. For example, to capture the selectional constraint that some verbs take only animate or only inanimate subjects, we could introduce new noun categories

```
<*animate-N>    (e.g., student, John)
<*inanimate-N>  (e.g., rock, cloud)
```

and verb categories

```
<*v-taking-animate-subject>    (e.g., sleep, invent)
<*v-taking-inanimate-subject>  (e.g., occur, result)
```

(many verbs take both animate and inanimate subjects, and so would be assigned both categories). We might then write rules such as

<N> ::= <*animate-N> | <*inanimate-N>
<V> ::= <*v-taking-animate-subject> / <*animate-N> __ |
    <*v-taking-inanimate-subject> / <*inanimate-N> __

to allow sentences like 'John invented the gizmo.' while excluding *'The cloud invented the gizmo.'. Unfortunately, in a grammar describing surface structure this won't work very well, since the 'logical subject' (which participates in subject selection) isn't necessarily just to the left of the verb. In a passive sentence the logical subject will be in a 'by' phrase following the verb ('The gizmo was invented by John.', *'The gizmo was invented by the cloud.'); in a relative clause the subject may be replaced by a relative pronoun ('. . . the students that invented the gizmo . . .', *'. . . the cloud that invented the gizmo . . .'). On the other hand, in deep structure the logical subject *is* always just to the left of the verb,[9] so such rules would work as part of the base component.

We could use such context-sensitive phrase-structure rules in the base to capture selection, count-noun, and subcategorization (verb – object string) constraints. Each additional constraint, however, would have a multiplicative effect on the number of terminal symbols and context-sensitive rules. For example, to incorporate object selection we would need to make <v-taking-animate-subject> and <v-taking-inanimate-subject> non-terminals and add four more productions,

<v-taking-animate-subject> ::=
    <v-taking-animate-subject-and-animate-object> / __ <*animate-N> |
    <v-taking-animate-subject-and-inanimate-object> / __ <*inanimate-N>

<v-taking-animate-subject> ::=
    <v-taking-inanimate-subject-and-animate-object> / __ <*animate-N> |
    <v-taking-inanimate-subject-and-inanimate-object> / __ <*inanimate-N>

This suggests that our formalism is inadequate – that there should be some way to represent these constraints independently and so avoid this combinatorial

---

[9] Actually, this isn't quite correct, since in our base grammar an AUX and possibly a COMP will intervene, so the rule would have to be

<V> ::= <*v-taking-animate-subject> /
        <*animate-N> <AUX> __ |
    <*v-taking-animate-subject> /
        <*animate-N> <COMP> <AUX> __ |
    <*v-taking-inanimate-subject> /
        <*inanimate-N> <AUX> __ |
    <*v-taking-inanimate-subject> /
        <*inanimate-N> <COMP> <AUX> __ |

To simplify our presentation, we shall ignore this complication; for further discussion of this problem, see Chomsky (1965), p. 155.

explosion. One way is to use *complex symbols* in place of these mile-long symbol names (Chomsky 1965, pp. 82 et seq.). A complex symbol is a collection of *features*, with each feature marked either + or −; for example, <*animate-N> would become the feature pair [+N, +Animate] while <*inanimate-N> would become [+N, −Animate]. Our modified base component would include the productions listed at the beginning of this subsection, with <*V> replaced by [+V], <*N> by [+N], etc. In addition, it would contain a new type of rule which can test and add individual features to a complex symbol; for instance,

$$[+V] \rightarrow [+[+\text{Animate}]\text{-Object}]/\underline{\quad}[+N, +\text{Animate}]$$

would add the feature +[+Animate]-Object to a verb if it is immediately followed by an animate noun. Thus the rules for animate / inanimate selection would become

$$[+V] \rightarrow [+[+\text{Animate}]\text{-Subject}]/[+N, +\text{Animate}]\underline{\quad}$$
$$[+V] \rightarrow [+[-\text{Animate}]\text{-Subject}]/[+N, -\text{Animate}]\underline{\quad}$$
$$[+V] \rightarrow [+[+\text{Animate}]\text{-Object}]/\underline{\quad}[+N, +\text{Animate}]$$
$$[+V] \rightarrow [+[-\text{Animate}]\text{-Object}]/\underline{\quad}[+N, -\text{Animate}]$$

Similar rules can be written for strict subcategorization, such as

$$[+V] \rightarrow [+V, +\text{Transitive}]/\underline{\quad}<\text{NP}>$$

Each word in the dictionary would be assigned one or more complex symbols. For example, 'teacher' would be entered as

$$[+N, +\text{Animate}]$$

while 'invent' would be

$$[+V, \text{Transitive}, +[+\text{Animate}]\text{-Subject}, +[-\text{Animate}]\text{-Object}]$$

2.5.3 *Transformational parsers – an overview*

The appeal of developing computational procedures for transformational analysis is clear. For one thing, the paraphrastic relations captured by transformational grammar should simplify subsequent stages of language processing. Perhaps more significant, adopting the formalism being used by theoretical linguists should make their insights and specific rules of analysis available to the computational linguist.[10]

On the other hand, since the generative process for transformational

---

[10] One might hope to use entire grammars developed by theoretical linguists, but in fact such linguists are, for the most part, not in the business of assembling grammars incorporating the 'best analysis' known at a given time of each of the myriad constructions of a natural language (one of the very few exceptions is the work by Stockwell, Schacter, and Partee (1973)).

grammar is so much more complex than for phrase-structure grammar, the task of building a recognition procedure is much more formidable. There are at least three basic problems in reversing the generative process:

(1) assigning to a given sentence a set of parse trees which includes all the surface trees which would be assigned by the transformational grammar
(2) given a tree not in the base, determining which sequences of transformations might have applied to generate this tree
(3) having decided on a transformation whose result may be the present tree, undoing this transformation

If we attack each of these problems in the most straightforward manner, we are likely to try many false paths which will not lead to an analysis. For the first problem, we could use a context-free grammar which will give all the surface trees assigned by the transformational grammar, and probably lots more; this context-free grammar is called a *covering grammar*. The superabundance of 'false' surface trees is aggravated by the fact that most English words have more than one category (play more than one syntactic role), although normally only one is used in any given sentence. For the second and third problems, we can construct a set of reverse transformations; however, since we are probably unable to determine uniquely in advance the transformations which produced a given tree, we will have to try many sequences of reverse transformations which will not yield a base tree.

Because of these problems, the earliest recognition procedure, suggested by Matthews, was based on the idea of synthesizing trees to match a given sentence. Although some checks were to have been made against the sentence during the generation procedure, it was still an inherently very inefficient procedure and was never implemented. Two major systems were developed in the mid 1960s, however, which did have limited success: the system of Zwicky *et al.* at MITRE and that of Petrick. We shall describe them here briefly, leaving some of the details to the next subsection.

The transformational generative grammar from which the MITRE group worked had a base component with about 275 rules and a set of 54 transformations (Zwicky, Friedman, Hall, and Walker 1965). For the recognition procedure they developed manually a context-free covering grammar with about 550 productions to produce the surface trees and a set of 134 reverse transformational rules. Their recognition procedure had four phases:

(1) analysis of the sentence using the context-free covering grammar (with a bottom-up parser)
(2) application of the reverse transformational rules
(3) for each candidate base tree produced by steps (1) and (2), a check whether it can in fact be generated by the base component

(4) for each base tree and sequence of transformations which passes the test in step (3), the (forward) transformations are applied to verify that the original sentence can in fact be generated

(The final check in step (4) is required because the covering grammar may lead to spurious matches of a transformation to the sentence in the reverse transformational process and because the reverse transformations may not incorporate all the constraints included in the forward transformations.) The covering grammar produced a large number of spurious surface analyses which the parser must process. The 1965 report, for example, cites a 12-word sentence which produced 48 parses with the covering grammar; each must be followed through steps (2) and (3) before most can be eliminated. The system was therefore very slow; 36 minutes were required to analyze one 11-word sentence.

Two measures were taken by the MITRE group to speed up the program: 'super-trees' and rejection rules (Walker, Chapin, Geis, and Gross 1966). 'Super-trees' was the MITRE term for a method of representing several parse trees in a single structure. They intended to apply the reverse transformations to these super-trees, thus processing several possible surface structures simultaneously; it is not clear if they succeeded in implementing this idea. Rejection rules were tests which were applied to the tree during the reverse transformational process (step (2) above), in order to eliminate some trees as early as possible in the parsing. The rejection rules incorporated some constraints which previously were only in the forward transformational component, and so eliminated some trees in step (2) which before had survived to step (4). The rejection rules had a significant effect on parsing times – the 11-word sentence which took 36 minutes before now took only $6\frac{1}{2}$.

The system developed by Petrick (Petrick 1965, 1966; Keyser and Petrick 1967) was similar in outline: applying a series of reverse transformations, checking if the resulting tree can be generated by the base component, and then verifying the analysis by applying the forward transformations to the base tree. There were, however, several differences from the MITRE system, motivated by the desire to have a parser which could be produced automatically from the generative formulation of the grammar. Petrick devised a procedure to generate, from the base component and transformations, an enlarged context-free grammar sufficient to analyze the surface sentence structures. He also automatically converted a set of forward transformations meeting certain conditions into pseudo-inverse (reverse) transformations. His parsing procedure also differed from the MITRE algorithm in the way in which the reverse transformations were applied. In the MITRE program reverse transformations operated on a sentence tree, just like forward transformations in a Chomsky grammar. Petrick, on the other hand, did not construct a surface tree in the analysis phase; when a particular reverse transformation came up for consideration, he built just enough structure above the sentence (using the enlarged context-free grammar) to determine if the transformation was applicable. If it was, the transformation was applied and the structure above the sentence then torn down again; what was passed from one reverse transformation to the next was only the string of word categories. In the verifying phase, of course, Petrick had to follow the rules of Chomsky grammar and apply the forward transformations to a sentence tree.

The price for generality was paid in efficiency. Petrick's problems in this regard were more severe than MITRE's for two reasons. First, the absence of a sentence tree during the application of the reverse transformational rules meant that many sequences of reverse transformations were tried which did not correspond to any sequence of tree transformations and hence would eventually be rejected. Second, if several reverse transformations could apply at some point in the analysis, the procedure could not tell in advance which would lead to a valid deep structure. Consequently, each one had to be tried and the resulting structure followed to a deep structure or a 'dead end' (where no more transformations apply). This produces a growth in the number of analysis paths which is exponential in the number of reverse transformations applied. This explosion can be avoided only if the reverse transformations include tests of the current analysis tree to determine which transformations applied to generate this tree. Such tests were included in the manually prepared reverse transformations of the MITRE group, but it would have been far too complicated for Petrick to produce such tests automatically when inverting the transformations.

Petrick's system has been significantly revised since it was first developed (Petrick 1973, Plath 1974a). In the current system the covering grammar and reverse transformations are both prepared manually. The transformational decomposition process works on a tree (as did MITRE's), and considerable flexibility has been provided in stating the transformations and the conditions of applicability. The transformations and conditions may be stated either in the traditional form (used by linguists) or in terms of elementary operations combined in LISP procedures. The resulting system is fast enough to be used in an information retrieval system with a grammar of moderate size (Plath 1976); most requests are processed in less than one minute (Damerau 1981).

2.5.4   Transformational parsers – some details

In this subsection we shall examine in somewhat greater detail the parsing procedures of MITRE and Petrick. Since these procedures are no longer used (while Petrick still employs a transformational parser, it is substantially different from his original one), our objective is not to present a full description of the parsing procedure but rather to show some of the problems of writing a transformational parser (for more details on Petrick's parser, see Grishman

(1976)). The two main phases in such a parser are the construction of the surface structure trees and the 'undoing' of the transformations; we shall deal with these two steps in turn.

Surface structure analysis. The surface structure parse tree will, in general, contain many structures which could not be directly generated by the base component. If we want to produce all the surface structure trees for a sentence using a context-free grammar, it will be necessary to augment the base component and create a covering grammar. For example, if the base component contains the production

<A> ::= <X> <Y>

and there is a transformation which interchanges x and y, the rule

<A> ::= <Y> <X>

must be included in the covering grammar which is used to produce the surface structure trees. Petrick has described (in his Ph. D. thesis) a procedure which can determine from the base and transformational components how the base must be augmented in order to obtain all surface structure trees.

Because a transformation can replace one node with two, it is possible for repeated application of such a transformation to produce a node in the surface structure with an arbitrary number of immediate descendents. This means that an infinite number of rules must be added to the base component. Petrick noted, however, that if a limit is placed on the length of sentences to be analyzed (and certain minimal assumptions are made about the grammar), only a finite number of rules are required. (Alternatively, a recursive transition network – which will be described in the next section – could be used to obtain the surface structure, since such a device allows a node to have an arbitrary number of immediate descendents.)

This augmented grammar will produce all the valid surface structure parse trees but it will also produce, in general, many spurious trees (trees not derivable from deep structures). This is unavoidable, since a context-free grammar is a much weaker computational device than a transformational grammar. Since each spurious surface analysis will have to undergo a lengthy reverse transformational process before it is recognized as invalid, this is a serious source of inefficiency, as was noted earlier.

These difficulties do not negate the inherent value of an automatic procedure, such as that described by Petrick, which will produce a covering grammar we can be sure is complete (which will produce all valid surface analyses). They do indicate, however, that if such a procedure is ever to be of practical value, it must be enhanced in order to produce 'tighter' surface grammars, perhaps by observing that certain sequences of transformations are impossible and hence suppressing the corresponding surface grammar productions. They also suggest that a more powerful device than a context-free grammar – such as the augmented context-free grammar which we will present in the next section – should be used to generate the surface analyses.

Reverse transformations. Armed with a covering grammar, we turn now to the construction of a reverse transformational component. This component should produce, from a surface structure, all deep structures which can generate the surface structure (and for a spurious surface structure, indicate that there is no deep structure).

The first problem is that it is not always possible to construct such a component. If a (forward) transformation simply deletes a portion of the parse tree, it will in general be impossible to reconstruct that portion when working backwards from the surface structure; there may be an infinite number of deep structures which produce one surface structure. Such a situation is called *irrecoverable deletion.* (This is in contrast to recoverable deletions, which either delete nodes specified as constants in the structural index, or nodes governed by an identity condition. If a transformation requires that two nodes have identical substructures, and then deletes one of them, the deletion is recoverable: the reverse transformational component may restore the deletion by copying the other node. An example of such a deletion is the embedding transformation of our tiny transformational grammar.) So, to be able to construct a reverse component at all, the grammar may contain no irrecoverable deletions.

Life would be relatively easy if, for each transformation, one could produce an inverse transformation which undoes the change wrought in the tree. Unfortunately, for the form of transformation which we have chosen, this is not possible. Consider, for example, a transformation with structural index

    A C D

and structural change

    1 0 3

Suppose that the only structure to which it ever applied in the generation of a sentence is as in figure 2.10, producing figure 2.11.

Reversing this transformation seems straightforward enough. The reverse transformation need not be a true inverse; it does not have to be able to reconstruct an arbitrary input which would match the forward transformation – it need only be able to reconstruct inputs which occur in the derivation of sentences. Thus, in this case, it must insert a B dominating a C below M. However, this operation cannot be performed using the transformational formalism described above. In terms of elementary changes to the parse tree, this formalism permits only deletion (of a node), replacement (of one node by another), and sister adjunction (insertion of one node next to another, with

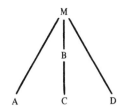

Figure 2.10

Figure 2.11

both dominated by the same node). It does not allow us to create new structures, and in particular does not allow insertion of one node below another. To circumvent this problem, the MITRE system and Petrick's later systems have allowed a larger set of elementary operations, capable of making an arbitrary change to a tree.

Even if the set of operations is sufficient to specify the reverse transformations, their formation is not trivial. In cases such as the one just considered, the reverse transformation cannot be generated from an examination of the forward transformation alone. One must examine the entire grammar to see how the transformation is used in sentence generation. This is a complex process which has (to the author's knowledge) never been programmed. In the MITRE system, the reverse transformations were all produced manually.

Petrick, seeking originally a procedure which would work automatically from the transformational grammar, took a different tack. He developed a reverse transformational component which mapped the surface string (the sentence) into a set of potential deep structure strings; the latter were then parsed by the base component. The individual transformations of the reverse component were string and not tree rewriting rules.

The advantage of this approach lies in the simplicity of forming the individual reverse transformations. The reverse transformations will be in one-to-one correspondence with the forward ones, and each reverse transformation T' can be computed on the basis of the corresponding forward transformation alone. These reverse transformations will satisfy the following property: for any tree t with frontier s, if T maps t into t' with frontier s', then T' maps s' into s.

Figure 2.12

Figure 2.13

Suppose we are given a forward transformation with structural index si and structural change sc. Since we are interested only in the frontier and not in the internal structure of the tree, we shall use a reduced structural change obtained by concatenating the elements of the structural change (so that, for example, the structural change $1\ 0\ 2+3$ would yield the reduced structural change $1+2+3$). The fact that a proper analysis exists for a tree with frontier s implies that s can be divided into substrings $s(1), \dots, s(n)$ such that, for all j from 1 to n, a tree can be built using the covering grammar with root $si(j)$ and frontier $s(j)$ (unless $si(j) = \text{'x'}$, in which case there is no restriction on $s(j)$) (see figure 2.12).

If r is the length of rsc, the reduced structural change, the transformation rearranges the string into a set of substrings $s'(j)$, $j = 1$ to r, given by

$$s'(j) = \text{if } rsc(j) \text{ is an integer then } s(rsc(j))$$
$$\text{else } rsc(j)$$

How can this shuffle be reversed? We begin by creating an *inverse structural index* $isi(j)$, $j = 1$ to r, according to

$$isi(j) = \text{if } rsc(j) \text{ is an integer then } si(rsc(j))$$
$$\text{else } rsc(j)$$

and an *inverse structural change* $isc(j)$, $j = 1$ to n, according to

$$isc(j) = \text{if there exists a } k \text{ such that } rsc(k) = j \text{ then } k$$
$$\text{else } si(j)$$

Then given a string s', we divide it into r substrings, requiring that the jth substring be the frontier of some tree with root $isi(j)$ (again, unless $isi(j) = \text{'x'}$). One of these divisions will be the $s'(j)$ produced by the forward transformation (there may be others). These substrings are then rearranged according to the *isc*, producing the original string *s*:

$$s(j) = \text{if } isc(j) \text{ is an integer then } s' \ (isc(j))$$
$$\text{else } isc(j)$$

If there are several matches to the *isi*, the transformation must be applied to all; we can only be sure that one of the resulting strings will be *s*. If the forward transformation is a recoverable deletion involving identity conditions, the formulas given above are somewhat more complicated.

Given a set of reverse transformations, we must finally specify the sequencing among them. The reverse transformations should be considered in precisely the reverse order from that of the corresponding forward transformations. The sequencing is again cyclic, with each iteration now creating an embedded sentence.

Even if a reverse transformation matches the sentence being decomposed, one cannot be sure that the corresponding forward transformation was involved in the generation of the sentence. Undoing the transformation may lead to a dead end (where no other reverse transformations apply), and another transformation may also have produced the current structure. Consequently, both possibilities – undoing and not undoing the transformation – must be followed. In analogy with the forward transformations, one can say that all reverse transformations are optional.

This implies, unfortunately, that parsing time can increase exponentially with the number of applicable transformations. Such a procedure has therefore proved impracticable for all but the smallest grammars and sentences. To avoid this exponential growth, the parser must have some way of determining directly from a tree the last transformation which applied to produce the tree. An analysis must be made of the possible intermediate structures which can arise in sentence generation, and the resulting information translated into conditions on the reverse transformations. Such an analysis has not been automated, but it is a straightforward and integral part of the manual construction of a reverse transformation component. The MITRE group was able to specify the appropriate conditions for all their reverse transformations; their system provided for optional reverse transformations but their grammar did not utilize this facility.

Eliminating optional reverse transformations is more difficult in a reverse component which uses string rewriting rules and does not retain any tree structure between transformations.[11] Most of the information which is needed to determine which transformation to undo is not available. In any case, the original impetus for using string rewriting rules – providing a procedure which

---

[11] Petrick's original system, using string rewriting rules, did retain some low-level tree structures between transformations, but his immediately subsequent systems did not.

can operate directly from the transformational grammar – is lost when we seek to add, for reasons of efficiency, restrictions which are not automatically generated from the grammar.

Petrick's current parser, part of the TQA system (the transformational question-answering system, originally called REQUEST), is much closer in overall structure to the MITRE design. A set of potential surface structure trees are operated on by a reverse transformational component consisting of tree rewriting rules. The reverse transformations are prepared manually, not obtained automatically from corresponding forward transformations. The conditions on the reverse transformations are sufficiently tight to obviate the need for optional reverse transformations. As a result, the question-answering system can operate efficiently with a moderately large set of reverse transformations (about 130).

Once all reverse transformations have been applied, the resulting structures must be checked to determine which are valid deep structures. If the reverse transformations work on trees, each tree must be examined for productions not in the base component. If the reverse transformations work on strings, each string must be parsed using the base component.

The original Petrick and MITRE procedures envisioned a final synthesis phase. This phase would apply to each deep structure produced by the reverse transformational component. It would apply the corresponding forward transformations to determine whether the original sentence can be recovered; if it cannot, the deep structure is rejected. Such a check is necessary if the reverse transformations can produce deep structures which do not lead back to the original sentence and perhaps do not lead to any sentence at all. This is certainly the case with the reverse transformations applied to strings; such transformations are unable to capture many constraints present when applying the forward transformations to trees. It can also be true with reverse transformations working on trees, if the constraints on the reverse transformations are too loose. With reverse transformations on trees, however, it should be possible to formulate constraints sufficiently tight as to obviate the need for a synthesis phase.

2.6   Augmented context-free parsers

One result of the early transformational systems was a recognition of the importance of finding an efficient parsing procedure if transformational analysis was ever to be a useful technique. As the systems indicated, there are two main obstacles to an efficient procedure. First, there is the problem of refining the surface analysis, so that each sentence produces fewer trees for which transformational decomposition must be attempted. This has generally been approached by using a more powerful mechanism than a context-free parser for the surface analysis. Second, there is the problem of determining the base structure (or kernel sentences) from the surface structure in a relatively direct fashion. This has generally been done by associating particular rules for building the deep structure with rules of the surface structure analysis. The approach here has generally been *ad hoc*, developing a reverse mapping without explicit reference to a corresponding set of forward transformations.

To get a higher quality surface parse, we want to incorporate additional grammatical constraints into the covering grammar. For the transformational systems just described, however, the covering grammar is a context-free grammar, and we have already considered (at the end of section 2.4.1) the difficulties of adding grammatical constraints to a context-free grammar. This suggests that we need a more powerful grammatical formalism. There are more powerful phrase-structure grammars (context-sensitive grammars and unrestricted rewriting rules), but, as we noted earlier, they have not proven particularly suitable for the statement of grammatical constraints in a surface grammar.

What then? When stuck a programmer does what he or she knows best – writes a program. We could write a single program embodying the entire grammar; this approach was used in some of the earliest natural language systems and is still seen occasionally today. If we weren't careful, however, the resulting program would be hard to read and modify. The structure imposed by using a formal system of grammar would be lost. In addition, the division between grammar and parsing algorithm would disappear, so that it would be very difficult to try the grammar with different parsing algorithms.

What we will consider instead in this section is the possibility of taking a context-free grammar and adding small procedures to individual productions of the grammar. The context-free grammar would continue to specify the constituent structure. The procedures would perform two functions: they would capture the grammatical constraints which do not easily fit into the context-free grammar. And they would determine the operations needed to recover the sentence's deep structure. Such combinations of context-free grammars and procedures are called *augmented context-free grammars.*

In the next two subsections, we shall present, by means of very small grammars, samples of two styles of writing augmented context-free grammars. The first is based on Restriction Language, developed by Sager and her co-workers at the New York University Linguistic String Project; the second is the augmented transition network (ATN) formalism introduced by Woods. Following this, we shall offer some brief historical and theoretical comment relating to these grammars.

2.6.1 Restriction Language

The Linguistic String Parser, and the Restriction Language used for writing grammars, were developed by a group at New York University led by Sager. In their system, the specifications of the surface grammar and transformations are separate, so we can consider these two components in turn.

A Restriction Language grammar (Sager and Grishman 1975) consists of a context-free component (written in BNF) and a set of *restrictions*. These restrictions are predicates on parse trees; a context-free analysis is accepted as a parse only if it passes all applicable restrictions. Some of these restrictions are constraints on the structure of the tree – how particular BNF productions are used in combination. Most, however, involve tests of *attributes* of particular words (comparable to the *features* used in transformational grammar, as discussed in section 2.5.2). The word classes (noun, tensed verb, adjective, etc.) provide only a first-order categorization of the grammatical properties of words. To implement some of the grammatical constraints cited earlier (number agreement, subcategorization, selection) we need a more refined classification. We achieve this by assigning attributes to words in the dictionary. For example, nouns and tensed verbs will be assigned the attributes SINGULAR or PLURAL; 'countable' nouns will be assigned NCOUNT; and verbs will be assigned attributes to indicate the types of object strings with which they can occur.

A crucial feature of linguistic string theory is that it singles out the relations between particular word pairs in a sentence. Two relations are central: the relation between two words that are elements of the same string (the *coelement* relation) and the relation between a host and its adjuncts. Most grammatical constraints (and, in fact, all of those we shall present below) involve words connected by these string relations.

Restrictions are associated with particular productions in the grammar; for instance, subject–verb number agreement is associated with the production for ASSERTION. When an ASSERTION is completed, the subject–verb agreement restriction is executed. The restriction tests the SINGULAR/PLURAL attribute of the subject and verb elements. If they match, parsing continues; if they don't this analysis is rejected.

Restriction Language is a high-level language specifically designed for writing natural language grammars. In its totality it is moderately complex, reflecting the wide variety of features available in the Linguistic String Parser. The examples below illustrate the three main features provided by the language:

* operations for traversing a tree to locate a particular node. These include operations for locating a named element of a string; operations for going from a host to its left and right adjuncts, and vice versa; and the CORE routine, which in general goes from a node to the sentence word associated with that node, exclusive of its left and right adjuncts (the 'x' of an LxR structure)
* operations for testing the names of nodes and testing the attributes of sentence words which are matched to leaf nodes in the tree

* logical connectives (BOTH. . .AND. . .,EITHER. . .OR. . .,IF. . .THEN. . .)
  for combining these tests to form the desired grammatical constraints

We shall consider three simple restrictions – those for count nouns, subject–verb number agreement, and subcategorization. In all cases what we shall present are highly simplified versions of the real restrictions in the Linguistic String Project grammar.

The count noun constraint requires that a singular countable noun (such as 'egg', but not 'milk') be preceded by an article ('the'), a linguistic quantifier ('each') or a possessive noun ('his', 'her'). The corresponding restriction reads

> WCOUNT = IN LNR:
>> IF THE CORE HAS THE ATTRIBUTE NCOUNT
>> THEN IN THE LEFT-ADJUNCT OF THE CORE, TPOS IS NOT EMPTY.

The restriction is named 'WCOUNT'; 'IN LNR' means that it is to be executed whenever an LNR node (a noun with its adjuncts) has been completed. The restriction first tests if the CORE (the noun underneath LNR) has the attribute NCOUNT (is a singular countable noun). If so, the restriction then looks to the LEFT-ADJUNCT of the CORE – in other words, the LN node – and checks that the element TPOS of LN (which includes articles, linguistic quantifiers, and possessive pronouns) is not EMPTY (in other words, matches at least one word of the sentence).

In its simplest form, number agreement requires that singular subjects take singular verbs and plural subjects plural verbs. This translates directly into Restriction Language:

> WAGREE = IN ASSERTION:
>> BOTH
>>> IF THE CORE OF THE SUBJECT HAS THE ATTRIBUTE SINGULAR
>>> THEN THE CORE OF THE VERB HAS THE ATTRIBUTE SINGULAR
>> AND
>>> IF THE CORE OF THE SUBJECT HAS THE ATTRIBUTE PLURAL
>>> THEN THE CORE OF THE VERB HAS THE ATTRIBUTE PLURAL.

(The restriction could be stated more succinctly by using additional features of the Restriction Language; we have limited ourselves to a minimal Restriction Language subset.)

Subcategorization restricts the object strings which can occur with a given verb. To implement this, we shall record as attributes of the verb the names of the object strings with which it can occur. For example, the verb 'begin' would be assigned the attributes NSTG ('I began the book.') and TOVO ('I began to read the book.'). We can then have a restriction which, for each option of OBJECT, verifies that the verb has the corresponding attribute:

> WSUBCAT = IN OBJECT:
>> IF THE VALUE OF THE OBJECT IS NSTG

THEN THE CORE OF COELEMENT VERB HAS THE ATTRIBUTE NSTG
ELSE IF THE VALUE OF THE OBJECT IS TOVO
THEN THE CORE OF COELEMENT VERB HAS THE ATTRIBUTE TOVO
ELSE [value must be NULLOBJ]
THE CORE OF COELEMENT VERB HAS THE ATTRIBUTE NULLOBJ.

The VALUE of a node is the node immediately below it. (Again, by using additional features of the Restriction Language, we could write a generalized restriction which works for all options of OBJECT.)

There are about 200 restrictions in the Linguistic String Project English grammar (Sager 1981). They combine to exclude almost all syntactically anomalous parses.[12] The surface analyses which are produced provide substantial guidance for the transformational analysis which follows, for two reasons. First, there is an inherent relation between string and transformational analysis – the strings into which the sentence is segmented generally correspond either to kernel strings or to the resultants of transformations. Second, the Linguistic String Project grammar incorporates an especially refined string classification (there are more than 50 object strings, for example). Specifically, in many cases different strings have been provided for similar surface constructions which arise from different transformational processes. As a result, the string name in the parse tree often determines the reverse transformation to be applied – relatively little pattern matching is needed during the decomposition process, in contrast to the procedures described in the last section.

The transformations are written in an extension of the Restriction Language (Hobbs and Grishman 1976). This extension allows the programmer to create new tree structures, insert them into the tree, and delete existing nodes from the tree. The new tree structures are specified as parenthesized lists with ' + ' signs connecting sibling nodes, so that for example

$a(b + c)$

specifies a tree structure with node a dominating nodes b and c (figure 2.14). New nodes can be created by giving the node name within ' < ... > ' brackets. A subtree of the current tree can be copied by specifying its root node. We shall illustrate these operations in a moment.

In Harrisian terms, the objective of the sentence analysis is to regularize the sentence structure by reducing the sentence to a composition of kernel sentences. We shall represent this target structure by a combination of ASSERTION strings, with the subjects and objects being simple nouns, pronouns, adjectives, or other ASSERTIONS. In some cases this just requires the insertion of

---

[12] This is not to say that this grammar usually yields just one parse corresponding to the intended reading of a sentence. Many sentences have several syntactically valid analyses, so that the 'correct' reading can only be selected using semantic information.

Figure 2.14

a subject or object into an otherwise complete string; in other cases it requires the construction of a completely new string around an element.

We shall consider two simple transformations. The first of these converts a TOVO object into a full ASSERTION (TOVO = *to* + infinitive verb + embedded object). In the sentence 'John wants to go.', the implicit subject of the verb 'to go' is 'John' (compare this with 'John wants Mary to go.'). To make this relation explicit, we shall copy the subject of the ASSERTION and insert it into the TOVO string, thus converting the TOVO to a full ASSERTION; the result is, in essence, 'John wants (John go)'.[13] In Restriction Language, the transformation to do this is

      T-TOVO = IN TOVO:
        REPLACE TOVO
          BY <ASSERTION> (<SA> (<NULL>)
                  + SUBJECT OF IMMEDIATE ASSERTION
                  + <SA> (<NULL>)
                  + <VERB> (LVR OF TOVO)
                  + FIRST SA OF TOVO
                  + OBJECT OF TOVO
                  + SECOND SA OF TOVO).

When this transformation is executed, we are 'looking at' the TOVO node. IMMEDIATE ASSERTION looks up in the tree for an ASSERTION node; SUBJECT OF IMMEDIATE ASSERTION then locates the SUBJECT element of the ASSERTION and copies the SUBJECT, along with the entire subtree it dominates, into the new structure being built. The constructs of the form ... OF TOVO similarly make copies of the elements of TOVO and the subtrees they dominate. We have included four SAs in the newly created ASSERTION so that it will have the same structure as ASSERTIONs created in parsing. The first two are newly created nodes with the value NULL specified; the last two are copies of the two SA nodes in the TOVO string.

For example, if we are analyzing the sentence 'John wants to eat pickles on his yacht.', the tree would have the structure shown in figure 2.15.

[13] Offering this as the transformation for all TOVO strings is an oversimplification. In cases where the original subject does not play the role of an agent, we may prefer a different analysis; for example, to decompose 'The rock began to fall.' as '(rock fall) began' rather than 'rock began (rock fall)'.

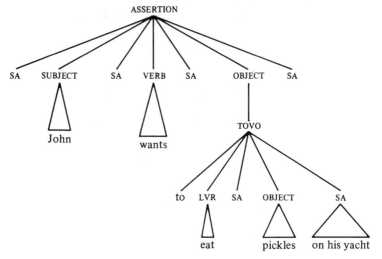

Figure 2.15

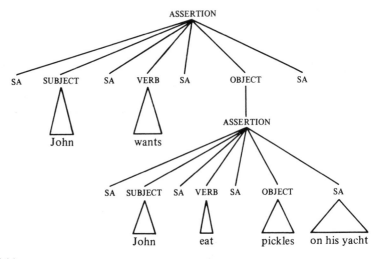

Figure 2.16

In this diagram, we have used triangles to indicate a node dominating some sentence words when we are not interested in the structures of the tree below that node. In addition, to avoid clutter we have omitted the NULLs beneath most of the SAs (sentence adjunct nodes). This tree would be changed by our T-TOVO transformation into figure 2.16.

The other transformation we shall consider concerns prenominal adjectives.

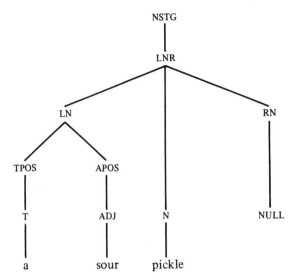

Figure 2.17

In our earlier presentation of transformational grammar, we indicated the desirability of deriving such adjectives from full sentence modifiers; in effect, deriving 'the red house' from 'the house (such that) house is red'. In our transformational grammar, the derivation proceeded through the intermediate stage of a relative clause; here, however, we shall map the adjective directly into a full ASSERTION. We have elected, somewhat arbitrarily, to place the resulting ASSERTION immediately to the right of the NSTG node. Also, to keep the transformation short, we have chosen this time to create a minimal ASSERTION structure, without any of the adjunct slots. The transformation, in Restriction Language, would be

```
T-APOS = IN LN:
    IF APOS IS NOT EMPTY
       THEN BOTH
          AFTER IMMEDIATE NSTG
          INSERT
             < ASSERTION >
             ( < SUBJECT >  ( < NSTG >  (CORE OF IMMEDIATE NSTG))
             + < VERB >  ('BE')
             + < OBJECT >  ( < ASTG >  (VALUE OF APOS)))
       AND
          REPLACE VALUE OF APOS
          BY  < NULL > .
```

This transformation would change 'a sour pickle', with the structure of figure 2.17, into 'a pickle (pickle is sour)' (figure 2.18).

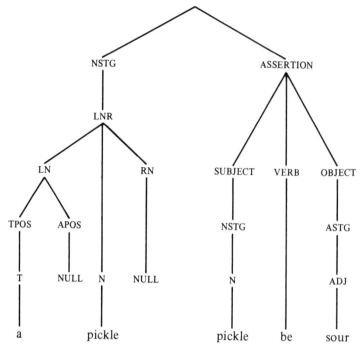

Figure 2.18

2.6.2 *Augmented transition networks*

The augmented transition network (ATN) formalism introduced by Woods in 1970 (Woods 1970b) has become one of the most popular forms for writing natural language grammars. Before we delve into some examples of ATNs, we must explain the underlying construct, the recursive transition network.

A transition network is a representation of a regular (or finite-state) grammar (see section 2.3.2). The network is a directed graph whose arcs are labeled by terminal symbols (words or word categories). One node of the graph is designated as the start state; one or more nodes are marked as final states. A sentence is in the language defined by the network if there is a path from the start state to some final state such that the labels on the arcs of the path match the words of the sentence.

For example, the network in figure 2.19 matches sentences consisting of either an '*a*' or a '*b*', followed by zero or more '*c*'s, followed by a '*d*'.

A recursive transition network is a transition network with the following extension: nodes of the graph are labeled, and arcs may be labeled with either node names or terminal symbols. These node names correspond to the non-

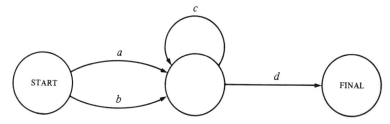

Figure 2.19

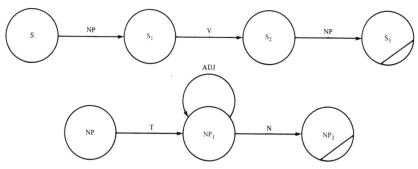

Figure 2.20

terminal symbols of a context-free grammar. An arc labeled with a node name can be traversed if there exists a path from the named node to a final state which matches some or all of the remainder of the sentence. For example, the recursive transition network of figure 2.20 (where a circle with a line through it designates a final state) defines an s as the sequence NP, V, NP, where an NP is a T followed by zero or more ADJs, followed by an N. In terms of weak generative capacity (the set of languages which can be defined), recursive transition networks are equivalent to context-free grammars. Recursive transition networks do have the advantage that repetitive patterns, such as the repeated adjective in the NP, can be captured without resort to recursion. (Recursive transition networks are thus essentially equivalent to an extension of context-free grammars in which regular expressions, not just finite sequences of symbols, are allowed on the right side of productions (LaLonde 1977).)

If we take a recursive transition network and add procedures (generally coded in LISP) for enforcing grammatical constraints and for generating a deep structure, we get an ATN (augmented transition network). Although the most apparent difference between ATNs and Restriction Language grammars is the difference between the recursive transition networks and the context-free grammars on which they are based, there are other differences which are more fundamental. The most basic difference is that surface analysis and deep structure generation, which are separate and sequential in the Restriction Language grammar, are performed concurrently in most ATNs. A related distinction is that most ATNs do not automatically construct an accessible representation of surface structure; instead, the programmer explicitly assigns values to 'registers' which are subsequently referenced in verifying grammatical constraints and building deep structures.

The parser for an ATN must find a path through the network from the start node to a final node. This is usually done by a top-down backtracking algorithm very similar to that used for context-free analysis. An ordering can be specified on the arcs leaving a node (just as the options of a rule are ordered in a BNF grammar), so that some paths will be tried before others.

Each arc of the network specifies

(1) the arc label (a word, word category, or node name)
(2) any conditions on traversing the arc
(3) the actions to be taken if the arc is traversed
(4) the new state reached when the arc is traversed

The specification for each state (node) of the network consists of a name and a series of such arcs (which have this node as their initial state).

In Woods' terminology, the arcs are classified according to their label type: WRD arcs, which match a specific word; CAT arcs, which match any word of a specified category; and PUSH arcs, which require traversal of another portion of the network starting at a specified node (and which begin by 'pushing' the current position in the network onto a stack). If a state is a final state, its specifications include a POP 'arc'. A state can have both POP 'arcs' and real arcs, so that (for alternative analyses) it may act as a final or intermediate state; such a state occurs in our example below.

The conditions are written as LISP predicates. Following Woods' notation, these predicates may test for particular features (attributes) in the definition of the current word using the function '(GETF feature)'.[14] The current word itself may be accessed by referencing the symbol '*' (in the case of tensed verbs, '*' returns the untensed (infinitive) form, which must be stored together with the tensed verb in the dictionary).

The actions associated with an arc involve chiefly the assignment of values to registers. The function '(SETR register value)' assigns the *value* to the specified *register* for the current level. Each time we try a PUSH arc and start traversing a new path, we create a new, deeper, level in the parsing process; when we POP, we return to a higher level. Each level of the parse has its own set of registers; register SUBJ at one level is distinct from register SUBJ at the level below. To permit communication between levels, the ATN provides the

---

[14] Function references in LISP have the form

(function-name arg₁ arg₂ . . .)

Thus '(GETF HAPPY)' invokes function GETF with argument HAPPY.

functions '(SENDR register value)', which sets the register at the level below the current one, and '(LIFTR register value)', which sets the register at the level above. The function '(GETR register)' retrieves the value of a register at the current level.

Finally, an arc must specify its final state. '(TO state)' directs the parser to go to *state* and to advance to the next word in the sentence; '(JUMP state)' goes to *state* without moving ahead in the sentence.

The POP arc may specify conditions under which this state can be a final state, and, in addition, a structure which is returned as the 'value' of this level. This value may be accessed by the '*' symbol in the PUSH arc which 'invoked' this level. The structure is built out of constant elements and the values of registers on that level. This mechanism is used to assemble the deep structure of a sentence, level by level.

Our example of an ATN will be a simplified version of one of the examples in Woods' original paper. The example includes only the top-level sentence network; it assumes the existence of an NP network such as the one shown above, suitably augmented. The network covers assertions and yes–no questions; simple and perfect verb forms ('John slept.', 'John has slept.'); intransitive verbs, verbs with noun objects, and verbs with 'N-to-v-object' objects ('John wants Jim to bake a cake.'). Verbs of these three types are distinguished by the LISP predicates INTRANS (intransitive), TRANS (transitive – takes either noun or 'N-to-v-object' objects), and S-TRANS (takes 'N-to-v-object' objects). The infinitive, tensed forms, and past participles of a verb are all placed in the category V, and are differentiated by the features UNTENSED for the infinitive and PPRT for the past participle.

The network is shown in figure 2.21. The conditions and actions on the arcs are given in table 2.3 ('T' means true – no conditions).

The nodes labeled Q_3, Q_4, and Q_6 have POP arcs. The POP arc on Q_3 has the condition.

(INTRANS (GETR V))

and returns the tree structure

(s type subj (TNS tns) (VP (V v)))

where the lower-case symbols are to be replaced by the values of the registers with those names. *Type* will be either DCL for declarative sentences or Q for questions; the remainder is similar to a Chomsky deep structure. Nodes Q_4 and Q_6 have a POP arc which has no condition and returns the structure

(s type subj (TNS tns) (VP (V v) obj)).

In this way, 'John has shot Leo.' will be transformed into

(s DCL (NP John)
        (TNS present perfect)
        (VP (V shoot) (NP Leo))).

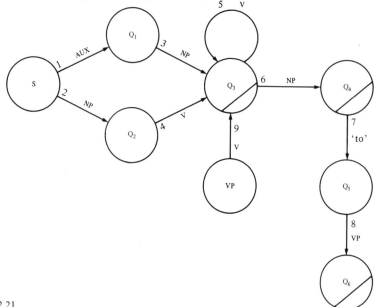

Figure 2.21

'N-to-V-object' will be transformed into an embedded s, so 'Iago wants Othello to stab Desdemona.' becomes

>(S DCL (NP Iago)
>   (TNS present)
>   (VP (V want)
>   (S DCL (NP Othello)
>   (TNS present)
>   (VP (V stab)
>   (NP Desdemona)))))

To help you in following the operations of the ATN, we give below a trace of the register assignments which occur in processing these two sentences. For 'John has shot Leo.', the path through the network is given in table 2.4. For 'Iago wants Othello to stab Desdemona.' there are two levels (top-level sentence and embedded sentence) and hence two sets of registers; the register assignments are as shown in table 2.5.

For further examples of ATNS, and a description of additional features of ATNS, see Bates (1978).

2.6.3 Some history

Augmented context-free grammar has been the dominant formalism for natural language processing since the early 1970s, and several dozen non-trivial grammars have been constructed in that period. We cannot hope to survey all these systems so, with due apology to those not mentioned, shall briefly describe a few of the earliest ones.

Table 2.3

Arc	Condition	Action
1	T	(SETR V *)
		(SETR TNS (GETF TENSE))
		(SETR TYPE 'Q)
2	T	(SETR SUBJ *)
		(SETR TYPE 'DCL)
3	T	(SETR SUBJ *)
4	T	(SETR V *)
		(SETR TNS (GETF TENSE))
5	(AND (GETF PPRT) (EQ (GETR V) 'HAVE))	(SETR TNS (APPEND1 (GETR TNS) 'PERFECT))
		(SETR V *)
6	(TRANS (GETR V))	(SETR OBJ *)
7	(S-TRANS (GETR V))	(SENDR SUBJ (GETR OBJ))
		(SENDR TNS (GETR TNS))
		(SENDR TYPE 'DCL)
8	T	(SETR OBJ *)
9	(GETF UNTENSED)	(SETR V *)

Table 2.4

Arc	Register assignments
2	SUBJ = (NP John)
	TYPE = DCL
4	V = have
	TNS = present
5	TNS = present perfect
	V = shoot
6	OBJ = (NP Leo)

Table 2.5

	Register assignments	
Arc	Top level	Embedded sentence level
2	SUBJ = (NP Iago)	
	TYPE = DCL	
4	V = want	
	TNS = present	
6	OBJ = (NP Othello)	
7		SUBJ = (NP Othello)
		TNS = present
		TYPE = DCL
8	– descend to lower level (PUSH) –	
9		V = stab
6		OBJ = (NP Desdemona)
	– return to top level (POP) –	
8	OBJ = (S DCL (NP Othello)	
	(TNS present)	
	(VP (V stab) (NP Desdemona)))	

Perhaps the oldest such system is the New York University Linguistic String Parser. This system can trace its roots back to the string analysis program at the University of Pennsylvania, which was mentioned in the section on context-free parsers. The system was developed for processing scientific and technical texts for information retrieval purposes, so an early emphasis was placed on creating a broad-coverage English grammar (systems for on-line dialog can normally get by with more restricted grammars). Their present grammar (Sager 1981), which has about 250 context-free rules and about 200 restrictions, has been used to analyze hospital records and journal articles in medicine and physiology. Because of the large size of their grammar, this group has been particularly concerned with techniques for organizing and specifying the grammar which will facilitate further development. One aspect of this is the Restriction Language described earlier in this section.

The system is based on the linguistic theories of Z. Harris (1962, 1968). Although Harrisian linguistic theory is little used today by theoretical linguists, it does provide two significant advantages for computational linguists. First, unlike Chomsky's theory, it provides a framework for surface analysis – linguistic string theory – which can be used in structuring a surface grammar. This framework singles out certain relations between constituents (string relations), and, as noted earlier, most grammatical restrictions can be stated in terms of these string relations. Second, there is a close correspondence between the string and transformational structure of a sentence, so that the string analysis provides a good guide for transformational decomposition.

The first two versions of the Linguistic String Parser, developed in the mid 1960s, used a low-level tree-and-list processing language to specify the restrictions (Sager 1967). In order to permit a more economical and perspicuous statement of the restrictions, the Restriction Language was introduced with the third version of the parser in the early 1970s (Grishman 1973; Grishman, Sager, Raze, and Bookchin 1973; Sager 1973; Sager and Grishman 1975). A mechanism for transformational analysis was added shortly thereafter (Hobbs and Grishman 1976).

(The groundwork for this approach to transformational analysis had been laid earlier by Joshi and Hiz (Joshi 1962; Hiz and Joshi 1967). Their proposed scheme involved a linguistic string analysis and a set of rules which constructed from each string a corresponding kernel-like sentence. It pointed out the value of linguistic string analysis in determining which reverse transformations need to be applied. Their proposal accounted for only a limited set of transformations, but it did lead to some theoretical studies of adjunct grammars and trace conditions (Joshi 1973) which laid a formal basis for their procedures. These studies indicated how it may be possible, starting from a transformational grammar not specifically oriented towards recognition, to determine the features of a sentence which indicate that a particular transformation applied in generating it, and hence to produce automatically an efficient transformational analysis procedure.)

An early version of the Linguistic String Parser, with a very restricted grammar, was used as the front end for an information retrieval system (Cautin 1969). The system is currently being used for the automatic structuring of natural language medical records (Sager 1978) and has been used for a natural language retrieval system which accesses these records (Grishman and Hirschman 1978).

Another broad-coverage augmented-context-free grammar is DIAGRAM (Robinson 1982), developed at SRI International. As in Restriction Language grammar, context-free rules are augmented by procedures which check syntactic constraints during the parse. Interpretations (analogous to deep structures) are computed after a parse is obtained, using rules similar in form to those in ATNS.

Recursive transition networks and ATNs also have a considerable history. The first system using such a network was developed by Thorne, Bratley, and Dewar at Edinburgh (Thorne, Bratley, and Dewar 1968; Dewar, Bratley, and Thorne 1969). They started with a regular base grammar, i.e., a finite transition network. The importance of using a regular base lay in their claim that some transformations are equivalent in effect to changing the base to a recursive transition network. Transformations which could not be handled in this fashion, such as conjunction, were incorporated into the parsing program. Parsing a sentence with this surface grammar should then also give some indication of the associated base and transformational structure. Their published papers do not describe, however, the process by which the surface grammar was constructed and so it is not clear just how the transformation and base structure was extracted from their parse.

The recursive transition network was extended into an ATN in the system of Bobrow and Fraser (1969). They allowed arbitrary LISP functions on arcs, and used these LISP functions for verifying constraints (by setting and testing flags) and for assigning deep structure labels to constituents. The ATN formalism was refined by Woods at Harvard and Bolt Beranek and Newman. In a paper which has significantly influenced subsequent work in natural language parsing (Woods 1970b), Woods sought to standardize the ATN formalism and separate it from the details of the parser implementation by introducing the set of operations for conditions and actions which we described above. This formalism, and variants thereof, is probably the one most widely used today, in part because it is relatively easy to implement 'on top of' a LISP system. At Bolt Beranek and Newman it has been used for several major systems, including the LSNLIS or LUNAR system (a natural language interface to a retrieval system for data about moon rocks – Woods, Kaplan, and Nash-Webber 1972; Woods 1973), the RUS system (which has also been used for natural language data base retrieval – Bobrow and Webber 1980), and their speech understanding research.

A somewhat different approach to integrating surface analysis and transformational decomposition was taken by Proto-RELADES, developed by IBM Cambridge (Culicover *et al.* 1969). Like the other systems we have described, their surface grammar was augmented by restrictions (in PL/I, this time). Like ATNs, the deep structure was built during the parse, but unlike ATNs, the rules which built the deep structure were in the form of reverse transformations acting on an (incomplete) surface tree. Proto-RELADES was tested as a restricted English language preprocessor for a library card catalog retrieval system (Loveman, Moyne, and Tobey 1971).

Some augmented context-free parsing systems do not construct a transformational deep structure but instead generate a semantic structure directly during the parse. One such system was developed by Winograd at MIT (Winograd 1971, 1972) for accepting English commands and questions about a 'blocks world' (a collection of blocks on a table which can be moved and stacked on command). Winograd's context-free grammar was encoded as a set of procedures instead of a data structure to be interpreted, but this is not a material difference; ATNs are now frequently compiled to increase efficiency. Winograd's grammar was based on Halliday's 'systemic grammar', which classifies sentences and noun phrases in terms of a large number of features; since Halliday's grammar is essentially descriptive rather than generative (it classifies sentences rather than trying to characterize the set of grammatical sentences), most of the detailed grammatical structure had to be supplied by Winograd. The primary distinctive feature of his system was the integration of the syntactic component with semantics and pragmatics (the manipulation of objects in the blocks world). By generating semantic structure during the parse, his parser was able to use not only syntactic constraints but also semantic and pragmatic information in selecting a proper sentence analysis.

2.6.4   Some comparisons

A basic distinction between the Restriction Language grammar and most ATNs is that in the ATNs the operations for enforcing grammatical constraints and building the deep structure are integrated and performed concurrently, while in the Restriction Language grammar they are separate and performed sequentially. The relative merits of the two approaches have been a source of discussion and dispute for at least a decade. It is part of the more general problem of serial versus parallel processing – should semantic analysis be done concurrently with syntactic analysis.

There are efficiency arguments in favor of each side. For all current large grammars, analysis of a sentence involves trying many false paths which are eventually blocked by syntactic or semantic constraints. The proponents of sequential processing argue: why waste time doing transformational and semantic analysis for paths which will eventually be blocked in the syntactic analysis? The proponents of parallel processing counter: why waste time on the further syntactic analysis of a path which we could have already eliminated through semantic constraints?

Parallel processing will do better if the added time required by the deeper analysis is outweighed by the fraction of incorrect analyses which can be eliminated early in the parsing process. This clearly depends on the relative complexity of the syntactic and semantic processing and the relative 'tightness' of the semantic constraints. For example, Winograd's system involved an extremely limited 'microworld' with simple semantics and pragmatics, so the application of semantic and pragmatic constraints during parsing turned out to be effective.

The parallel/serial balance also depends on the extent to which syntactic and semantic constraints can be projected onto the surface analysis. If most constraints can only be expressed at the level of deep or semantic structure, parallel processing is probably more efficient. This may depend in turn on the type of surface analysis; for example, the relationships exhibited by linguistic string analysis are suitable for expressing many of these constraints, so there is less motivation in the Restriction Language grammar for concurrent transformational decomposition. In the next chapter (section 3.3) we shall consider in detail how certain semantic constraints can be readily incorporated into the surface grammar.

Separating the grammatical constraints from the construction of deep structure also offers the advantage of *modularity*. Very large natural language systems will be more comprehensible and manageable if they can be divided into components which interact only through limited, precisely defined interfaces – in this case, the parse tree. Generally when these components are separated they are designed to be executed sequentially. However, it is possible to arrange these components so that they can be specified separately and then run either sequentially or concurrently. One such organization is Woods' 'cascaded ATNs' (Woods 1980), which has been used for the RUS grammar (Bobrow and Webber 1980).

2.6.5 *PROLOG*

In general in this volume we have paid little attention to the choice of programming language used to implement language analysis procedures (in matter of fact, most of the systems we have discussed are implemented in LISP, which has become the standard programming language for artificial intelligence applications in the United States). In giving examples of specific approaches, we have examined some special-purpose languages and notations, such as Restriction Language and Woods' ATN notation. We have, however, tried to keep our focus on the linguistic, organizational, and algorithmic issues which we believe to be primary.

Having stated this principle, we shall now proceed to violate it. We shall examine in this subsection the programming language PROLOG.[15] PROLOG, like LISP, is suitable as a general-purpose symbol-manipulation language; at the

---

[15] Readers wishing a more leisurely and far more thorough introduction to PROLOG can consult Clocksin and Mellish (1981).

same time, it permits a very simple, direct implementation of augmented context-free grammar. Context-free analysis, in effect, is available as a special case of the general control structure provided by PROLOG.

PROLOG is very different in its control structure from the usual programming languages. The basic element of a PROLOG program is a particular type of predicate calculus formula called a *Horn* or *definite* clause.[16] Executing a PROLOG program consists of finding a proof for one formula using the other formulas in the program.

The simplest type of PROLOG clause is a 'fact' or 'assertion', which asserts some predicate of one or more individuals. For example,

>   mother(mary,alex).

asserts that Mary is the mother of Alex (following the conventions of DEC-10 PROLOG, names of predicates and constants like 'mary' begin with a lower-case letter; variables begin with a capital letter). A PROLOG program will typically have a 'data base' with many such facts:

>   mother(mary,alex).
>   mother(mary,jane).
>   mother(jane,henry).
>   father(adam,alex).
>   father(horatio,henry).

To get a PROLOG program to do something, we ask a question:

>   ?- mother(mary,jane).

and PROLOG will reply

>   yes

So far, not too exciting – PROLOG just checked whether the question was in the data base. We can include a variable in the question

>   ?-mother(jane,X).

This means 'is there some value of X such that mother(jane,X) is true?' In our data base there is, so PROLOG responds with the value

>   X = henry

This is still not much more than a retrieval system. The power of PROLOG is derived from its ability to state rules or implications. For example, the rule

>   parent (X,Y) :- father(X,Y).

states that (for all X and Y) X is a parent of Y *if* X is the father of Y; in other words, a PROLOG rule is an assertion that the right side of the rule implies the

---

[16] A brief exposition of predicate calculus is given in section 3.1.2.

left side of the rule. By itself, this rule is discriminatory, so we add a second rule[17]

parent(X,Y) :- mother(X,Y).

The effect of these two rules together is to assert that if either *X* is the father of *Y* or *X* is the mother of *Y* then *X* is the parent of *Y*. We can make use of these rules by asking the question

?-parent(mary,jane).

PROLOG responds by looking for clauses relevant to the question – either facts in the data base or rules whose left-hand side matches the question. The first such clause it finds is the rule 'parent (X,Y) :- father (X,Y)'. PROLOG *binds* the variables X and Y in this rule to the corresponding arguments in the question:

parent(mary,jane).
     ↕ ↕
parent(X , Y) :- father (X,Y).

producing the rule

parent(mary,jane) :- father(mary,jane).

PROLOG then tries to verify the right side of this rule, 'father(mary,jane)'. No rule or fact matches 'father(mary,jane)', however, so this rule fails. PROLOG thereupon *backtracks*, trying to find another rule to match the question, 'parent(mary,jane)'. There is another rule, 'parent(X,Y):-mother(X,Y)', so X and Y are bound in that rule, yielding

parent(mary,jane) :- mother(mary,jane).

Now 'mother(mary,jane)' is in the data base, so this rule succeeds, thus verifying the initial question 'parent(mary,jane)'. PROLOG responds by printing

yes

The right side of a rule may also contain a conjunction of goals (a *goal*, usually called an *atom* in predicate logic, is a predicate symbol along with its arguments). A rule of the form

A :- *B, C.*

where *A*, *B*, and *C* are goals, asserts that *A* is true if both *B* and *C* are true. For example,

sibling(X,Y) :- parent(Z,X), parent(Z,Y).

---

[17] Variable names are local to an individual rule, so we could just as well have chosen different variable names for the second rule, such as I and J:
    parent(I,J) :- mother(I,J).

means that X is a sibling of Y if there exists a Z such that Z is the parent of X and the parent of Y. If we then ask

?- sibling (alex,jane).

PROLOG will locate this rule and bind X and Y, producing

sibling(alex,jane) :- parent(Z,alex), parent(Z,jane).

Next, it will try to verify the first goal on the right side, 'parent(Z,alex)'. It finds the first rule for parent,

parent(X,Y) :- father(X,Y).

and binds X to Z and Y to alex to get

parent(Z,alex) :- father(Z,alex).

'father(Z,alex)' will succeed by matching 'father(adam,alex)' in the data base, binding Z to adam. This verifies 'parent(Z,alex)'. Returning to the rule for sibling, PROLOG can now proceed to the second goal, which (now that Z has been bound to adam) is 'parent(adam,jane)'. This goal will eventually fail, after trying both rules for parent. PROLOG will now backtrack and try to find another match for the first goal with a different binding for Z. There are no other values (besides Z = adam) which satisfy 'father(Z,alex)', so PROLOG tries the next rule for parent:

parent(X,Y) :- mother(X,Y).

With variables suitably bound, this becomes

parent(Z,alex) :- mother(Z,alex).

which is satisfied with Z bound to mary. We proceed once again back to the rule for sibling and on to the second goal, which is now 'parent(mary,jane)'. This term eventually succeeds, thus verifying 'sibling(alex,jane)'.

If you have managed to wade through all this binding and backtracking, you may be wondering what all this has to do with augmented context-free analysis. The answer is simply that the task of analyzing a sentence with respect to a grammar can be stated directly in terms of PROLOG rules such as the ones just considered (Colmerauer 1978). Such a formulation of a grammar is called a *definite clause grammar* (Pereira and Warren 1980).

We can view a production such as

<S> ::= <NP> <VP>

in the following terms: a sequence of words constitutes an s if there exists some division of the sequence such that the words before the dividing point constitute an NP and those after the dividing point constitute a VP. We will make each grammar symbol (s, NP, VP) a PROLOG predicate, so that the PROLOG rule will have the basic form s(...) :- np(...),vp(...).

We must still decide what to put into the argument slots in order to capture the notion of a sequence being split into two subsequences. There are several possibilities; the one usually adopted associates two arguments with each predicate:

np(W,R)

is true if W is a sequence of words, if there is a subsequence constituting an NP at the beginning of W, and if the remainder of W following the NP is R. For example, we would expect

np([the,brown,fox,eats,chickens],[eats,chickens])

to be true if *np* is suitably defined (in PROLOG, a sequence of elements is enclosed in brackets: [...]). This argument structure may seem a bit convoluted, but it makes it easy to assemble rules. For example,

<S> ::= <NP> <VP>

would become

s(X,Y) :- np(X,Z), vp(Z,Y).

You can think of this as follows: to see if X is a sentence (with 'leftover' Y), we first send it to *np*, which chops off the words corresponding to an NP and returns the remainder in Z; *vp* takes Z, chops off the words which correspond to a VP, and returns what's left in Y. If the BNF rule has several options,

<VP> ::= <VERB> <NP> | <VERB> <PP>

we write several PROLOG rules

vp(X,Y) :- verb(X,Z), np(Z,Y).
vp(X,Y) :- verb(X,Z), pp(Z,Y).

and PROLOG will try each one in turn. Rules involving terminal symbols must be translated somewhat differently. For example,

<VERB> ::= eats

would become

verb([eats|X],X).

This rule says that *verb* will succeed if the first argument consists of the word 'eats' followed by some sequence of words 'X'; this remainder will be returned as the value of the second argument.

Using these techniques, we can take a simple context-free grammar such as

<S>	::= <NP> <VP>
<NP>	::= <NOUN> | <ARTICLE> <ADJ> <NOUN>

```
<VP>        ::= <VERB> <NP> | <VERB> <PP>
<PP>        ::= <PREP> <NP>
<ARTICLE> ::= the | a
<ADJ>       ::= brown
<NOUN>    ::= chicken | chickens | fox | foxes
<VERB>::=::= eat | eats | yearn | yearns
<PREP>      ::= for
```

and convert it into a set of PROLOG rules:

```
s(X,Y)   :- np(X,Z), vp(Z,Y).
np(X,Y):- noun(X,Y).
np(X,Y):- article(X,W), adj(W,Z), noun(Z,Y).
vp(X,Y):- verb(X,Z), np(Z,Y).
vp(X,Y):- verb(X,Z), pp(Z,Y).
pp(X,Y):- prep(X,Z), np(Z,Y).
article    ([the      |X],X).
article    ([a        |X],X).
adj        ([brown  |X],X).
noun       ([chicken |X],X).
noun       ([chickens|X,]X).
noun       ([fox      |X],X).
noun       ([foxes   |X],X).
verb       ([eat      |X],X).
verb       ([eats     |X],X).
verb       ([yearn   |X],X).
verb       ([yearns  |X],X).
prep       ([for      |X],X).
```

Once we have rewritten the context-free grammar in this form, we can test it by asking a question such as

?- s([the,brown,fox,eats,chickens],[ ])

(here [ ] denotes the empty list; this indicates that the sequence of words is to be analyzed as an s with no words left over). PROLOG will analyze the sentence by matching, advancing, and backtracking as we described in our 'sibling' example. The procedure is exactly the same as that followed by the top-down parser described in section 2.4.2. If an analysis is found (as it should be for this grammar), PROLOG will respond

yes

and we can go home satisfied.

What's so great about this? After all, people were writing context-free parsers long before PROLOG came on the scene. Well, for one thing, it's quite elegant. Here we have a programming language with a simple control structure which turns out to be just sufficient for context-free language analysis without requiring us to write our own parsing procedure.[18] Because the grammar is a PROLOG program which can be compiled, it's potentially quite efficient. Perhaps most important, the fact that the grammar is a program provides a natural way of augmenting the grammar, by adding arguments to the predicates or by adding goals to a rule. We don't have to have one formalism for the context-free grammar and a separate one for the augmentations.

Consider, for example, augmenting a PROLOG grammar to check for number agreement between subject and verb. We would add to the predicates *np* and *vp* a third argument whose value would be either 'singular' or 'plural';

   np(X,Y,singular)

would match an NP with a singular noun, for instance. We would similarly add a third argument, with value 'singular' or 'plural', to *noun* and *verb*. The rules for *np* would insure that the value of this 'number' argument for the *np* is the same as that for the *noun* it contains:

   np(X,Y,NUM) :- noun(X,Y,NUM).
   np(X,Y,NUM) :- article(X,W), adj(W,Z), noun(Z,Y,NUM).

(so that a singular noun phrase must contain a singular noun, for example). Likewise for *vp* and the *verb* it contains:

   vp(X,Y,NUM) :- verb(X,Z,NUM), np(Z,Y).
   vp(X,Y,NUM) :- verb(X,Z,NUM), pp(Z,Y).

The noun and verb definitions would explicitly specify 'singular' or 'plural' as their third argument:

   noun   ([fox |X],X,singular).
   noun   ([foxes|X],X,plural).
   verb   ([eat |X],X,plural).
   verb   ([eats |X],X,singular).
      etc.

We can then enforce number agreement simply by associating the same variable with this argument to *np* and *vp* in the rule for *s*:

   s(X,Y) :- np(X,Z,NUM), vp(Z,Y,NUM).

The PROLOG rules can also be extended in order to build structure during the parsing process. This structure could be a parse tree, with grammatical constraints tested by operations on this tree, in the manner of Restriction

---

[18] This is not accidental. Colmerauer, who was instrumental in the development of PROLOG, had been concerned with natural language analysis, and the relation between parsing and proof procedures (Colmerauer 1978).

Language grammar (Hirschman and Puder 1982); transformations would then be implemented by a separate set of PROLOG rules. Alternatively, the parsing rules can immediately generate a deep structure, in the manner of most ATN grammars (Pereira and Warren 1980), or even a logical form (Colmerauer 1978); most PROLOG grammars have taken one of these approaches.

PROLOG is a relatively new language. Work over the past several years has demonstrated that it is an effective vehicle for the development of small natural language grammars. It remains to be seen whether it offers sufficient flexibility for very large natural language systems.

2.7   Other phrase-structure grammars

Think back a moment over where we have come in the last three sections. After reviewing the various types of phrase-structure grammars, we considered context-free grammar in detail but found it inadequate for capturing all of natural language grammar. We then turned to transformational grammar, which was difficult to implement, and to augmented context-free grammar, which was less elegant but computationally more tractable. In taking this path we neglected another alternative – using more powerful (context-sensitive or unrestricted) phrase-structure grammars. We shall consider that alternative, and others relating to phrase-structure grammar, in this section.

2.7.1   Context-sensitive grammar

After context-free grammar, the next more powerful class in the Chomsky hierarchy is context-sensitive grammar. We have considered context-sensitive grammar briefly in connection with the base component of transformational grammar (section 2.5.2). We noted there that the contextual constraints of context-sensitive grammar, while effective at deep structure, have not proven effective in capturing grammatical constraints and regularities in terms of surface structure trees. As a result, context-sensitive grammars have been little used by themselves for natural language description and analysis.

As far as we know, only one major parsing system has been developed using a context-sensitive phrase structure grammar. This was DEACON, Direct English Access and Control, which was designed as a natural language interface to a command, control, and information retrieval system for the Army and was developed at General Electric (Craig *et al.* 1966). DEACON is notable not so much for using a context-sensitive grammar as it is for being one of the first systems to provide a flexible, systematic interaction between the parser and the semantic component. Woods has noted (Woods 1970a) that the parser used in the DEACON project may produce redundant parses, and has given a parsing algorithm for context-sensitive languages which remedies this deficiency.

2.7.2   Unrestricted phrase-structure grammar

A number of natural language systems have used grammars composed of unrestricted phrase-structure rewriting rules. Since unrestricted rewriting rules, like transformational grammars, can be used to define any recursively enumerable language, they may be sufficient for analyzing both surface and deep structure. As with transformational grammars, it will in practice be necessary to impose some constraint (such as ordering) on the rules, so that the language defined is recursive; otherwise a parser will never be able to determine whether some sentences are grammatical or not.

One parser for unrestricted rewriting rules was described by Kay (1967). This parser included a number of mechanisms for restricting the application of rules, such as rule ordering, specifying part of the structure dominated by one element of the rule, or requiring the equality of the structures dominated by two elements. These mechanisms do not increase the generative power of the grammars, but are designed to make grammars easier to write. Kay described how his parser could be used to effect some reverse transformations.

Kay's parser was incorporated into a system called REL (Rapidly Extensible Language) developed by Thompson, Dostert, *et al.* at the California Institute of Technology (Thompson *et al.* 1969; Dostert and Thompson 1971). Kay's original parser was augmented by allowing a set of binary features to be associated with each node, including feature tests as part of the rewrite rules, and permitting more general restrictions where the features were inadequate. The REL system was designed to support a number of grammars, each interfaced to its own data base. One of these is REL English, which analyzes a subset of English into a set of subject-verb-object-time modifier deep structures; this grammar has 239 rules. In support of the use of general rewrite rules with features, they note that only 29 of the 239 rules required constraints which could not be conveniently stated in terms of feature tests. This is also a factor in efficiency, since binary feature tests can be performed very quickly.

Another system which uses unrestricted rewriting rules with optional conditions on the elements is the 'Q' system developed by Colmerauer (1970). This system has been used in a machine translation project at the University of Montreal (Kittredge *et al.* 1973).

2.7.3   Grammar and metagrammar

As an alternative to having more powerful grammars, we can consider more powerful ways of *specifying* grammars. Until now we have taken for granted that the way to specify a phrase-structure grammar is to write down its productions, one by one. Instead of this, we could imagine a set of rules which generate the productions of the grammar, in the same sense that the grammar generates the language. We could call these rules *metarules*, and the set of metarules a *metagrammar*. As a simple example of such a metarule, recall that in the BNF version of the linguistic string grammar (section 2.4.1) we had the rules

$$<LNR> ::= <LN> <*N> <RN>$$

and

$$<LVR> ::= <LV> <*V> <RV>$$

These represented a noun and an untensed verb, respectively, with their left and right adjuncts. These rules fit the pattern

$$<LxR> ::= <Lx> <*x> <Rx>$$

for word category x with its left and right adjuncts. We could give formal recognition to this regularity by allowing in our grammar a specification such as

$$<LxR> ::= <Lx> <*x> <Rx>, \quad x = N, V$$

This type of metarule, which becomes an actual production of the grammar when a value is substituted for x, is called a production *schema*. In our tiny grammar, this schema doesn't save much – one schema replaces two rules – but in a full linguistic string grammar, with lots of LxRs, the savings would be substantial.

Metarules may take many forms, but they have a common ultimate objective – to capture regularities in the language. We noted early on that context-free grammars were unable to capture many of the regularities of natural language; we may be able to characterize English (to a fair approximation) by a context-free grammar, but the grammar required would be enormous and unrevealing. Transformational grammar overcomes this by introducing rules (transformations) which interrelate sentences (or phrase-structure trees). Metagrammars try to capture the same regularities through metarules which interrelate productions in a context-free grammar. We shall consider a specific example of this in a moment.

The interest in using metagrammars for describing *programming* languages was sharply stimulated by the work on ALGOL 68. The type of grammar used to specify ALGOL 68 was called a Winjgaarden or W-grammar. Roughly speaking, a W-grammar consists of a set of rule schemata such as the one given above; however, the values which may be substituted for the variables in a schema (x in the example above) may themselves be specified by a context-free grammar. The result is a potentially infinite set of context-free rules. W-grammar is a very powerful formalism – like unrestricted rewriting rules, W-grammar can define any recursively enumerable language.

de Chastellier and Colmerauer (1969) investigated the possibility of using

W-grammars for natural language analysis and machine translation. They showed how portions of transformational grammars of English and French may be rewritten as W-grammars, with metarules in the W-grammar taking the place of the transformations. Such W-grammars, however, do not appear to have been used in any operational natural language system, presumably because of the difficulty of parsing with respect to a W-grammar.

More recently, Gazdar has proposed a system of metarules for describing natural language grammar (Gazdar 1981; Gazdar, Pullman, and Sag 1982). His approach, which has been taken up by a number of linguists, is called Generalized Phrase Structure Grammar (GPSG). In GPSG, as in W-grammar, the metarules generate a context-free grammar which in turn generates the language of interest. Care has been taken in GPSG to insure that the context-free grammar will be finite, so that the task of sentence analysis will be tractable. Specifically, there is a 'natural' (but not necessarily very efficient) approach to parsing GPSGs: generate the context-free grammar and then use a context-free parser.

Gazdar distinguishes in his formalism between rule schemata and metarules. A rule schema is a production with variables, such as the example with $<\text{L}x\text{R}>$ we gave above. A metarule, on the other hand, is a command of the following form: for every production P in the grammar matching a specified pattern, add a new production P' which is obtained by modifying P in a specified way. These metarules are in several ways analogous to transformations, but while transformations operate on trees to create new trees, metarules operate on productions to create new productions.

An example may clarify this analogy. Suppose we wanted to include in our grammar agentless passives – passive sentences without a 'by' phrase (e.g., 'Lincoln was shot.'). Within the small transformational grammar presented in section 2.5.2, we could do this by modifying the passive transformation we gave there. The agentless passive transformation would be

	NP	AUX	V	NP
structural index:	NP	AUX	V	NP
structural changes:	4	2	be + en + 3	0

The net effect of this rule on the set of allowable surface structures is to delete one NP from the VP. We can capture this effect within GPSG by the following metarule:

> For every production of the form
> $<\text{VP}> ::= <^*\text{V}> <\text{NP}> \text{X}$
> add a production of the form
> $<\text{VP}> ::= \text{be} <^*\text{VEN}> \text{X}$

(where VEN is the word class for past participles). The 'X' in the metarule matches any sequence of zero or more symbols. Thus if our initial set of productions includes

$$<VP> ::= <*V> <NP>$$

and

$$<VP> ::= <*V> <NP> <PP>$$

the metarule will add the productions

$$<VP> ::= be <*VEN>$$

and

$$<VP ::= be <*VEN> <PP>$$

thus generating sentences such as 'Lincoln was shot.' and 'A book was given to Mary.'. (The fact that the subject of the passive sentence plays the same role as the direct object of the active sentence is accounted for by a corresponding semantic metarule, which we shall not discuss here.)

GPSG has been used as the basis for a language analysis system being developed by Hewlett-Packard (Gawron *et al.* 1982). Their system takes the 'natural' approach of expanding out the context-free grammar before analyzing any sentences. A recent version of the grammar has an initial set of 40 productions and 10 metarules; applying the metarules yields a grammar of 283 productions. A standard context-free parser is then used to analyze sentences with this grammar. The system has been applied as a natural language front-end for querying a relational data base.

2.8 Analyzing adjuncts

We turn now from our general survey of parsing procedures to an examination of some specific features of natural language. The features we shall be concerned with are ones which do not fit naturally into the standard syntax analysis procedures we have described, but rather call for some systematic change to either the parsing procedure or the form of the grammar, or to both.

The first class of constructions we shall look at are adjuncts or modifying phrases. We shall be concerned in particular with certain classes of adjuncts which give rise to a high degree of syntactic ambiguity. For example, in the sentence

I saw the man in the park with a telescope.

it isn't clear whether 'with a telescope' modifies 'park', 'man', or 'saw', or whether 'in the park' modifies 'man' or 'saw' (not to mention the ambiguity of whether 'saw' is the past tense of 'see' or means 'am sawing'). More prepositional phrases make the situation even worse, as in the sentence

I fixed the pipe under the sink in the bathroom with a wrench.

In such sentences, the host of a prepositional phrase (the word it modifies) may be either the verb, the object, or the noun in any of the preceding prepositional phrases. A similar situation arises with other adjuncts which may end in nouns, such as relative clauses. When such adjuncts appear in sequence, the degree of syntactic ambiguity goes up at least as the factorial of the number of adjuncts.

If no semantic or pragmatic restrictions are applied during parsing, and we have our system generate all possible syntactic analyses of a sentence, we will end up with dozens of parses for sentences of moderate size; this is hopelessly inefficient. If we do apply such restrictions during syntactic analysis, the parser will still have to generate a number of partial sentence analyses (with the adjuncts in the various possible positions), most of which will (hopefully) be knocked out by the restrictions; this is feasible but still moderately inefficient.

Another, potentially more efficient solution has the parser identify the adjuncts and list for each adjunct the words it could be modifying, without generating a separate parse for each possibility. The ambiguities associated with the adjuncts are thus factored out. Semantic and pragmatic information may then be used to select for each adjunct its most likely or acceptable host. This may be done either during the syntax analysis (Woods 1973; Simmons and Bennett-Novak 1975) or after the syntax phase is complete (Borgida 1975; Hobbs and Grishman 1976).

In most cases where the ambiguities have been factored out, this has been done by augmenting a traditional parse tree structure with special links to connect an adjunct with the various words it might modify. More recently there have been suggestions for basically different representations of the output of syntactic analysis, representations which – unlike parse trees – do not unambiguously specify the position of each phrase within the overall sentence structure (Marcus, Hindle, and Fleck 1983). Such representations fit naturally with an approach which postpones the resolution of adjunct placement ambiguities until after parsing.

2.9   Analyzing coordinate conjunction

Coordinate conjunction (constructions involving 'and', 'or', etc.) poses two types of problems for the computational linguist. First, it greatly increases the number of possible structures which may appear in a parse tree. Second, like adjunction, it frequently leads to a high degree of syntactic ambiguity.

Let us consider first the problem of the new structures introduced by conjunction. The allowed patterns of conjoinings in a sentence are quite regular. Loosely speaking, a sequence of elements in the sentence tree may be followed by a conjunction and by some or all of the elements immediately preceding the conjunction. For example, if the top-level sentence structure is subject–verb–object and an 'and' appears after the object, the allowed patterns of conjoinings include subject–verb–object–and–subject–verb–object ('I drank milk and Mary ate cake.'), subject–verb–object–and–verb–object ('I drank milk and ate cake.'), and subject–verb–object–and–object ('I drank milk and seltzer.'). There are certain exceptions, known as gapping phenomena, in which one of the elements following the conjunction may be omitted; for example, subject–verb–object–and–subject–object ('I drank milk and Mary seltzer.').

We can extend the context-free component of our surface grammar to account for these patterns. For example, in place of the production

$$<SENTENCE> ::= <SUBJECT> <VERB> <OBJECT>$$

we would have the set of productions

$$<SENTENCE> ::= <SUBJECT> <CA_1> <VERB> <CA_2> <OBJECT>$$
$$<CA_3>$$

$$<CA_1> \quad ::= \text{and} <SUBJECT> <CA_1> \mid$$
$$\textit{null}$$

$$<CA_2> \quad ::= \text{and} <SUBJECT> <CA_1> <VERB> <CA_2> \mid$$
$$\text{and} <VERB> <CA_2> \mid$$
$$\textit{null}$$

$$<CA_3> \quad ::= \text{and} <SUBJECT> <CA_1> <VERB> <CA_2>$$
$$<OBJECT> <CA_3> \mid$$
$$\text{and} <VERB> <CA_2> <OBJECT> <CA_3> \mid$$
$$\text{and} <OBJECT> <CA_3> \mid$$
$$\textit{null}$$

(this does not include gapping). The trouble with coordinate conjunctions is that they can occur almost anywhere in the structure of a sentence. Thus the same changes which we made above to the definition of SENTENCE would have to be made to all (or at least many) of the productions in the grammar. Clearly, such an extension to the grammar could increase its size by perhaps an order of magnitude.

Instead of adding all these productions to the grammar, we could use a mechanism which automatically generates the additional elements and productions needed to account for conjunction as required during the parsing process. When a conjunction is encountered in the sentence, the normal parsing procedure is interrupted, a special conjunction node is inserted in the parse tree (such as the CA_n nodes above), and the appropriate definition is generated for this conjunction node. This definition allows for all the alternative conjoined element sequences, like the definitions of the CA_n shown above. Conjoinings not fitting the basic pattern, such as gappings, are still included explicitly in the grammar. An interrupt mechanism of this sort is part of the Linguistic String Project parser (Sager 1967). A similar mechanism is included in Woods' augmented transition network parser (Woods 1973) and a number of other systems.

This solves the problem of correcting the context-free grammar for conjunction, but in an augmented context-free system the context-free component is generally only a small part of the total system. The task remains of modifying both the routines which enforce grammatical constraints and the transformations (or the structure-building operations of the ATN) to account for conjunction. Since practically every routine which examines a parse tree is potentially affected by conjunction, this task may be enormous. Fortunately, many of these modifications follow a fixed pattern: most grammatical constraints apply distributively to conjoined structures. That is, if we have a grammatical constraint between two elements A and B in a parse tree, and in a particular sentence A is conjoined (producing the structure $(A$ and $A')$), the constraint will be satisfied if it is separately satisfied for the pairs A B and A' B. In the Linguistic String Project grammar, elements of the parse tree are located by a set of routines; if an element is conjoined, the routine returns a set of values, and a non-deterministic programming mechanism executes the remainder of the restriction for each one of these values (Raze 1976). In this way most of the restrictions do not have to be rewritten for conjunction; only those restrictions which are specially affected by conjunction, such as number agreement, have to be modified.

In addition to these problems of generating the appropriate structures, conjunction gives rise to many problems of syntactic ambiguity which may be difficult to resolve. Unless there is an explicit scope marker in the sentence ('both', 'either', 'neither'), the scope of a conjunction may be hard to determine. Consider for example

> The victim was struck on the left hand and neck.

– does 'left' modify 'neck' or only 'hand'? Or how about

> The patient reported shortness of breath and chest pain.

– did the patient report 'shortness of chest pain'?

2.10   Parsing with probability and graded acceptability

In all the systems described above, a sharp line was drawn between correct and incorrect parses: a terminal node either did or did not match the next word in the sentence; an analysis of a phrase was either acceptable or unacceptable. There are circumstances under which we would want to relax these requirements. For one thing, in analyzing connected speech, the segmentation and identification of words can never be done with complete certainty. At best, one can say that a certain sound has some probability of being one phoneme and some other probability of being another phoneme; some expected phonemes may be lost entirely in the sound received. Consequently, one may associate some number with each terminal node, indicating the probability or quality of match; non-terminal nodes will be assigned some value based on the values of the terminal nodes beneath. Another circumstance arises in natural language systems which are sophisticated enough to realize that syntactic and semantic restrictions are rarely all-or-nothing affairs, and that some restrictions are stronger than others. For example, the nominative–accusative distinction has become quite weak for relative pronouns (?'The man who I met yesterday') but remains strong for personal pronouns (*'The man whom me met yesterday'). As a result a parser which wants to get the best analysis even if every analysis violates some constraint must associate a measure of grammaticality or acceptability with the analyses of portions of the sentence, and ultimately with the analyses of the entire sentence.

In principle, one could generate every sentence analysis with a non-zero acceptability or probability of match, and then select the best analysis obtained. Hobbs (1974) has described a modification to the bottom-up nodal spans parsing algorithm which uses this approach. Wilks (1975) uses an essentially similar technique in his language analyzer based on 'preference semantics'.

In a speech-understanding system, however, there are too many possible matches to make such an approach (generating all possible parses and selecting the best) practical. In consequence, the research in speech under-standing (and particularly the ARPA-funded efforts of 1971–76) stimulated the development of several new algorithms.

An early effort was the 'best-first' parser developed by Paxton and Robinson of SRI (Paxton and Robinson 1973). Their procedure involved a modification of the standard top-down serial parsing algorithm for context-free grammars. The standard algorithm generates one possible parse tree until it gets stuck (generates a terminal node which does not match the next sentence word); it then 'backs up' to try another alternative. The best-first procedure instead tries all alternatives in parallel. A measure is associated with each alternative path, indicating the likelihood that this analysis matches the sentence processed so far and that it can be extended to a complete sentence analysis. At each moment, the path with the highest likelihood is extended; if its measure falls below that of some other path, the parser shifts its attention to that other path.

This early parser gradually developed into a more dynamic system which was used in the later SRI speech-understanding systems. It was capable of working left-to-right, right-to-left, or middle-out and able to merge common parts of alternative theories.

When a standard top-down parser moves forward through the sentence, building the parse tree, it alternates between two types of operation: working top-down, it creates the nodes of the parse tree; working bottom-up, it matches words of the sentence and 'completes' nodes of the tree. In the parser of the later SRI speech-understanding systems, these two operations were performed by two tasks which are scheduled in alternation: the 'predict task' and the 'word task'. Incomplete parse tree nodes – nodes not yet checked against the sentence – are called *predictions*; completed nodes, which match a portion of the sentence, are called *phrases*. Given a phrase, the predict task can create predictions to extend the phrase to the left or right. To extend a phrase to the left (right), the task identifies all productions which contain that phrase and looks at the symbol preceding (following) that phrase in those productions. It creates predictions for those symbols and for symbols derived by expanding those symbols, continuing until a terminal symbol is reached. Given a prediction of a terminal symbol, the word task can compare it with the utterance and, if it matches, create a corresponding phrase. Whenever a 'complete phrase' is created (one equal to the right-hand side of a production), a new phrase can be started (equal to the left-hand side of that production). If the analysis is successful, a phrase will ultimately be created corresponding to the root node and subsuming the entire sentence.

Two values are computed for each phrase. The *score* represents the quality of the phrase. For a terminal phrase, it indicates how well the terminal symbol matches the utterance. For other phrases, the score is computed by a function associated with the production which combines the scores of its constituents with various linguistic factors (the score is reduced if grammatical constraints are violated). The score is independent of a phrase's context in the parse tree. The *rating* of a phrase is an estimate of the best score of an analysis of the complete sentence which uses that phrase. It is computed using the scores of other phrases which may combine with this one in forming a complete sentence analysis. The phrase ratings are used to determine task priorities – to select which predictions to make or which words to try to match next.

3   Semantic analysis

What is the objective of semantic analysis? We could say that it is to determine what a sentence *means*, but by itself this is not a very helpful answer. It may be more enlightening to say that, for declarative sentences, semantics seeks to determine the conditions under which a sentence is true or, almost equivalently, what the inference rules are among sentences of the language. Characterizing the semantics of questions and imperatives is a bit more problematic, but we can see the connection with declaratives by noting that, roughly speaking, questions are requests to be told whether a sentence is true (or to be told the values for which a certain sentence is true) and imperatives are requests to make a sentence true.

People who study natural language semantics find it desirable (or even necessary) to define a formal language with a simple semantics, thus changing the problem to one of determining the mapping from natural language into this formal language. What properties should this formal language have (which natural language does not)? It should

> *be unambiguous
> *have simple rules of interpretation and inference, and in particular
> *have a logical structure determined by the form of the sentence

We shall examine some such languages, the languages of the various logics, shortly.

Of course, when we build a practical natural language system our interest is generally not just finding out if sentences are true or false. We usually want the system to do something in response to our input – retrieve some data, move a robot arm, etc. In general, this will mean translating the natural language input into the formal language of a data base retrieval system, a robot command system, etc. In comparison with natural language, these formal languages will have the properties just cited, although their rules of interpretation will not be as simple as those of a logic. Thus we can expect considerable similarity between the tasks of translating into such a 'practical language' and translating into a logical formalism.

Furthermore, as natural language interfaces become more sophisticated, the amount of inferencing they do in the course of processing an input increases. This increases the motivation for using a logical formalism (or something equivalent) as an internal representation, and having the semantic analyzer translate from natural language (or from the output of the syntactic analyzer) into the formalism.

3.1 Formal languages for meaning representation

Since classical times, philosophers have studied logical argumentation in order to see what characterizes sound arguments, such as

> given that: All men are mortal.
>   Socrates is a man.
> we may conclude: Socrates is mortal.

in contrast to unsound arguments, such as

> given that: No man is mortal.
>   Snoopy is not a man.
> we may conclude: Snoopy is mortal.

These studies have led to the development of *symbolic logic*, with formal rules of inference.

In this section we shall examine various types of logic, and see how the formal languages associated with these logics may be used to represent the meanings of sentences. We shall also examine alternative representations used in computational linguistics programs (e.g., semantic networks) and their relation to logical expressions. Many texts are available with a rigorous treatment of symbolic logic; for a less formal, broader treatment we particularly recommend the book by Allwood, Andersson, and Dahl (1977).

3.1.1 *Propositional logic*

We shall begin by examining the simplest symbolic logic, propositional logic. Propositional logic aims to characterize arguments such as

> given that: If it is raining you will get wet.
>   It is raining.
> we may conclude: You will get wet.

We observe that, as long as we preserve the general structure of the argument, including the 'if . . . then . . .' connective in the first line, we may change the sentences making up the argument and still have a valid argument. For example,

> given that: If it is noon then Jon is sleeping.
>   It is noon.
> we may conclude: Jon is sleeping.

is a valid argument.

From such examples we may abstract a general rule of inference. A *proposition* is a declarative sentence which may be either true or false (e.g., 'It is raining.', 'Jon is sleeping.'). Let P and Q represent propositions. Let '$P \rightarrow Q$' represent 'if P then Q'. Then the following is a valid inference:

given that: $P \rightarrow Q$
                     P
we may conclude: Q

(This rule is called *modus ponens*.) Similarly, from arguments such as

given that: It is sunny or it is cloudy.
                     It is not sunny.
we may conclude: It is cloudy.

we can abstract the pattern:

given that: $P \vee Q$
                     $\sim P$
we may conclude: Q

where '$\vee$' represents 'or' and '$\sim$' represents 'not'.

'$P \rightarrow Q$', '$P \vee Q$', and '$\sim P$' are all examples of formulas in propositional logic; we shall also use the symbol '$\wedge$', representing 'and'. Formulas of propositional logic are formed according to the following rules:

(1) A proposition is a formula.
(2) If G is a formula, $(\sim G)$ is a formula.
(3) If G and H are formulas, $(G \wedge H)$, $(G \vee H)$ and $(G \rightarrow H)$ are formulas.
(4) All formulas are generated by applying the above rules.

The semantics of these formulas is quite simple. Given the truth value of the propositions in a formula, we can determine the truth value of the formula by the following rules:

(1) The value of $\sim G$ is false if G is true, and true if G is false.
(2) The value of $G \wedge H$ is true if both G and H are true, otherwise false.
(3) The value of $G \vee H$ is true if either G or H is true, otherwise false.
(4) The value of $G \rightarrow H$ is true if either G is false or H is true, otherwise it is false.

The $\sim$, $\wedge$, $\vee$, and $\rightarrow$ operators correspond to at least some uses of 'not' (or 'it is not the case that'), 'and', 'or', and 'if...then...' to combine complete English sentences into larger sentences. We used these correspondences in formalizing the arguments given above. Some of the meaning of the English connectives is not captured, however (for example, the use of 'and' to mean 'and then', or the usual use of 'if A then B', which conveys some causal connection between A and B – so-called strict implication rather than material implication).

3.1.2 Predicate logic

Recall the argument with which we began this section:

> given that: All men are mortal.
>   Socrates is a man.
> we may conclude: Socrates is mortal.

We cannot capture the structure of this argument in propositional logic. Why? At the level of propositional logic, each of these sentences is a separate proposition – we cannot represent what these sentences have in common. In order to formalize this argument, we must be able to represent the fact that 'Socrates is a man.' asserts some predicate 'is a man' of some object 'Socrates' and that 'Socrates is mortal.' asserts another predicate, 'is mortal', *about the same object*. In order to do so, we must turn to a more powerful logic, predicate logic.

In predicate logic we have *terms* and *predicates*. A term is something whose value is some object in the universe; for example, 'Socrates' is a term. Predicates are functions from terms to the values *true* and *false*. For example, if 'M' represents the predicate 'is mortal', M(Socrates) represents the sentence 'Socrates is mortal.'. We say that 'Socrates' is the argument of the predicate 'M', and we call the expression 'M(Socrates)' an *atom*. An atom in predicate logic corresponds to a proposition in propositional logic.

We will want to retain the logical connectives we had in propositional logic: $\sim$, $\wedge$, $\vee$, $\rightarrow$. In addition, we need a mechanism for representing general statements such as 'All men are mortal.' or 'Every man has a father.' For this purpose we introduce *universal* and *existential quantifiers*. Let '$e(x)$' be a predicate logic expression in which the variable 'x' appears in place of a constant term (such as 'Socrates') as the argument of one or more predicates. Then

$$(\forall x)\ e(x)$$

is true if, for every object, if we assign that object as the value of 'x', the expression '$e(x)$' is true. Similarly,

$$(\exists x)\ e(x)$$

is true if there is some object such that, if we assign that object as the value of 'x', the expression '$e(x)$' is true. For example, if 'M' represents 'is mortal',

$$(\forall x)\ M(x)$$

means 'everything is mortal'. 'All men are mortal' can be represented as 'for all x, if x is a man then x is mortal':

$$(\forall x)\ P(x) \rightarrow M(x)$$

where 'P' represents 'is a man'. To represent 'every man has a father' we first introduce the predicate of two arguments $F(x,y)$ to mean 'x is the father of y'. We can then rephrase the sentence as 'for every y, if y is a man then there exists an x such that x is the father of y':

$$(\forall y)\ P(y) \rightarrow (\exists x)\ F(x,y)$$

If a variable appears in an expression as an argument of a predicate, but does not appear in a quantifier, we say that the variable is *free* or *unbound*; thus 'x' is free in the expression '$P(x)$'. If the variable does appear in a quantifier, we say that it is *bound* by that quantifier.

We can summarize the rules for forming predicate logic expressions as follows. A term is either a constant or a variable.[1] If P is a predicate which takes n arguments, and $t_1, ..., t_n$ are terms, then $P(t_1, ..., t_n)$ is an atom. A formula can then be defined by

(1) An atom is a formula.
(2) If F and G are formulas, $(\sim F)$, $(F \wedge G)$, $(F \vee G)$, and $(F \rightarrow G)$ are formulas.
(3) If F is a formula and x a variable free in F (not already bound to a quantifier), then $(\forall x)\ F$ and $(\exists x)\ F$ are formulas.
(4) All formulas are generated by applying the above rules.

To return to our original argument, we can now present it in predicate logic as follows:

given that: $(\forall x)\ P(x) \rightarrow M(x)$
                   $P(\text{Socrates})$
we may conclude: $M(\text{Socrates})$

The proof of this argument proceeds in two steps: from the universally quantified formula

$$(\forall x)\ P(x) \rightarrow M(x)$$

we may infer the specific case

$$P(\text{Socrates}) \rightarrow M(\text{Socrates})$$

(this is called *universal instantiation*). We may then use the rule of *modus ponens* (as we did in one of our propositional logic examples) to combine this with

$$P(\text{Socrates})$$

and obtain the desired conclusion

$$M(\text{Socrates})$$

---

[1] Most formulations of predicate logic also allow functions from terms to terms, but we shall not require them for our presentation.

3.1.3   *Restricted quantification*

The basic existential and universal quantifiers range over the entire universe of
the domain. We may define restricted quantifiers in several essentially
equivalent ways.

$$(\exists x\!: F) \quad \text{and} \quad (\forall x\!: F)$$

where F is a predicate of one argument, are quantifiers which range over those
values of x for which $F(x)$ is true. They may be defined in terms of the standard
(unrestricted) quantifiers as follows:

$$(\exists x\!: F)\ G\ =\ (\exists x)\ (F(x) \wedge G)$$
$$(\forall x\!: F)\ G\ =\ (\forall x)\ (F(x) \rightarrow G)$$

We may also think of a predicate of one argument as defining a set – the set of
elements for which the predicate is true – and write

$$(\exists x \in F) \quad \text{and} \quad (\forall x \in F)$$

To provide further flexibility, we may define new sets by a set-former
operation:

$$\{x \in F | G\}$$

where G is a formula and x a variable free in G, defines those elements of F for
which G is true.

Restricted quantification does not make the formalism any more powerful;
any formula using restricted quantifiers may be rewritten as an equivalent
formula involving only unrestricted quantification. However, restricted
quantifiers will make it easier to describe the correspondence between syntax
and semantics, so we shall include them in our semantic representation.

3.1.4   *Semantic nets*

Ever since the 'early days' of work on the automatic semantic analysis of
natural language, there has been a strong inclination to use graphical
representations of semantic structures (for example, PROTOSYNTHEX
(Schwarcz, Burger, and Simmons 1970) and TLC (Quillian 1969)). These
representations have come to be called *semantic networks*. An excellent
overview of these networks was written by Woods (1975).

There is no standard for semantic networks (as there is for predicate
calculus), so the best we can do is to give some characteristics of typical
systems. A network consists of labeled nodes and labeled arcs; the number of
different arc labels is usually limited to a small set. Constants (individuals) are
represented by nodes. Some unary functions and binary predicates are
represented directly as arcs connecting the nodes involved, so the predicate

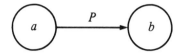

Figure 3.1

$P(a,b)$ could be represented as shown in figure 3.1. In all other cases, each instance of a predicate applied to a set of arguments is represented by a node. One arc leads from this node to each of its arguments. These arcs may be labeled 'argument 1', 'argument 2', etc. or more likely be assigned more mnemonic names like 'agent', 'instrument', etc. An additional arc, labeled 'predicate', leads from this node to a node labeled with the name of the predicate. Thus hit (John,Mary,bat) might be represented as shown in figure 3.2. Some arbitrary label (in this case act_{27}) is assigned to the node. If several atoms use the same argument or the same predicate name, they will have arcs leading to the same node. Thus there is one node for each individual constant ('John') and for each predicate ('hit'), plus one node for each atom.

Logical connectives and quantifiers can be represented as operators whose arguments are atoms or other instances of logical operators. The *partitioned semantic net* (Hendrix 1978) adds the notion of a *space*, which is a subset of the nodes and arcs in a net. Spaces are convenient for indicating the scope of logical and quantificational operators.

By such devices, semantic nets can obtain the power of predicate calculus. We may thus regard semantic nets (or, at least, some implementations of semantic nets) as an alternative notation for predicate calculus. By having a single node for each individual, the net emphasizes the connection between predicates referring to the same object. A predicate calculus notation makes indexing of atoms by their arguments and discussing 'chains' of predicates connecting two objects less natural. On the other hand, predicate calculus representations are quite standard, so their semantics is readily understood in isolation; the same cannot be said for semantic nets. We have therefore chosen to use predicate calculus for our discussion of natural language semantics.

3.1.5   Notions not captured in predicate logic

Although much of the work in computational linguistics (and much of our subsequent discussion) uses semantic representations with the power of predicate calculus, it is important to recognize that much more will be required for full natural language systems. We note briefly below some of the areas in which extensions are required.

3.1.5.1   Modality, tense, and belief
Predicate calculus is designed to describe permanent, necessary, universal facts. It is correspondingly limited in the operations which can be applied to

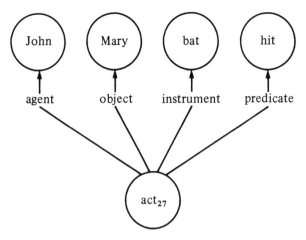

Figure 3.2

formulas – logical connectives and quantifiers. Natural language is used to discuss notions of possibility, belief, and time, and any semantic representation must be able to capture such notions. These operations differ from predicates in that some of their arguments are formulas. Among the operators which have been considered by logicians are

*modal operators: possible(F), necessary(F)
*epistemic operators: believe(x,F)
*temporal operators: true-at-some-time-in-the-future(F), ...

where x is a term and F a formula. Many computational linguistic systems have at least a partial implementation of temporal logic, with time being made a distinguished argument of a subset of the predicates, instead of a separate operator applied to the predicate. Much less work has been done on modal and epistemic operators.

In our discussion of predicate calculus, we were free to use interchangeably a function and its values, a predicate and the set it defined, or a formula and its truth value. For these higher-order operators, we must be careful to distinguish the two. For example,

The price of a Big Mac is $10.

may be evaluated by replacing 'the price of a Big Mac' by its value, say $2, to obtain

$2 is $10.

and then replacing this by its value, to obtain

false

On the other hand, within the scope of believe,

I believe the price of a Big Mac is $10.

one can no longer replace 'the price of a Big Mac' by its value; it clearly isn't the same to say

I believe $2 is $10.

Thus, once we use modal and epistemic operators we must be careful to distinguish between the *intension* of an expression – the description itself – and its *extension* – the value or set determined by that description.

3.1.5.2   Presupposition

Another notion of natural language which is not captured by predicate logic is exemplified by the sentence

The moon of Jupiter has orange stripes.

The problem is that Jupiter has more than one moon, so this sentence really does not refer to anything (we exclude for the moment the possibility of anaphora, in which we refer back to some moon of Jupiter that we were discussing previously). Some linguists have suggested that, to account for such sentences, we no longer require that every sentence be true or false, but rather allow a sentence to be true, false, or have no truth value. The sentence above would then have no truth value.

'The moon of Jupiter' is an example of a *definite description*. We can add a corresponding notion to predicate calculus by introducing a *definite quantifier*, ι, such that

$$(\iota\ x{\in}S)\ P(x)$$

is true if set S has precisely one element and $P(x)$ is true for that element; is false if S has precisely one element and $P(x)$ is false for that element; and otherwise has no truth value.

A definite description may be considered a special type of *presupposition*. A presupposition is something which must be true in order for the sentence under consideration to have a truth value. For the example above, the presupposition is

Jupiter has precisely one moon.

Another type of presupposition involves so-called *factive* verbs, such as 'regret'. Such verbs can occur with an embedded sentence in object position, and have the property that, whether asserted or negated, they imply the truth of the embedded sentence. For example, both

Sam regrets that he studied computational linguistics.

and

> Sam does not regret that he studied computational linguistics.

imply

> Sam studied computational linguistics.

If the embedded sentence is false (if Sam did *not* study computational linguistics), the larger sentence is meaningless – it has no truth value. Thus 'Sam regrets that he studied computational linguistics.' *presupposes* 'Sam studied computational linguistics.'.

Definite descriptions are handled quite easily, and are included in many natural language systems. More elaborate means for checking presuppositions were used in the CO-OP system, a natural language data base retrieval system, to identify a user's misconceptions about the data and provide helpful responses (Kaplan 1983). Presupposition tests were also used in a small foreign-language instruction system as a means of detecting student errors (Weischedel, Voge, and James 1978).

3.1.5.3 *Fuzziness*

The predicates of predicate logic are either true or false. Many predicates of natural language, however, are not so clear cut:

> John is young.

doesn't define a precise range of ages which John might have. Furthermore, many constructions of English are explicitly imprecise, such as

> Most linguists like licorice.

To account for such imprecision in a formal way, the notion of a 'fuzzy logic' was introduced by Zadeh and has been substantially elaborated over the last decade (Zadeh 1978). In a fuzzy logic, the truth value of a proposition is replaced by a *possibility distribution*.

As a simple example of a possibility distribution, consider the sentence

> X is a small integer.

We can define the fuzzy set 'small integer' as in table 3.1. We then say that 'X is a small integer.' defines a possibility distribution, with

> possibility$(X=0) = 1$
> possibility$(X=1) = 1$
> possibility$(X=2) = 0.8$
>   etc.

Fuzzy logic provides rules for computing the possibility distribution obtained by combining fuzzy predicates with logical connectives or by modifying fuzzy

Table 3.1

Value	Grade of membership
0	1
1	1
2	0.8
3	0.6
4	0.4
5	0.2

predicates. For example, the theory suggests that 'very' corresponds to squaring the original possibility distribution, so that

X is a very small integer.

yields the possibility distribution

possibility$(X=0) = 1$
possibility$(X=1) = 1$
possibility$(X=2) = 0.64$
    etc.

Although many modifiers, fuzzy quantifiers, and other constructions have been analyzed in fuzzy logic, no natural language application systems have yet been constructed incorporating fuzzy logic.

3.1.6   Choice of predicates

In addition to choosing the type of logic to be used in our semantic representation, we must select the predicates to be used in our logical form. What choices do we have? One alternative is to choose predicates in close correspondence with the words of our natural language input, possibly mapping a word with several clearly different meanings into several distinct predicates, but otherwise maintaining a one-to-one relationship. On the other hand, we might try to decompose the meanings of many words into combinations of more 'elementary' predicates. A classic example is to decompose 'kill' into 'cause to die'. What is the value of such a decomposition? For one thing, it means that we have fewer predicates to deal with in subsequent stages of semantic analysis. For another, it permits some inferences to be made quite directly, without having special rules for each word. For example, if we decomposed 'kill', we could deduce that someone who has been killed is dead (using knowledge of the semantics of 'cause', but not requiring any further information about 'kill'). Such inferences may be crucial to understanding the coherence of a sentence. Consider

John sold his melons at the fair, but he lost the money on his way home.

To understand what 'the money' refers to, we must know that 'to sell X' is 'to give someone X in exchange for money'.

Schank's semantic representation embodies an extreme view regarding predicate decomposition. Because his sentence analysis is primarily semantic rather than syntactic, he finds such decomposition (which makes explicit the roles of all the 'participants' in an action or predicate) particularly important. In particular, he wants a semantic representation such that any two synonymous sentences will have the same semantic representation. To achieve this, he has proposed a *conceptual dependency* network based on a small number of primitive actions (Schank 1975). The primitive actions of conceptual dependency are:

(1) ATRANS – the transfer of an abstract relationship such as possession, ownership, or control.
(2) PTRANS – the transfer of physical location of an object.
(3) PROPEL – the application of physical force to an object.
(4) MOVE – the movement of a bodypart of an animal by that animal.
(5) GRASP – the grasping of an object by an actor.
(6) INGEST – the taking in of an object by an animal.
(7) EXPEL – the expulsion from the body of an animal into the world.
(8) MTRANS – the transfer of mental information between animals or between the conscious processor, long-term memory, and sense organs of an animal.
(9) MBUILD – the construction by an animal of new information from old information.
(10) SPEAK – the action of producing sounds.
(11) ATTEND – the action of attending or focusing a sense organ towards a stimulus.

In addition, the graphical representation of conceptual dependency networks provides notation for causation, possession, containment, and a few other relationships (adjectives and nouns are not decomposed to primitives, so the objective of a canonical semantic representation is clearly not entirely achieved). As an example of his decomposition (without using his graphical representation),

John hit Mary.

would become

John's propelling a physical object from John to Mary caused a state of physical contact between that object and Mary.

Although the idea of decomposing into elementary actions is appealing, it does have several problems. First, it is not always evident what the proper decomposition is for a verb, whether the decomposition is unique, or whether the given 'primitive actions' are the appropriate ones for a semantic decomposition. Schank points out (Schank and Riesbeck 1981, p. 26) that the conceptual dependency representation was intended for stories about simple physical events and human interaction and may be inadequate for other domains. Both Schank and others have augmented the set of primitive acts in order to analyze richer texts. For complex technical vocabularies, very different decompositions may be needed.

The second objection is a strategic one. Even if such a reduction is possible, it is not clear that it should always be done. Decomposition should be done to the degree needed for inferencing; unnecessary decomposition produces unnecessarily large structures for subsequent processing. Just how this can be done will become clearer as the role and means of inferencing in natural language is better understood.

To simplify the following sections we shall use a set of predicates closely tied to the natural language vocabulary. In doing so, we do not preclude subsequent expansion to more elementary predicates if needed for later processing.

3.2   Translation to logical form

Having chosen a somewhat extended predicate calculus (with restricted quantifiers and the definite quantifier ι) for our semantic representation, we must now consider the task of translating natural language sentences into this logical form. We assume that the input to this translation procedure is the output of syntax analysis – sentences which have been parsed and transformationally decomposed.

How should such a translation procedure be organized? It will be convenient if the translation can be done compositionally: if we can assign a logical form to each node of the decomposition tree, and compute the logical form of each non-terminal as a function of the logical form of its immediate constituents. The translation of the entire sentence would then be the logical form associated with the root of the tree. We shall adhere rather closely to this compositional approach, although we shall not follow it religiously.

3.2.1   The input to the translation

The first step in planning a translation process is to establish a correspondence between the types of syntactic constructs in the input and the types of semantic constructs in the output. Intuitively, for example, we may expect that sentences will be mapped into formulas, and noun phrases into terms. In order to establish the correspondence more precisely, we must specify the output of the syntactic analyzer in more detail.

As we noted at the beginning of our discussion of syntax analysis, one objective of transformational decomposition within an overall system is to reduce the number of structures which must be processed during semantic analysis. We thus have a trade-off between the complexity of our transformations and the complexity of the translation procedure we are now considering. If we have fewer transformations, and are left with a larger variety of syntactic structures, we will have to analyze a larger number of different patterns in our translation procedure. For the presentation which follows, we shall assume a high degree of transformational decomposition, and hence relatively few structures to be dealt with by our translation procedure.

At the heart of our decomposition tree are two structures, the elementary assertion (s) and the noun phrase (NP). As far as possible, we will expand adjuncts (modifiers) into full assertions. For example, 'men who eat potatoes' will be transformed into the noun 'men' with the adjunct 'men eat potatoes'; 'young men' will be transformed into 'men' such that 'men are young'.[2] Furthermore, it will facilitate our translation if we eliminate the copula ('be') from assertions of the form *N be Adj* and *N be P N*, and treat adjectives and prepositions as verbs in our decomposition tree. Our decomposition tree structures can be described by the BNF

$$
\begin{aligned}
<\text{S}> &::= <\text{SUBJECT}> <\text{VERB}> <\text{OBJECT}>^* <\text{ADJUNCT}>^* \\
<\text{SUBJECT}> &::= <\text{NP}> \mid <\text{S}> \\
<\text{OBJECT}> &::= <\text{NP}> \mid <\text{S}> \\
<\text{NP}> &::= [\, <\text{DET}> \,] <\text{NOUN}> <\text{ADJUNCT}>^* \\
<\text{DET}> &::= <\text{ARTICLE}> \mid <\text{QUANTIFIER}> \\
<\text{ADJUNCT}> &::= <\text{S}>
\end{aligned}
$$

Here '*a**' denotes zero or more instances of *a*, and <NOUN>, <VERB>, <ARTICLE>, and <QUANTIFIER> are terminal symbols. For example, the sentence

Joan met several young men from Ohio.

would be transformed into figure 3.3.

We shall proceed to develop the translation rules in several stages. Let us begin by considering a very simple sentence.

Joan met Otto.

---

[2] There are some adjectives for which this would be inappropriate; for instance, 'alleged' ('alleged criminal' but not 'criminal who is alleged'); we ignore such adjectives in our simplified presentation here.

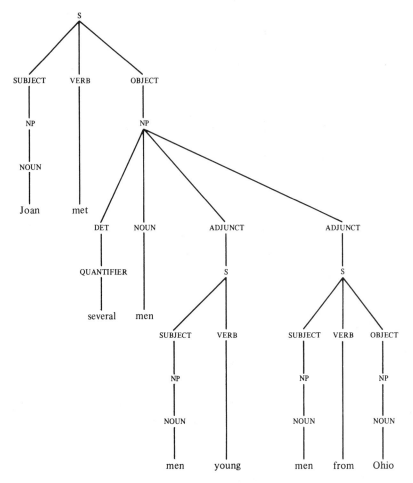

Figure 3.3

which is transformed into figure 3.4. We would expect this to translate into the atom

met(Joan,Otto)

This suggests that the translations of the NPs are terms (Joan and Otto, respectively) and that the translation of the s is obtained by applying the predicate corresponding to the verb to the terms which are the translations of the subject and object(s).

If we consider an NP other than a proper name, however, we see that it cannot be translated into a term. For example,

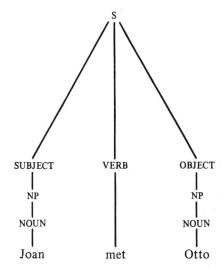

Figure 3.4

Every teacher likes Otto.

could be translated as

($\forall\, t \in teachers$) likes(t,Otto)

where *teachers* is the set of all teachers.[3] In this case the first NP translates into a quantifier over a set, where the set is obtained from the noun and the quantifier from the determiner. In order to have a more uniform translation, where each NP contributes a quantifier binding one argument of the predicate, we may find it convenient to introduce a 'dummy' quantifier for proper names:

($\forall\, t \in teachers$) ($\iota\, u \in$\{Otto\}) likes(t,u)

For simplicity, we shall not include these dummy quantifiers in the subsequent examples of this section, but we will make use of them in later sections (e.g., in anaphora resolution).

The next complication involves adjuncts of NPs, such as

Every teacher in Texas likes Otto.

Transformations will expand the adjunct 'in Texas' into 'teacher is in Texas'. We can regard this, like most adjuncts, as specifying a restriction of the base set

---

[3] If we did not have restricted quantifiers, we could still provide a translation of the sentence, as

($\forall\, t$) (teacher(t) $\rightarrow$ likes(t,Otto))

but the first NP would not correspond to a natural component of this formula.

(the set of teachers). The restricted set, the set of teachers who are in Texas, could be expressed as the set-former

$$\{v \in teachers \mid in(v,Texas)\}$$

Thus the adjunct contributes the restriction 'in(v,Texas)' to the set-former; note that 'teacher' is bound to the variable v in the set-former, so we do not need to generate a quantifier for v when translating the adjunct into predicate calculus. The whole sentence, 'Every teacher in Texas likes Otto.', then gets translated into

$$(\forall t \in \{v \in teachers \mid in(v,Texas)\}) \, likes(t,Otto)$$

If there are several adjuncts on a noun phrase, the restrictions are conjoined in logical form. For instance,

> Every young teacher in Texas likes Otto.

would get translated into

$$(\forall t \in \{v \in teachers \mid in(v,Texas) \wedge young(v)\}) \, (likes(t,Otto))$$

We can summarize these observations regarding the translation procedure as follows. The input tree has two principal structures, s and NP. Each s is translated into a formula (specifically, an atom preceded by quantifiers). Each NP is translated into a variable and (in most cases) a quantifier over that variable. The translation of the NP may be divided into three cases:

(1) the noun is a copy (copied during transformational decomposition) of a noun already bound to a variable in an outer context (this is the case for nouns in adjuncts which are copies of the host (the word being modified)); the translation of the NP is the variable previously bound to the noun

(2) the noun is a name n (which, we assume, uniquely identifies an individual); select a previously unused variable u; the translation of the NP is the variable u, quantified by

$$(\iota u \in \{n\})$$

(or, if we do not require that each NP translate into a quantifier, we can simply return n as the translation of this NP)

(3) for other NPs, the translation is generated in two stages – first the set-former, then the quantifier:

(a) select a previously unused variable v and 'bind' it to the noun; compute the translation of all the adjuncts of this NP; let $R =$ the conjunction of these translations (if there are no such adjuncts, $R = true$); form the set-former $\{v \in B \mid R\}$, where B is the set characterized by the noun itself

(b) select a previously unused variable *u*; select a quantifier *q* based on the determiner and the number of the noun, as follows:[4]

$$
\left.\begin{array}{l}
\text{each} \\
\text{every} \\
\text{all [the]} \\
\text{the + plural noun}
\end{array}\right\} \forall
$$

$$
\left.\begin{array}{l}
\text{a} \\
\text{some} \\
\text{any}
\end{array}\right\} \exists
$$

the + singular noun − ι
if no determiner is present, use $\exists$

if the set-former computed by (a) is *G*, the translation of the NP is the variable *u* quantified by

$$(q\, u \in G)$$

The translation of an s is obtained by applying the predicate corresponding to the verb to the variables which are the translations of the subject and object(s), and prefixing the resulting atom with the quantifiers generated by the subject and object.

We have so far avoided the issue of sentence adjuncts, primarily because we are not aware of any treatment of these adjuncts comparable in breadth and simplicity to that just offered for NP adjuncts. A typical treatment identifies certain types of adjuncts – those involving time, location, and instrument, for instance – and introduces additional predicate arguments corresponding to these types.[5] The adjuncts are then mapped into restrictions on the quantifiers for these arguments. As a simple example, we could introduce an extra argument to indicate the year in which an action occurred. The sentence

Steve shot Peter.

would then translate into

$(\exists\, t \in years)$ shot(Steve,Peter,t)

where *years* is the set of all years up to the present; the sentence

Steve shot Peter before 1978.

[4] Although this selection is typical of that used in many natural language systems, it is a crude approximation to the actual semantics. For example, we do not differentiate between 'a' and 'some', and we neglect generic usages such as 'The lion is a dangerous animal.' and 'Man is mortal.'.

[5] If arguments are identified by keyword rather than position, it is possible to omit the argument if no corresponding adjunct is present, with the understanding that the argument is implicitly existentially or universally quantified.

would translate into

$$(\exists \, t \in \{ u \in \mathit{years} \mid u < 1978\}) \, \mathrm{shot(Steve,Peter,}t)$$

3.2.2   Historical notes

The idea of computing semantic interpretation by rules of composition applied to a syntax tree was a natural extension of interpretation rules for formal logics. DEACON, one of the first natural language interfaces for data base manipulation, used this approach, although the translation was made directly into objects in and operations on the data base (Craig *et al.* 1966).

Two relatively early systems which used semantic representations quite close to our extended predicate calculus were the systems of Woods (1968) and Petrick (1972, 1975). Our approach in particular represents an adaptation of that of Woods. Woods has published a review article (Woods 1978), primarily describing semantic interpretation in the LUNAR system, but also addressing some general problems of semantic interpretation.

The development of formal rules of semantic interpretation has until recently not been a major line of research. Logicians have been primarily concerned with the characterization of formal logical systems adequate to capture certain classes of argument. Transformational generative linguistics, particularly under the influence of Chomsky, has emphasized syntax as a separate discipline, and the ability to study issues of grammaticality independent of considerations of semantics. Only recently has there been increasing interest in the nature of the rules for translation to logical form.

The most extensive formal work on semantic interpretation has been done by Montague and his disciples (Montague 1974). Montague himself developed an intensional logic for the representation of natural language semantics and formulated precise rules for the interpretation of a limited subset of English, focusing in particular on problems of quantification. These rules operated in a compositional fashion from the parse tree. More recent work has extended the range of constructs covered and incorporated grammatical transformations into his system. The complexity of his logical system prevented its immediate application in computational linguistics, but the influence of his work is now being increasingly felt. In particular, several recent natural language analyzers have bypassed transformational decomposition and instead associated a rule of semantic interpretation with each production of the surface grammar, so that semantic interpretation can be done directly from the parse tree (see, for instance, Gawron *et al.* 1982).

3.2.3   Quantifier ordering

In our previous discussion of semantic interpretation we studiously avoided the issue of quantifier ordering (or quantifier scope). In building the interpretation of an s, we did not specify the order in which quantifiers should be combined. This order is definitely significant, as evidenced by jokes such as the following which play on the order of the existential and universal quantifiers

> A woman gives birth in the United States every five minutes, and if we can just find her and stop her, we've got the population problem licked.

All things being equal – that is, if the two readings are equally plausible – the preferred reading of a sentence will be the one in which the quantifier ordering corresponds to the surface ordering of noun phrases. A classic example of this is the pair of sentences

(1) Everyone in the room speaks two languages.
(2) Two languages are spoken by everyone in the room.

Note that the second sentence is the passive of the first; otherwise the sentences are identical (and thus have the same deep structure, except for a possible passive marker). These sentences, however, do not have the same interpretation. Sentence (1) is usually interpreted with the quantifier for 'everyone in the room' given wider scope (so the two languages may be different for different people), while sentence (2) is usually interpreted with the quantifier 'there exist two languages' given wider scope (so that the languages are the same for everyone).

This observation implies that while functional relationships (operator–operand or predicate–argument relationships) are best determined from deep structure, the quantifier scopes are best determined from surface structure. While this is not a severe computational problem, it does upset the overall structure of the 'Standard Theory' of transformational grammar (in which semantic interpretation is based exclusively on deep structure). Not long after the Standard Theory was proposed, it became evident that several aspects of the semantics, including quantifier scope, scope of negatives, and focus, were functions of surface structure. This led to the development of Extended Standard Theory (in which the semantic interpretation is based on the entire transformational derivation) and Revised Extended Standard Theory (in which the semantic interpretation is based on the surface structure, and some mechanism or set of rules is provided for determining the deep structure relationships from the surface structure).

In addition to the surface ordering, the quantifier scoping of the 'preferred' or 'most likely' interpretation is affected by the actual English word chosen to express the quantifier. In particular, the word 'each' is more likely to be interpreted as a quantifier of wide scope –

> Two languages are spoken by each person in the room.

probably means that the two languages can be different for different people. The SRI speech understanding system went so far as to assign a strength to each English quantifier, and to use these strengths to determine quantifier scoping, relying on surface order only to break ties (Walker 1978, p. 220).

The comments made above about surface order were offered with the proviso that the readings with the different scopings were equally plausible. In many cases, however, the two readings are not equally plausible, and the plausible (and intended) reading often does not correspond to the surface order. The sentence

A woman gives birth in the US every 5 minutes.

is a good example of this phenomenon. As in the case of syntactic ambiguity, resolving quantifier scope may involve arbitrary knowledge about the world and about the relation of the current sentence to the prior discourse.

None the less, as was the case for syntactic ambiguity, it is possible to identify particular information about the domain which is useful in resolving some of these scope ambiguities. In the present instance, one relevant piece of information is the identification of some predicates as functional relations. If for each value of x there exists at most one value of y for which $P(x,y)$ is true, then P determines a (partial) function from its first to its second argument. For instance,

$$F(x,y) = y \text{ is the father of } x$$

determines such a function; so does

$$T(x,y) = x \text{ is an X-ray of patient } y$$

(because patients do not sit for group X-rays). This information can be used to resolve scope ambiguities when one variable is bound by an existential quantifier or set former and the other is bound by a universal quantifier. For example,

The X-rays of the patients show metastases.

might be translated (using the quantifier order corresponding to surface order) as

$$(\forall x \in \{ y \in X \mid (\forall p \in P) \, T(y,p)\}) \; \text{show}(x, \text{metastases})$$

where X is the set of X-rays, P the set of patients, and T was defined just above. However, we know from the functional property of T that $(\forall p \in P) \, T(y,p)$ is not true for any y, so we must select the alternative analysis,

$$(\forall p \in P)(\forall x \in \{ y \in X \mid T(y,p)\}) \; \text{show}(x, \text{metastases})$$

A slightly different case arises in

I met the fathers of the students.

Here the reading with the quantifier for students inside the set-former,

$$(\forall f \in \{\, g \in M \mid (\forall s \in S)\, F(s,g)\}) \text{ met } (I,f)$$

(where M is the set of all fathers, S the set of students and F is as defined above) will be rejected because $\{\, g \in M \mid (\forall s \in S)\, F(s,g)\}$ must be a set of at most one element, whereas the sentence says *fathers*. We are thus left with the reading

$$(\forall s \in S)\,(\forall f \in \{\, g \in M \mid F(s,g)\}) \text{ met } (I,f)$$

In order to handle such analyses we would require a more complicated semantic interpretation procedure which is able to move quantifiers out of adjuncts into the matrix sentence.

In natural language data base retrieval systems, where the information specified by the input questions is fixed and readily available, an alternative approach is possible. Instead of inferring that a set is empty or a singleton, one can determine this information by actually computing the set. Either way, the information can be used to rule out one reading. This approach has been advocated by Harris and is used in his ROBOT system (L. Harris 1977).

3.3   Semantic constraints

3.3.1   *The nature of the constraints*

Most sequences of words do not constitute grammatical sentences. In the previous chapter we examined some of the (syntactic) constraints which are satisfied by grammatical sentences, and some of the formalisms for representing these constraints. It is similarly true that many grammatical sentences are not meaningful sentences. Most people would balk at saying that sentences such as

> Freedom is dark green.
> My closet is well behaved.

are either true or false (i.e., have a truth value), except perhaps in some poetic, non-literal sense. Now that we have discussed the semantic representation of sentences, we shall examine some of the (semantic) constraints satisfied by meaningful sentences.

Why are we interested in such constraints? For language analysis applications, our motives are similar to those for studying syntactic constraints. We don't expect that the input will contain lots of meaningless sentences which our program should be able to identify and reject. However, a single sentence may give rise to several semantic analyses (often arising from several syntactic analyses); some of these may be meaningless. If we assume that the input was intended to be meaningful, we can use the semantic constraints to identify the meaningless analyses and exclude them from consideration (just as syntactic constraints may be used to eliminate other analyses). For example,

I noticed a man on the road wearing a hat.

has two syntactic analyses and correspondingly two semantic analyses (with the man wearing the hat in one analysis and the road wearing it in the other). If we can determine that 'the road is wearing the hat' is meaningless, we can exclude that reading and home in on the other.

Such syntactic ambiguities are not isolated examples; they are pervasive in spoken and written language. In listening and reading, we usually perceive only one analysis for a sentence and remain unaware of the ambiguities. A little practical experience with automatic syntactic analysis, however, will make one realize how common the ambiguities are, and consequently how important it is to resolve these ambiguities in order to be able to understand the text.

The examples we have given of meaningless sentences have a common characteristic: they apply a predicate to an object for which the predicate is not meaningful. Abstract objects (such as 'freedom') don't have colors; inanimate objects don't have good or bad manners; roads don't wear clothes. We can put this more formally by saying that most predicates are well-defined (i.e., take on the value 'true' or 'false') only for a subset of the universe of possible argument values. This subset is called the *domain* of the predicate. For example, the domain of 'green(x)' is the set of all concrete objects. A sentence is meaningful only if, in its logical form, the argument of each predicate belongs to the domain of the predicate.

This is not the only semantic constraint a sentence must satisfy in order to be meaningful. For example, a meaningful sentence should be free of contradictory predicates ('He drank the colorless red liquid.'). A meaningful text (or a meaningful sentence with several clauses) must also satisfy *text coherence* constraints, such as the constraint violated by the sentence 'Mary baked cookies, but John baked cookies.'. However, the constraint on the domain of predicates is important for two reasons. First, this constraint by itself is sufficient to disambiguate a large portion of syntactically ambiguous sentences (particularly within a sublanguage, as we shall discuss shortly). Second, this constraint is relatively easy to check, in part because it is a *local* constraint. (By *local* we mean that it operates at logical form between a predicate and its arguments, at syntactic structure between a verb and its subject and object, rather than operating between predicates or between sentences.) For these reasons, we will focus in this section on this type of constraint.

This class of semantic constraints has aspects in common with both syntactic and semantic constraints we considered earlier.

Earlier on in this chapter (in section 3.1.5.2, to be precise) we introduced some semantic constraints called *presuppositions*. A proposition p presupposes a proposition q if q must be true in order for p to have a truth value. We mentioned there two types of presuppositions. The first type arose from definite noun phrases; for example,

The present king of France is bald.

presupposes that 'There is, at present, a (exactly one) king of France.' The second type arose from factive verbs; for example,

John realized that Fred was a Canadian.

presupposes that 'Fred was a Canadian'. The semantic constraints we are interested in in this section can be viewed as a third class of presuppositions: a sentence whose logical form contains '$P(t)$', for some predicate P and term t, presupposes that t is in the domain of P. For example,

Curriery is usually dark brown.

presupposes that 'curriery' is a concrete substance. In logic, the sets which constitute the domains of predicates are called *sorts* or *categories*, and hence this type of presupposition has been called *sortal* or *categorical presupposition* (Allwood, Andersson, and Dahl 1977, p. 150).

On the other hand, we may note that these constraints relating to predicate domain are directly reflected in the ways in which words may combine to form (meaningful) sentences. In simple sentences, for example, these predicate–argument constraints determine what subjects and objects can occur with a particular verb. They are similar in this regard to grammatical 'co-occurrence' constraints, such as subcategorization. It is natural, therefore, to consider the predicate domain constraints as part of the grammar of a language. In fact, we did so in the previous chapter in the guise of *selectional constraints*. We considered there only a few classes of nouns – human and non-human, animate and inanimate – but the same approach could be readily applied to more refined classes. Harris has stressed this parallel between grammatical constraints and predicate domain constraints in sublanguages, a topic which we shall turn to next.

In keeping with common usage, we shall borrow the grammatical term and henceforth refer to the semantic constraints relating to predicate domains as selectional constraints.

3.3.2 Sublanguages

When natural language is used to discuss a restricted domain, and in particular when used by a community of speakers sharing specialized knowledge, the language frequently takes on characteristics different from the language as a whole. It may be more restricted in its lexical, syntactic, semantic, or discourse properties; it may also include constructs not present in the language as a whole. The resulting language is called a *sublanguage*.[6] Examples of sublanguages are the languages used in weather reports, in patient summaries

---

[6] For a brief overview and extensive bibliography on sublanguages, see Kittredge (1983); for a more detailed exposition, see Kittredge and Lehrberger (1981), and Grishman and Kittredge (1986).

by physicians, in maintenance manuals for electronic equipment, and in the journal articles from a single field of science or engineering.

The property of sublanguages which interests us here is the following: in most sublanguages, the selectional constraints are much sharper and make finer distinctions than they do for the language as a whole. The language as a whole includes imaginary contexts (fairy tales, science fiction) and figurative and metaphorical usages, which may violate ordinary selectional constraints. Sublanguages, particularly scientific and technical sublanguages, generally do not permit such usages. In consequence, these semantic constraints are likely to be strictly observed in such sublanguages.

Harris has pointed out (Z. Harris 1968, p. 152) the parallel between the grammatical/ungrammatical distinction for a language as a whole and the acceptable/nonsensical distinction for the language of a field of science. For example, 'The polypeptides were washed in hydrochloric acid.' is a sentence in the language of biochemistry, whereas 'Hydrochloric acid was washed in polypeptides.' is not; the latter sentence would be regarded as nonsense by a biochemist. Harris has shown how the sentences of a science sublanguage can be characterized by methods analogous to those for characterizing the language as a whole. 'In describing the sentences of biochemistry we can define particular subclasses of words, such as names of solutions, reagents, etc., and verbs for classes of reaction or laboratory activities that are carried out on the molecules. Of these specially defined subclasses, only particular sequences will be found in (true or false) well-formed sentences in biochemistry discourses.' [*op cit.*, p. 153] Continuing our example, we would define the classes N_{mol} (nouns naming molecules, such as 'polypeptides'), N_{sol} (nouns naming solvents, such as 'hydrochloric acid'), and V_{sol} (verbs involving solvents, such as 'wash'). We would then include the sequence 'N_{mol} is V_{sol}-en in N_{sol}' in our sublanguage grammar, but not 'N_{sol} is V_{sol}-en in N_{mol}'. Such sublanguage grammars have been developed for subfields of biochemistry (Sager 1975) and medicine.

Because the semantic constraints in most sublanguages are both detailed and strictly observed, we can expect them to contribute significantly to resolving syntactic ambiguity. Furthermore, as a practical matter, restricting ourselves to a limited domain with a limited vocabulary and range of concepts makes it feasible to accumulate a fairly complete set of semantic constraints. For unrestricted natural language, with its wide range of concepts and less sharply defined predicate domains, it is not clear whether effective constraints could be constructed using the relatively simple notion of predicate domains.

The structure of the sublanguage for a domain reflects the structure of people's knowledge about the domain. Investigating the semantic patterns and constraints in the sublanguage can lead us to discover these 'knowledge' or 'information structures' (Sager 1972). In particular, the semantic constraints we are studying in this section can yield a classification of the objects and relations in the domain. The sets which are the predicate domains can serve as a classification of the objects; these classes – such as N_{mol} and N_{sol} in the biochemistry example above – correspond in most cases to the basic concepts of the domain as they might be elicited from a domain expert. Similarly, it is possible to classify the predicates by grouping together those with the same predicate domain. We shall return to this idea of discovering the organization of knowledge through linguistic analysis in the next chapter.

3.3.3 Specifying the constraints

In the first subsection we gave a formal characterization of the semantic constraints we are interested in: they specify what combinations of predicate and arguments are meaningful. Our discussion now turns to a more practical issue: how can we collect and organize these predicate–argument patterns for a realistic domain?

In principle what we need to do is specify, for each argument position of each predicate and for each object in the domain, whether that object can meaningfully appear in that argument position.[7] For any realistic domain, however, this is an overwhelming amount of data. Ways must be found of specifying this data in more compact form.

Our first observation is that, in tabulating the domains of the various predicates, we find the same set of objects appearing repeatedly. Rather than enumerate the set each time, we give each set a name and use the names in specifying the predicate domains. This is what Harris did (previous subsection) in creating the classes N_{mol} and N_{sol}.

To make the ideas of this section more concrete, we shall follow a small example through the next several pages. Suppose we have a 'microworld' in which the only objects are

Jack   (a man)
Jill   (a woman)
Fuzzy (a bear)

---

[7] In practice the meaningful values for one argument of a verb may depend on the value of the other argument. For example,

> John raised his leg.
> The bear raised his leg.

are OK, and so is

> John raised the issue of linguist's rights.

but it is hard to imagine that

> The bear raised the issue of linguist's rights.

In such cases either we must specify the allowable argument *pairs* (rather than each argument separately), or we must say that the verb corresponds to several different predicates (in this case, raising physical objects and raising topics of discussion), for each of which the subject and object domains can be independently specified.

Snoopy (a dog)
berries
nuts

and the only predicates are

laugh (x) = x is laughing
cry (x) = x is crying
sleep (x) = x is sleeping
eat (x,y) = x is eating y
feed (x,y) = x is feeding y
disappear (x) = x has disappeared

and the predicate domains are

laugh: Jack, Jill
cry: Jack, Jill
sleep: Jack, Jill, Fuzzy, Snoopy
eat (1st arg.):   Jack, Jill, Fuzzy, Snoopy
    (2nd arg.):   berries, nuts
feed (1st arg.): Jack, Jill
    (2nd arg.):   Jack, Jill, Fuzzy, Snoopy
disappear: Jack, Jill, Fuzzy, Snoopy, berries, nuts

We can give names to the following sets:

people   = {Jack, Jill}
animals = {Jack, Jill, Fuzzy, Snoopy}
foods   = {berries, nuts}
things   = {Jack, Jill, Fuzzy, Snoopy, berries, nuts}

and then specify the predicate domains as follows:

laugh: *people*
cry: *people*
sleep: *animals*
eat (1st arg.):   *animals*
    (2nd arg.):   *food*
feed (1st arg.): *people*
    (2nd arg.):   *animals*
disappear: *things*

Just as we have created classes of objects, we can create classes of predicates, grouping two predicates together if they have the same domain in all argument positions. The domains then need be specified only once for the class rather than separately for each predicate. In our example this is only a small benefit, since there are only two predicates ('laugh' and 'cry') which we can group in this way.

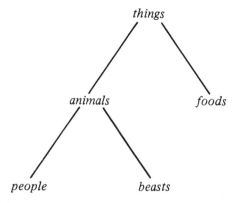

Figure 3.5

Suppose now that we have to add a third person, 'Donald', to our microworld. In order to specify the predicate domains correctly, we have to add 'Donald' to three sets: *people, animals,* and *things.* We can see that this is wasteful: we 'know' that if x is a person, he is also an animal and a thing. We can incorporate this knowledge into our representation by changing the way we specify sets:

> *people*   = {Jack, Jill}
> *beasts*   = {Fuzzy, Snoopy}
> *foods*   = {berries, nuts}
> *animals* = *people* ∪ *beasts*
> *things*   = *foods* ∪ *animals*

Now to add 'Donald' we only have to add him to the *people* set; the other changes follow from the equations.

What we have created here is a *hierarchical* taxonomy or classification of the objects in the domain. Such a taxonomy is conveniently represented by a tree (figure 3.5). In this tree node *a* dominates node *b* if *a* is a superset of *b*. We may 'annotate' this tree by introducing nodes corresponding to the microworld predicates and adding arcs (represented by -----) from the predicate nodes to the object class nodes which are the domains of the predicate's arguments as in figure 3.6. (For two-argument predicates, we have labeled the arc to the domain of the first argument with a 1 and the arc to the domain of the second argument with a 2.) Figure 3.6, with its arcs connecting predicates and arguments, bears considerable resemblance to the semantic network shown in section 3.1.4; in fact, this diagram is also referred to as a semantic network. Note, however, that the significance of the two networks is quite different: the earlier network signified that a predicate applied to particular arguments is *true,* whereas the similar structure just below signifies that a predicate applied to a member of a class is *meaningful.* These two types of network and their relation

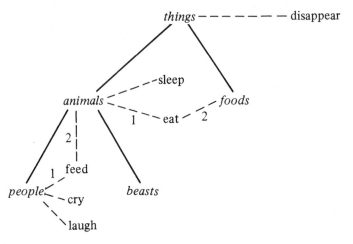

Figure 3.6

and elaborations are discussed in detail in Findler (1979).

3.3.4   *Enforcing the constraints*

Now that we have discussed how to specify the constraints for a domain, we may consider how to enforce them; that is, at what point in the analysis process should we check that the analysis satisfies these constraints?

Since we have stated them as constraints on logical form, it seems most natural to verify them after the sentence has been mapped into logical form. However, the relations we would be checking at logical form – between a predicate and its arguments – correspond directly to the *functional relations* available at deep structure – between a verb and its 'logical' subject and object. These constraints can thus be checked just as well in deep structure. Other things being equal, we will prefer to check the constraints, and thus block bad analyses, as early as possible. We will, therefore, generally prefer to apply these constraints at deep structure.

Among the systems which verify these constraints at deep structure is the PSI-KLONE system at Bolt Beranek and Newman (Bobrow and Webber 1980). PSI-KLONE is based on the RUS grammar, which is organized as a syntactic–semantic cascade, following the cascaded ATN organization suggested by Woods (see section 2.6.4). As the input is being parsed, pieces of deep structure are assembled and sent, as a stream of symbols, to the semantic component. The semantic component incorporates a taxonomy of the objects and relations in the domain being discussed. When a piece of deep structure (specifying, for example, two constituents and their relation at deep structure) is received by the semantic component, it uses 'relation mapping rules' to determine whether there is a corresponding meaningful semantic relation. If there isn't, the semantic component informs the syntactic component and the syntactic component seeks an alternative analysis.

It is also possible to enforce these constraints at surface structure. This is considerably more difficult, however, because the functional relations are not directly available at surface structure. We must take account of such constructs as passives (which interchange subject and object), relative clauses (which omit the subject or object), and aspectual verbs such as 'begin' (which may intervene between the subject and main verb). If it's so difficult, why should we bother?

Recall our earlier comment that selectional constraints can play a major role in eliminating incorrect sentence analyses. Suppose we are using a system in which the stages of language analysis – parsing, transformational analysis, semantic analysis – are performed *sequentially*. If the constraints are not applied until deep structure or logical form is generated, many incorrect analyses will have to be followed through much of the analysis process. By applying the constraints during the parse, we can 'head off' these wrong analyses much sooner, and thus probably[8] speed the analysis process.

As we said, applying these constraints is more complex at surface structure, since the functional relations are not directly available. They must be computed by, in effect, undoing some transformational operations. Restriction Language grammar provides a set of 'extended scope' routines which do some of this work (Sager and Grishman 1975; Sager 1981). For example, DEEPEST-VERB looks through aspectual verbs and adjectives to find the main verb of the sentence; the DEEPEST-VERB of 'John is unable to stop laughing.', for instance, is 'laughing'. Once the verb and its logical subject and object have been identified in the parse tree, the constraints may be verified by comparing the semantic classes of these words against the list of meaningful patterns, just as would be done in checking the constraints at deep structure.

A quite different approach to enforcing these constraints at surface structure is to incorporate the constraints into the phrase-structure component. Instead of stating the phrase-structure rules in terms of grammatical categories such as noun and noun phrase, they are stated in terms of semantic categories of the sublanguage being captured. This approach is known as *semantic grammar* (Burton 1976).

Suppose we wanted a grammar of simple declarative sentences which captured the semantic constraints of the microworld of people and animals we described above. Instead of rules like

---

[8] We must say 'probably' because the verification of semantic constraints does slow the parse, and the net increase in speed therefore depends on the relative speed of the various stages and the number of bad parses blocked by these constraints.

```
<SENTENCE> ::= <SUBJECT> <VERB> <OBJECT>
<SUBJECT>  ::= <NP>
<NP>       ::= <*NOUN> | <*ARTICLE> <*NOUN>
               etc.
```

our grammar would look something like

```
<SENTENCE> ::= <PERSON> is <EMOTING> |
               <ANIMAL> is sleeping |
               <ANIMAL> is eating <FOOD> |
               <PERSON> is feeding <ANIMAL> |
               <THING> has disappeared
<PERSON>   ::= Jack | Jill
<BEAST>    ::= Fuzzy | Snoopy
<ANIMAL>   ::= <PERSON> | <BEAST>
<FOOD>     ::= a berry | a nut
<THING>    ::= <ANIMAL> | <FOOD>
<EMOTING>  ::= laughing | crying
```

This approach has been used quite heavily, particularly in the mid and late 1970s, in developing natural language interfaces. Its appeal is immediate: it avoids the need for a separate apparatus for enforcing the semantic constraints. If a context-free or augmented context-free parser is available, it is possible to bring up small natural language systems very quickly using this approach. More recently, however, this approach has fallen a bit from favor, especially for larger applications, for two reasons: it isn't portable and it fails to capture linguistic generalizations. The lack of portability – the ability to move a system to a new domain with minimal modifications – is apparent: when we go to a new domain we have to rewrite the semantic grammar pretty much from scratch. The inability to capture linguistic generalization is evident if we consider the task of adding a syntactic construct, such as plurals or passives, to this grammar. If we added plurals we would have to specify number agreement separately for each option of SENTENCE. To add passives we would have to add a new option for each active sentence form which could passivize (for our small example, we would add the options

<FOOD> is being eaten by <ANIMAL>

and

<ANIMAL> is being fed by <PERSON>

to the definition of SENTENCE). Furthermore, if we employed transformations we would require a separate transformation for each passive form.

These deficiencies in semantic grammar arise from the attempt to merge two different kinds of knowledge – grammatical and semantic (selectional). In small systems, where the creation of mechanisms for handling the knowledge is a major factor, this merging (and consequent reduction in mechanism) may be desirable. In larger systems the knowledge itself dominates the system-building task, so we must look for the most efficient way of representing this knowledge. This is generally best achieved by separating disparate types of knowledge; trying to merge them will often yield a much larger representation, one growing as the product of the sizes of its components.

3.4   Conceptual analyzers

We have presented so far in this book two levels of representation – syntactic and semantic – and constraints on acceptable structures at each level. All of the analyzers we have described begin by creating (explicitly or implicitly) a syntactic structure, apply syntactic and sometimes also semantic (selectional) constraints, and then translate this into a semantic representation. It has struck many people that this is an inherently inefficient way of doing things. If our ultimate objective is the generation of a semantic representation of the sentence, why don't we do so directly, and use the syntactic constraints to guide this process?

The largest 'school' of computational linguists to adopt this approach was started by Roger Schank. In addition to the approach of analyzing text directly into semantic structures, this school is tied together by a common semantic representation, called Conceptual Dependency ('CD') networks (see section 3.1.6). The language analyzers of this school are in consequence often called 'conceptual analyzers'. This title subsumes a variety of procedures, differing in their algorithm (top-down, bottom-up, or mixed) and their grammatical coverage. What these conceptual analyzers share is the use of skeletal semantic structures to guide the analysis. These skeletons are incomplete CD networks – networks which specify the primitive actions and the type of objects (people, foods, etc.) involved, and have places for filling in the specific objects involved in a particular instance. These skeletons are comparable to the selectional patterns we studied in the previous section (although one such skeleton may subsume several selectional patterns). Roughly speaking, then, we can characterize these analyzers as being guided by semantic (selectional) patterns and then applying (limited) syntactic checks, whereas most parsers are guided by syntactic patterns and then apply semantic checks. For this reason, we have included our presentation of conceptual analyzers here following the discussion of semantic constraints.

Consider for example the sentence 'John eats berries.'. The verb 'eat' corresponds to the primitive act INGEST. The skeleton for INGEST has two slots: one for an ACTOR (an animate being) and one for an OBJECT (an edible thing). A conceptual analyzer would find the word 'eat', create an INGEST skeleton, and then look for items in the sentence to fill the slots. It would find 'John', which satisfies the requirements for an ACTOR, and 'berries', which satisfies the requirements for an OBJECT of INGEST. Once these slots are filled in, the skeleton becomes a complete semantic representation.

Because it relies primarily on semantic factors, this approach has no trouble with syntactically ill-formed sentences, such as 'John eat berries.' or 'Berries John eats.'. However, the analyzer must sometimes make use of word order in order to produce the correct semantic analysis. For instance, 'give' is represented in CD by the primitive act ATRANS (transfer possession). ATRANS has four slots: the ACTOR (a person), the OBJECT (which is transferred), the person it is transferred FROM and the person it is transferred TO. The definition of 'gives' includes a skeletal ATRANS structure; it specifies that the same entity will fill the ACTOR and FROM slots; and it specifies that this entity normally precedes the verb, whereas the TO and OBJECT entities normally follow the verb. This word order information enables the analyzer to figure out who ATRANSed what to whom in a sentence such as 'Jack gave Jill some berries.'.

This approach lends itself quite naturally to a mixture of bottom-up and top-down analysis, with the selection of the skeleton done bottom-up (data-driven) and the filling of the slots done top-down (goal directed). To see how this works, we shall examine very briefly, and with some simplifications, how a recent conceptual analyzer, CA, goes about analyzing a sentence (for a more detailed description of CA see Birnbaum and Selfridge (1981)). CA makes a single left-to-right scan of the sentence. It maintains a concept list, or C-LIST, of conceptual structures which have been built from words already scanned but which have not yet been incorporated into larger CD structures. It also maintains a list of *requests* which have not yet been satisfied. When CA creates a semantic skeleton, it also creates requests to fill the slots in the skeleton; these requests remain active until they find something to fill their slot (this use of requests was inherited from CA's predecessors, MARGIE and ELI, both written by Riesbeck).

Suppose CA is given the sentence 'Jack gave Jill a berry.'. CA will retrieve the dictionary entry for 'Jack', which gives the CD representation of 'Jack':

(PP CLASS (HUMAN) NAME (JACK))

('PP' stands for Picture Producer, which is used in CD notation to designate a concrete object.) This structure is placed on the C-LIST. CA now advances to the word 'gave', whose dictionary entry includes the CD skeleton

(ATRANS ACTOR (NIL)
         OBJECT (NIL)
         TO (NIL)
         FROM (NIL))

(where NIL signifies an unfilled slot). This structure is added to the C-LIST. The definition of 'gave' also includes three requests:

(1) If you can find a human on the C-LIST preceding the ATRANS structure, put it in the ACTOR and FROM slots of the ATRANS.

(2) If you can find a human on the C-LIST following the ATRANS structure, put it in the TO slot of the ATRANS.

(3) If you can find a physical object on the C-LIST following the ATRANS structure, put it in the OBJECT slot of the ATRANS.

Request (1) is immediately satisfiable; it puts the representation of 'Jack' into the ACTOR and FROM slots and then removes the representation of 'Jack' from the C-LIST. Requests (2) and (3) cannot be satisfied at present, so they are placed on the request list, and CA moves on. It gets the definition of the next word, 'Jill', and puts its CD representation on the C-LIST:

(PP CLASS (HUMAN) NAME (JILL))

CA then examines the request list and sees that request (2) can be satisfied. This request moves the representation of 'Jill' into the TO slot of the ATRANS. The definition of the next word, 'a', has no independent CD representation; it contains only the request

> If a new structure has been added to the C-LIST, mark it as an indefinite reference.

This is placed on the request list as request (4). Finally CA reads the word 'berry', gets its definition, and places its representation on the C-LIST:

(PP CLASS (PHYSOBJ) NAME (BERRY))

We can then execute request (4), which adds REF (INDEFINITE) to this structure. Request (3) is then executed, inserting this structure into the OBJECT slot of the ATRANS. This completes the analysis; the completed CD structure is

(ATRANS ACTOR (PP CLASS (HUMAN) NAME (JACK))
        OBJECT (PP CLASS (PHYSOBJ) NAME (BERRY) REF (INDEFINITE))
        FROM (PP CLASS (HUMAN) NAME (JACK))
        TO (PP CLASS (HUMAN) NAME (JILL)))

As we noted earlier, this conceptual analysis procedure is distinguished by the direct translation of the text to a semantic representation and by the absence of an autonomous syntactic component. The integration of syntax and semantics is evident in the 'requests', which incorporate both semantic (word class) and syntactic (word order) constraints. Because the requests are procedural in nature, they provide a great deal of flexibility. Data directed and goal directed analysis are readily combined, and other knowledge sources can be readily used in the analysis procedure. The latter is particularly important since a major issue in the development of these analyzers has been the utilization of other types of knowledge, such as 'scripts' and 'plans' (discussed in the next chapter).

On the other hand, this integration of syntax with semantics, and of specification with procedure, has several practical difficulties, some of which were cited earlier (section 2.2). As in the case of semantic grammar, the merging of syntax and semantics makes it difficult to capture syntactic generalizations, such as the relation of active and passive forms. This is especially true of a system like CA where rules are associated not with syntactic or semantic patterns but with individual words. The absence of an explicit syntactic structure further complicates the task of capturing some syntactic phenomena, such as the relative clause (a relative clause is characterized by the omission of a single element in syntactic structure, but this may correspond to the omission of one, two, or more elements in CD representation). In addition to these practical difficulties, the integration of syntactic, semantic, and procedural knowledge makes it harder to precisely characterize this knowledge and thus develop a more formal model from experimental programs.

3.5   Anaphora resolution

One of the powers of natural language and one of the reasons that it is difficult to analyze is that much of what is communicated is implicit in the discourse. In particular, the connections between sentences and between sentence constituents are often implicit. Consider the following scene in a fancy restaurant:

> Sipping the last of his cordial, the customer was presented with the check. A look of incredulity crept over his face.

Although it is not stated explicitly, we infer a cause-and-effect relationship between the two sentences. We also understand certain references which are made to entities mentioned elsewhere in the discourse, or to entities somehow related to those mentioned explicitly in the text. Such references are sometimes called *contextual references* because they are references to entities explicit or implicit in the context established by the prior discourse.

In our example, both instances of 'his' refer to 'the customer'. This is an example of *anaphora* – reference to an entity explicitly mentioned in the text. The (usually prior) mention of the entity to which the anaphoric phrase refers is termed the *antecedent*. Another instance of contextual reference in our example is 'the check'. Although no mention has been made of any kind of check, we know that what the customer receives is not his paycheck but the bill. We know this because we know that receiving a check of this type is part of the normal sequence of events in a restaurant.

In the current section we shall examine the process of anaphora resolution – determining the entity to which an anaphoric phrase refers. Anaphora has been extensively studied by linguists and computational linguists, and a number of precise observations have been made about the phenomenon (for a survey of the field, see Hirst (1981)). More particularly, we shall restrict ourselves to noun phrase anaphora (where the anaphoric phrase and antecedent are both noun phrases (or pronouns)) because this form of anaphora has been most extensively studied and is best understood. More general contextual reference has been the object of increasing study by computational linguists during the past few years, but the results to date are of a more tentative and general nature. We shall discuss some of these results in the next chapter, as a part of text analysis.

3.5.1 *When to do anaphora resolution*

Anaphora resolution is a process of substitution: we replace the anaphoric phrase by a (more) complete description – a description sufficient to permit interpretation of the noun phrase by subsequent stages of semantic processing. At what point in the processing of a sentence should this substitution be done? After parsing? After translation to logical form? In doing anaphora resolution, we would like to use a representation of the text in which the possible values which may be substituted for the anaphoric text can be readily computed. Thus we must consider what kinds of values may be substituted for an anaphoric phrase.

What do anaphoric expressions refer to? The first answer one might offer is that such expressions refer to previous noun phrases in the discourse. One would then suppose that, to resolve the anaphora, one would replace the anaphoric expression by the noun phrase to which it refers. For example, if we have the sequence

> Mary bought several shirts at the store.
> She paid $20.

'she' must refer to a previous animate noun phrase; we look for such a noun phrase and find 'Mary', so we proceed to substitute 'Mary' for 'she' to get

> Mary paid $20.

We can now continue processing the sentence (transformational analysis, semantic analysis) just as we would a sentence without pronouns.

Now consider

> Mary bought several shirts at the store. They cost $20.

We want to find an antecedent for 'they', so we look for a previous plural noun phrase. We find 'several shirts' and substitute this phrase for the pronoun:

> Several shirts cost $20.

As you may notice, this isn't quite right. It isn't any old bunch of shirts that costs $20; it's the shirts which Mary bought at the store. Thus 'they' refers to the set of shirts which Mary bought at the store. This set description does not correspond to any natural constituent of the parse tree. However, as we shall show in the next section, it is readily computable from the logical form. This suggests that the substitutions required for anaphora resolution are best performed after translation to logical form.

This argument is buttressed by the observation that the number (singular/plural) associated with an antecedent may depend on the quantifier structure of the sentence containing the antecedent. Compare

>   Each student bought an ice-cream cone. They were delicious.

and

>   The students bought an apple pie. It was delicious.

Since (in our analysis scheme) the quantifier scoping is not explicit until the translation to logical form, it would be difficult to capture the distinction between these examples at an earlier stage of processing.

We shall begin by considering the task of anaphora resolution for definite pronouns. We will divide this task into two parts – identifying the set descriptions which can be referred to anaphorically (the 'discourse entities'), and selecting the correct discourse entity to be substituted for a pronoun. After that we shall turn to the problems raised by other anaphoric noun phrases.

3.5.2 *Computing discourse entities*

The discourse entities, then, are set descriptions associated with each noun phrase in the discourse. In the following exposition we will follow closely the rules for computing discourse entities which were developed by Webber (1979). In our formalism, the set descriptions will be represented by set-former expressions.

In computing the discourse entities, we differentiate between noun phrases giving rise to universal ($\forall$) and definite (ι) quantifiers and those translated into existential ($\exists$) quantifiers. If a noun phrase is translated into a quantifier

> $(\forall x \in G)$

or

> $(\iota x \in G)$

then the associated discourse entity is simply G. For example,

>   All the magnolias in Central Park were in bloom. They looked magnificent.

The logical form for the first sentence (with the proper noun translated into an explicit definite quantifier) would be

> $(\forall m \in \{n \in magnolias \mid (\iota p \in \{\text{Central Park}\}) \, in(n,p)\}) \, \text{in-bloom}(m)$

so that 'Central Park' would have the discourse entity {Central Park} and 'all the magnolias in Central Park' would have the discourse entity $\{n \in magnolias \mid (\iota\, p \in \{\text{Central Park}\})\, in(n,p)\}$. If a noun phrase is translated into an existential quantifier

$$(\exists x \in G)\, P(x)$$

where $P(x)$ is the translation of the portion of the sentence within the scope of the existential quantifier, it gives rise to the discourse entity[9]

$$\{x \in G \mid P(x)\}$$

For example, in the sentence

A magnolia in Central Park is in bloom.

which has the logical form

$$(\exists m \in \{n \in magnolias \mid (\iota\, p \in \{\text{Central Park}\})\, in(n,p)\})\, \text{in-bloom}(m)$$

the phrase 'a magnolia in Central Park' will give rise to ('evoke') the discourse entity

$$\{m \in \{n \in magnolias \mid (\iota\, p \in \{\text{Central Park}\})\, in(n,p)\} \mid \text{in-bloom}(m)\}$$

which can be simplified to

$$\{m \in magnolias \mid (\iota\, p \in \{\text{Central Park}\})\, in(m,p) \wedge \text{in-bloom}(m)\}$$

i.e., the magnolia in Central Park which is in bloom.

In the semantic analysis of a sentence containing a pronoun, we could place the pronoun itself in the position normally occupied by the set to quantify over, and use the quantifier ι for singular pronouns, $\forall$ for plural pronouns. For example,

It was magnificent.

could be translated into

$$(\iota\, x \in it)\, magnificent(x)$$

This representation may seem peculiar, but it makes anaphora resolution quite simple: replace the pronoun in logical form by the discourse entity of the antecedent. For instance, in the sequence

A magnolia in Central Park was in bloom. It was magnificent.

---

[9] Strictly speaking, the discourse entity should also be qualified by the restriction 'which was mentioned (or *evoked*, to use Webber's term) in the *n*th sentence of the discourse'. To simplify our formulas, however, we shall not include this qualification in our set descriptions.

anaphora resolution would convert the logical form of the second sentence from

$$(\iota\, x \in \text{it})\ \text{magnificent}(x)$$

to

$$(\iota\, x \in \{m \in magnolias \mid (\iota\, p \in \{\text{Central Park}\})\ \text{in}(m,p)$$
$$\wedge\ \text{in-bloom}(m)\})\ \text{magnificent}(x)$$

These basic rules are adequate to handle the most common situations where pronouns are used. To simplify matters further, in many systems employing natural language interfaces there is a unique identifier (or 'name') associated with each individual in the domain. If this is the case, we may be able to 'evaluate' the discourse entity and record for each discourse entity its extension – the list of individuals – rather than the set-former expression. For example, if we have a data base of trees, in which the magnolias are labeled mag_1, mag_2 etc. we may be able to determine that the magnolia in Central Park which is in bloom is mag_{17}, and so record the discourse entity as $\{mag_{17}\}$ instead of the complex expression given just above. In natural language interfaces for data base retrieval, computing the extensions of the discourse entities can often be made part of the process of retrieving the requested information, with little extra effort.

In order to have a complete procedure for computing discourse entities, several elaborations are required to these basic rules; we will mention two of these complications here.

If an existential quantifier $(\exists x \in G)$ is in the scope of some other quantifier $(\exists y \in H)$, $(\forall y \in H)$, or $(\iota y \in H)$, then the discourse description, instead of being $\{x \in G \mid P(x)\}$, will be

$$\{x \in G \mid (\exists y \in H)\ P(x)\}$$

For example, in the sentence

Every student bought a book.

which has the logical form

$$(\forall s \in students)\ (\exists b \in books)\ \text{bought}(s,b)$$

the phrase 'a book' will give rise to the discourse entity

$$\{b \in books \mid (\exists s \in students)\ \text{bought}\ (s,b)\}$$

i.e., the set of books which had been bought by some student. This would be the referent of 'they' in 'They cost $5 each.'.

Another problem arises when a pronoun in the scope of a quantifier has as its antecedent the noun phrase corresponding to the quantifier; for example,

Every customer bought the cat she liked best.

If 'every customer' is translated as $(\forall x \in C)$, the discourse entity associated with this noun phrase is C, the set of customers. However, the referent for 'she' should not be C but rather the bound variable x; i.e., the analysis should have the form

$$(\forall x \in C) \ x \text{ bought the cat which } x \text{ liked best}$$

We can account for such sentences in our anaphora resolution procedure by saying that the discourse entity associated with a noun phrase depends on the context of the referring (anaphoric) phrase. If a noun phrase is translated into a quantifier $(\forall x \in G)$ or $(\exists x \in G)$ then within the scope of the quantifier the discourse entity associated with the noun phrase is x; outside the scope of the quantifier it is as given above $(G \text{ or } \{x \in G \mid P(x)\})$.

3.5.3 Selecting the referent

Selecting the correct referent is the most difficult part of anaphora resolution. Many systems have developed relatively *ad hoc*, system-specific heuristics to attack this problem. Along with these, a number of more systematic criteria have gradually developed. We can divide these into syntactic and semantic criteria.

Syntactic constraints on intrasentential anaphora have been intensively studied by generative linguists. We will mention here the earliest and simplest form of these constraints, which accounts for 'most' of the cases. These rules have since been repeatedly refined, and are still a source of considerable debate.

The first constraint, enunciated by Langacker (1969), says that a pronoun may not both precede and command its antecedent. The *command* relation is defined as follows: node A commands node B if (1) neither A nor B dominates the other; and (2) the s-node that most immediately dominates A also dominates B. This constraint may be illustrated by the following four sentences (Jackendoff 1972, p. 118):

(1) Jake left town after he robbed the bank.
(2) He left town after Jake robbed the bank.
(3) After Jake robbed the bank, he left town.
(4) After he robbed the bank, Jake left town.

In which of these sentences can 'he' refer to 'Jake'? These sentences consist of two clauses, a main clause ('__left town') and a subordinate clause ('__robbed the bank'). The subject of the main clause commands the subject of the subordinate clause. Sentence (2) is therefore the only sentence in which 'he' both precedes and commands 'Jake'. Thus, according to Langacker's rule, 'Jake' *may* be the antecedent of 'he' in all of the sentences except sentence (2). This constraint can exclude certain noun phrases as possible antecedents of a pronoun, but it cannot (by itself) tell us that a particular noun phrase must be the antecedent of a pronoun. Note also that, like the rule for quantifier scoping, this rule depends on the surface ordering of constituents.

The other constraint concerns reflexive pronouns (myself, himself). It says that a pronoun and its antecedent are in the same clause if and only if the pronoun is reflexive (Lees and Klima 1963). This constraint can serve us two ways: for sentences like

> Jack likes him.

it tells us that the antecedent of 'him' cannot be 'Jack'; for a sentence such as

> Jack likes himself.

it tells us that the antecedent of 'himself' must be 'Jack'.

Few natural language systems handle reflexive pronouns and few incorporate the command-and-precede constraint or anything similar. These constraints exclude only a few of the possible antecedents within the same sentence as a pronoun, and impose no restriction on antecedents in prior sentences. Their net effect in narrowing the range of possible antecedents is therefore less than that of the semantic constraints.

The semantic constraints ask what antecedents would make sense in place of the anaphoric expression. As in previous cases where we took recourse to semantic information – to resolve syntactic ambiguity, to select quantifier scope – there is no limit to the world knowledge which may be required. An example of this (Winograd 1971, p. 11) is the following pair of sentences:

> The city councilmen refused to give the women a permit for a demonstration because they feared violence.
> The city councilmen refused to give the women a permit for a demonstration because they advocated revolution.

The antecedent of 'they' is different in the two sentences, and the inferences required to make the proper choice are quite complex.

As in the case of syntactic ambiguity, however, we can use sublanguage word classes to capture a substantial part of our knowledge about which word sequences are meaningful and which are meaningless. For purposes of anaphora resolution, we would determine from the immediate context of a pronoun and the sublanguage (semantic) grammar the sublanguage word class or classes which could meaningfully occur in place of the pronoun. We would then limit our antecedent search to words of that class. This is very similar to the approach used by some systems for completing sentence fragments, and in fact some systems use the same procedure for both functions. For example, in the sequence

> The new fighter took off from the *Kennedy*. It flew beautifully.

sublanguage information tells us that the subject of 'fly' can be a plane but not a ship (such as the carrier *Kennedy*), so we are able to select 'the new fighter' as the proper antecedent of 'it'.

In a later chapter, on text analysis, we will consider more sophisticated criteria for antecedent selection, which seek not only to make the individual sentences meaningful but to have the sequence of sentences fit some coherent pattern. Thus in the previous example, the sentence about the plane's taking off could reasonably be followed by some comment on its flight (whereas 'The new fighter was loaded aboard the *Kennedy*. It flew beautifully.' is more peculiar).

3.5.3.1 Search order

Clearly the discourse entities mentioned in a long text are not all equally likely antecedents of an anaphoric noun phrase. We want to take into account the factors of *recency* and *focus* in selecting among antecedents which pass the syntactic and semantic tests. This is typically accomplished by specifying a search order, an order in which the potential antecedents are to be considered.

Hobbs (1976) has proposed a search order which is quite successful in finding the 'correct' antecedent. His algorithm examines first the syntactically allowed positions of the current sentence, then the noun phrases of the previous sentence, then the sentence before that. The parse trees of prior sentences are searched breadth-first, top-down, left-to-right, so that the subject and objects of the main clause are considered first. In a very simple way this accounts for the observation that the subject is most likely to be the focus of the current discourse, and hence more likely to be referred to anaphorically. Sidner (1979, 1983) has considered the role of focusing in more detail. A more sophisticated analysis of focus and of anaphora resolution in general will require a better overall understanding of text (as opposed to sentence) analysis.

3.5.4 *Other anaphoric noun phrases*

Up to now we have restricted our consideration of anaphoric noun phrases to definite pronouns. There are also indefinite pronouns, which we shall discuss shortly.

Which other[10] noun phrases are anaphoric? Noun phrases with zeroed

---

[10] Even pronouns are not always anaphoric. There is the generic use of pronouns:

> He who laughs last laughs best.
> One must pay all fees to graduate.

Also, in conversation, the referent may be in the physical context:

> [pointing] He did it.

nouns ('*The last three* were beautiful.') usually are, although sometimes the zeroed noun is recoverable from another source ('He only buys the best.').

Beyond these, almost any noun phrase *may* be anaphoric. A noun phrase with *the* (definite noun phrases) may identify a unique object in and of itself, or it may be anaphoric. Thus it is necessary to try to perform anaphora resolution in such cases; if the resolution procedure is unsuccessful, the non-anaphoric reading is taken. The same is true of noun phrases with universal quantifiers, which may be anaphoric ('Jack bought five houses. Every house had a garage.'). Noun phrases with existential quantifiers are less likely to be anaphoric, except for the case of zeroed noun phrases mentioned earlier ('Jack bought five houses. Some houses had garages.' may sound peculiar, but '. . . Some had garages.' is OK).

3.5.5   Definite noun phrases

In this section we shall deal with sequences such as

> J.D., aged 58, was admitted to BH on 5-29-84. *The patient* complained of chest pain and nausea.

or

> Fifty students gathered in front of the president's office. *The men* were wearing their official beanies.

The overall process of anaphora resolution is much the same as it is for definite pronouns. However, the additional information in the anaphoric noun phrase (the noun and possible modifiers) affects the antecedent search and the substitution process.

In the antecedent search, conflicts between information in the anaphoric noun phrase and information in the candidate antecedent can be used to exclude some potential antecedents. These conflicts can be of two types. A definite contradiction arises if the cores of the two noun phrases are not in a superset–subset or set–member relation (with either antecedent or anaphor being the subset); a contradiction can also arise between a modifier of the anaphor and a modifier of the antecedent. Subset relations can be detected by maintaining a hierarchical word classification. Detecting contradiction between modifiers in general would require a full theorem prover, but some success can be obtained by more limited means, such as observing that some attributes of an object must be single valued.

Even in cases where an attribute can be multi-valued, the presence of an explicit attribute with different values in the anaphor and candidate antecedent is generally an indication that a contrast between the two values was intended, and hence that this is not the correct antecedent.

Once an antecedent has been selected, we combine the information from anaphor and antecedent. This can be done by conjoining the predicates in the set descriptors of the discourse entity and the anaphoric phrase. For instance, in the sequence

> I entertained some men from Milwaukee. The old men wore slacks and the young ones wore jeans.

'some men from Milwaukee' will have the discourse entity

$$\{m \in men \mid from(m,\text{Milwaukee}) \wedge entertained(I,m)\}$$

'the old men' will translate to the quantifier

$$(\forall x \in \{n \in men \mid old(n)\})$$

which should be replaced during anaphora resolution by

$$\{\forall x \in \{m \in men \mid old(m) \wedge from(m,\text{Milwaukee}) \wedge entertained(I,m)\}\}$$

In the common case that the anaphoric phrase uses a generic noun ('I met some linguists from Philadelphia. The scientists were wearing . . .') the conjoining will not change the original discourse entity.

3.5.6 Indefinite pronouns and noun phrases

Compare the following two sequences:

> John bought 10 apples. Several were rotten.

and

> John bought 10 apples. Mary bought several too.

The first sequence is similar to examples of anaphora we have considered previously. The zeroed noun following 'several' acts like a pronoun; anaphora resolution will replace it by the discourse entity for '10 apples', producing the equivalent of 'several of the 10 apples which John bought'.

In the second sequence, the antecedent for 'several' is also '10 apples'. However, in contrast to the previous example, 'several' does *not* refer to the particular apples which John bought but rather to some other individuals satisfying the description 'apple'. We shall distinguish these two types of anaphora by calling the first *entity anaphora* and the second *description anaphora* (called by Webber *one anaphora*). Any pronoun or noun phrase can be used for entity anaphora, but only phrases with zeroed nouns or the pronoun 'one' can be used for description anaphora.

The processes of antecedent selection and of substitution are quite different for the two types of anaphora. For description anaphora, we begin with the *discourse description* associated with each noun phrase. The discourse description is simply the set quantified over in the logical form (for the ∀ and ι quantifiers, the discourse description and discourse entity are the same). In selecting the antecedent, we do *not* consider conflicts between modifiers in the anaphoric noun phrase and those in the discourse description. However, when a substitution value is formed by conjoining the modifiers of the discourse description and anaphor, any modifiers in the discourse description which conflict with modifiers of the anaphor are deleted. For example, in

> Jack bought a red rubber ball. Mary bought a green one.

the discourse description for 'a red rubber ball' will be

> $\{b \in balls \mid red(b) \wedge \text{made-of}(b,rubber)\}$;

'a green one' might be translated into logical form as

> $(\exists x \in \{y \in one \mid green(y)\})$

In combining the two set descriptions, the predicate 'red' is dropped because it conflicts with 'green' leaving the quantifier

> $(\exists x \in \{y \in balls \mid green(y) \wedge \text{made-of}(y,rubber)\})$

The difference between the antecedent selection rules for entity and description anaphora can be used to discriminate between entity and description anaphora where both are possible. For example, in the interchange

> Did John have any chest X-rays?
>   Yes, three.
> Did Mary have *any*?

we can determine that 'any' in the second question is an instance of description anaphora, because the discourse entity for 'any chest X-rays' (viz., the chest X-rays which John had) has a predicate *has(John,x)* which contradicts the context of the anaphoric phrase.

3.6   Analyzing sentence fragments

A large amount of natural language input consists of sentence fragments. Unless people are constrained by the obligations of formal writing to use complete, grammatical sentences, they will be inclined to leave out parts of the sentence which they believe the reader will be able to reconstruct. For example, some types of medical records consist primarily of sentence fragments, and our very limited experience with natural language question-answering suggests that users will use fragmentary questions if the system will let them. The use of fragments, like the use of anaphoric phrases, provides a way of omitting information which will be understood by the listener or reader, and thus making communication more efficient.

We face two problems in adapting techniques designed for complete sentences to handle sentence fragments. First, we must be able to parse these sentence fragments. Second, at some stage of the processing we must reconstruct the missing information in the fragment. The sources for this reconstructed material can be divided into two classes: information about the language and the domain ('real-world knowledge') and information from the immediately preceding discourse or dialog. We shall consider three different approaches to these problems, and examine their relative advantages and disadvantages.

The New York University Linguistic String Project has been processing medical records which consist primarily of sentence fragments. An analysis was made of the fragments in a substantial corpus of patient care histories (approximately 50 histories of several pages each). This analysis showed that the deleted material in the fragments is mainly of a small class of sentence parts:

    (1) tense and the verb *be* ('Wound healing well.')
    (2) subject, tense, and the verb *be* ('To be seen by gynecologist.')
    (3) subject ('Found osteochondritis in rib.')
    (4) subject, tense, and verb ('No bone pain.')

The fragments were further classified according to the sublanguage classes of the deleted material. The String Project chose to parse these sentences by adding productions to the grammar corresponding to the classes of fragments which had been identified. For example, to account for deletion of tense + *be*, a production was included to expand the sentence as subject + object of *be*. Since the deleted material fell into the few patterns listed above, relatively few productions had to be added to the grammar (Anderson, Bross, and Sager 1975; Marsh 1983).

The medical records were automatically mapped into a tabular structure called an *information format*, which will be considered in more detail in the chapter on discourse analysis. Very roughly, each sentence corresponded to a row of this table, while each column held words conveying a particular type of information (normally words from a particular sublanguage class); for example, columns might be labeled 'patient', 'test performed', 'part of body tested', 'medical finding', etc. Deleted material was restored only after the record had been translated into this tabular form. If a particular entry in a row is empty but should be filled (certain columns should always be filled, others need not be), the system will look upward in that column for the missing information. This corresponds to looking at earlier sentences of the same record for the information omitted from the current sentence. If an appropriate entry is found, it is copied into the missing entry; if not, the system checks if there is a default value for this column. For example, in the radiologist's report 'X-ray' is assumed if no test is specified. If such is the case, the default value is filled in, otherwise an error is reported (unable to reconstruct missing information) (Grishman and Hirschman 1978; Marsh 1983).

An outwardly very different approach is taken by the LIFER system at SRI, a natural language interface for data base retrieval (Hendrix 1977, 1978). LIFER's mechanism is designed to handle the situation where the user first asks a full-sentence question, e.g.,

> What is the length of *Santa Inez*?

and, after receiving an answer, types a fragmentary or elliptical question such as

> Of the *Kennedy*?

The basic assumption is that the intended question has a structure which parallels the previous question. The question may therefore be reconstructed by identifying the substring of the previous question which corresponds to the fragment and replacing the substring by the fragment, to obtain in this case

> What is the length of the *Kennedy*?

The correspondence is established by finding an analysis of the fragment as a series of (terminal and non-terminal) symbols which occurs in the parse of the original question (more precisely, occurs as a substring of a cut of the parse tree). In our example, both 'of *Santa Inez*' and 'of the *Kennedy*' can be analyzed as 'of < SHIP >'. The expansion of < SHIP > in the full question and fragment need not be the same, so the system would also correctly process 'Of the fastest nuclear carrier?' LIFER uses a semantic grammar, so the match of symbols implies a correspondence in the type of information, not just its form. To employ this technique with a conventional grammar (with categories such as noun, verb, noun phrase, etc.) we would have to match both the symbols in the tree and the sublanguage classes of some of the words.

The obvious main strength of the LIFER approach is that it is a *procedural* account of a class of ellipsis. In contrast to the Linguistic String Project's approach, it does not require the user to enumerate the fragments to be accepted. On the other hand, the SRI algorithm works only if there is a parallel between the preceding question and the full question from which the current fragment is derived. Although this may account for a substantial class of fragments in a question-answering environment, it doesn't account for all of them, for example,

> Did Smith have any X-rays?
> Yes, a chest X-ray on 2-24-83.
> Any clouding or thickening?

It would not account for many of the fragments in the medical record corpus (where most often even the first sentence of a record is a fragment).

Yet a third approach was taken by Waltz in his PLANES system, also a natural language data base retrieval system (Waltz 1978). Like LIFER, it uses a semantic grammar and an ATN formalism. Unlike most ATN systems, however, there is no top-level, sentence network. Instead, the grammar consists of a set of ATNs (called 'subnets'), each defining phrases with a specific meaning, such as plane types, malfunctions, and dates. A question will be accepted if it matches any sequence of these subnets. Such a scheme will accept fragments just as readily as full sentences, so long as the fragments match one or more complete subnets. In fact, relaxing the constraints on the ordering of sentence constituents allows the system to accept various grammatical sentence strings ('Did plane 3 make any flights?', 'Were any flights made by plane 3?') as well as ungrammatical ones ('Make plane 3 any flights?') without any special provision in the grammar.

Missing material is reconstructed using *concept case frames* and *context registers*. The context registers hold the most recent items matched by each type of subnet – the most recently mentioned plane, date, etc. The concept case frames are the semantic sentence patterns; each frame specifies an 'act' (usually a verb) together with one possible combination of subnets which can occur meaningfully with that verb (e.g., require plane-type maintenance-type). The concept case frames and the subnets together are roughly equivalent to a semantic grammar (except that they do not specify the order of major sentence constituents). If the subnets matched in processing a question are not equal to a concept case frame but are a subset of precisely one frame, PLANES assumes that the question is an instance of that frame with some cases (subnets) omitted. The omitted cases are then filled in from the corresponding context registers. If there are several possible frames, PLANES tries to make a choice based on the constituents present in the previous question.

The systems we have considered have one significant feature in common: they rely heavily on the division of words and phrases into semantic classes. In effect, prior sentences are searched for a phrase of a particular class (omitted from the fragment) or a phrase of the same class as one in the fragment. (This was somewhat refined in the SRI speech understanding system (Walker 1978). This system used a large number of classes arranged in a hierarchy, so that a distance can be defined between classes. Prior sentences are then searched for a phrase *closest* in class to the class of the fragment.)

The systems differ greatly in the way they determine the structure of the fragment and of the omitted material. The LIFER and PLANES systems have the virtue of accounting for a class of fragments in procedural terms. The class handled by LIFER, however, is limited to fragments paralleling the previous question. PLANES handles a broader class, but at the cost of ignoring in the grammar the order of sentence constituents. When order is important (for example, to bracket relative clauses) PLANES must resort to *ad hoc* procedures not needed in other systems. We may hope that a more comprehensive view of the syntactic and semantic information available to reconstruct omitted information will yield a broader-coverage procedure for fragment analysis in the near future.

3.7   Using the logical form

Fragment processing and anaphora resolution have now filled in omitted material and references to entities previously mentioned in the text. More general discourse analysis mechanisms (such as will be presented in the next chapter) would fill in other information, including implicit relations between sentences, leaving us with a 'complete' logical representation of the information in the text. Now what?

In the introduction we considered several applications for natural language processing, including machine translation, question-answering, and command systems. What we do with the logical form depends on the application:

* for machine translation, we would reverse the language analysis process to generate text in the target language[11]
* question-answering, starting from logical form, can be viewed as a slightly modified form of theorem-proving, with the answer corresponding to the value bound to some variable in the question (Green 1969)
* a command system can also be viewed as a form of theorem-proving, in which some of the axioms correspond to basic operations of the system being commanded

Strictly speaking, one might consider these theorem-proving tasks to be outside the realm of computational linguistics. As a practical matter, however, they are an integral part of computational linguistic systems and thus of direct concern to the computational linguist.

For question-answering systems, a general-purpose theorem-prover would be too inefficient for all but the tiniest data bases. Instead, the logical form is translated into the query language of some data base retrieval system, which retrieves the required information. For the LUNAR system, Woods used a representation of logical form quite close to our predicate calculus with restricted quantifiers; for retrieval, the quantifiers were directly interpreted as iterations over the corresponding sets. Other question-answering systems have used existing data base systems and query languages; the translation from our logical form to the relational calculus is particularly straightforward.

In principle, the translation to query language can be preceded by stages for inferencing and for simplification of the logical form, but these stages are very limited or entirely absent in most practical question-answering systems. The chief use of inferencing is for mapping the set of relations which may appear in questions (and hence in the logical form) into a more limited set of relations which actually appears in the data base.

---

[11] Most current translation systems do not analyse their input to the level of logical form (Slocum 1985).

Some natural language command systems, although very limited in scope, have come closer to the model of using a theorem-prover to process the logical form. The best known example is Winograd's blocks-world program (Winograd 1971, 1972). His system used PLANNER, in effect a Horn-clause theorem-prover, to bridge the gap between his logical form and the basic operations of moving blocks in his microworld.

In describing these natural language systems as a series of stages – syntax analysis, semantic analysis, deduction – we must not lose sight of the feedback from later to earlier stages. In many cases the results of deduction are needed to resolve ambiguities of syntactic or semantic analysis. Winograd's blocks-world system is a prime example of the interaction possible in a highly integrated system, and this demonstration of the interaction was probably the prime contribution of his doctoral research.

4   Discourse analysis and information structuring

Up to now, we have restricted ourselves to determining the structure and meaning of individual sentences. Although we have used limited extrasentential information (for anaphora resolution), we have not examined the structure of entire texts. Yet the information conveyed by a text is clearly more than the sum of its parts – more than the meanings of its individual sentences. If a text tells a story, describes a procedure, or offers an argument, we must understand the connections between the component sentences in order to have fully understood the story. These connections are needed both *per se* (to answer questions about why an event occurred, for example) and to resolve ambiguities in the meanings of individual sentences. *Discourse analysis* is the study of these connections. Because these connections are usually implicit in the text, identifying them may be a difficult task.

As a simple example of the problems we face, consider the following brief description of a naval encounter:

> Just before dawn, the *Valiant* sighted the *Zwiebel* and fired two torpedoes. It sank swiftly, leaving few survivors.

The most evident linguistic problem we face is finding an antecedent for 'it'. There are four candidates in the first sentence: 'dawn', '*Valiant*', '*Zwiebel*', and 'torpedoes'. Semantic classification should enable us to exclude 'dawn' (*'dawn sinks'), and number agreement will exclude 'torpedoes', but that still leaves us with two candidates: 'the *Valiant*' and 'the *Zwiebel*' (which are presumably both ships of some sort). Our syntactic and semantic tools will not enable us to choose between these two candidates. In order to decide that it was the *Zwiebel* which sank, we must recognize the causal relationship between the firing of the torpedoes and the sinking of the ship: that the *Valiant* fired at the *Zwiebel* (since one does not normally fire at oneself), and hence that it was probably the *Zwiebel* which sank. Recognizing this causal relationship would also allow the system to answer such questions as 'What did the *Valiant* fire at?' and 'Why did the *Zwiebel* sink?'. If the system has a slightly more detailed model (in which a torpedo causes a ship to sink by hitting the ship, exploding, and making a hole in the hull below the water), it would also be able to answer such questions as 'Did a torpedo explode?'. The writer of this passage would have known all these causal relationships, but he would also have realized that such facts and connections can readily be inferred by the reader, and so would not have bothered to include them explicitly in the narrative. Since so much of the information conveyed by this (and most other) texts is implicit, we cannot claim that we have adequately understood the text unless this implicit information has been recovered. This is the role of the discourse analysis component.

Conceptually, we may view discourse analysis as receiving a series of predicate calculus formulas produced by the semantic analysis of a text. (If there are as yet unresolved syntactic or semantic ambiguities, discourse analysis will receive several alternative series of formulas.) Discourse analysis will supplement this series with formulas representing the connections between the input formulas and additional facts which had to be inferred in order to establish these connections. (If alternative analyses are received, some will be rejected because they are 'incoherent': because satisfactory connections cannot be established between the sentences as analyzed.) In practice, discourse analysis is likely to be more tightly integrated with the other components. For example, when the anaphora component is unable to identify or select an antecedent, it can invoke discourse analysis at that point to try and resolve the ambiguity.

4.1   Text grammar

We shall use the term *discourse* to mean any multi-sentence text. Discourse comes in many forms. A discourse may tell a story, describe a scene, give instructions, or present an argument.

Given this wide variety, it may be hard to imagine any general statements we can make about discourse structure. There have, however, been a number of efforts at defining conditions which must be satisfied for a text to be coherent. Much of this work comes under the heading of *text grammar* (see, for example, van Dijk (1973), Bellert (1973), and Brown and Yule (1983)). A number of very general conditions have been developed, with different conditions being proposed by different workers. One condition, the condition of introduction, requires that an individual entity must be 'introduced' (e.g., either explicitly by an existential quantifier or indirectly as a consequence of another introduction) before it can be used as a discourse referent (e.g., in a definite noun phrase). Another requirement is that the consequences of any sentence in a text must have non-null intersection with the consequences of the other sentences. Hobbs (1982) has identified four general classes of coherence relations between the sentences in a text.

What these various coherence criteria have in common is that they involve substantial inferencing and require access to relevant world knowledge. Text grammar is thus not a neatly closed problem in the way that sentence grammar is. As a practical matter it tells us that text analysis will depend critically on our ability to organize this relevant world knowledge.

4.2   Organizing world knowledge

Once we have selected a logical formalism (see section 3.1), we can take all of our world knowledge and encode it as a vast collection of theorems in this formalism. As sentences of a text are received, we can translate them into this same formalism using the methods introduced in chapter 3. We can then use some powerful theorem-prover to draw the necessary inferences (for example, to eliminate some semantic interpretations by showing that they contradict world knowledge).

This may sound very neat but it ignores a host of practical problems. It doesn't provide us any guidance in collecting all the world knowledge we need (imagine trying to write down everything you know about buying groceries). Even worse, perhaps, it provides no guidance to the theorem-prover in selecting which theorems to use and which inferences to draw. It is hard to imagine an inference system (or the human brain) finding its way through an unorganized collection of hundreds of thousands of theorems. Therefore the primary challenge of text analysis, as it has been perceived since the early 1970s, is how to identify and organize the requisite world knowledge so that it can be effectively brought to bear on the problems of text analysis. The remainder of this chapter will consider a number of efforts at meeting this challenge.

4.2.1   Grouping facts by topic

One of the earliest efforts at procedural text analysis was Charniak's investigation of children's stories. Charniak was particularly concerned with the way in which relationships between sentences could be used to resolve pronominal reference. Consider for example the following paragraph (Charniak 1972, p. 7):

> Janet and Penny went to the store to get presents for Jack. Janet said 'I will get Jack a top.' 'Don't get Jack a top' said Penny. 'He has a top. He will make you take it back.'

The problem for anaphora resolution is what does *it* refer to – the top Jack has or the one Janet plans to buy? Making a correct choice involves several inferences – that for some possessions X, if someone already has an X he probably won't want another X; and that, if you buy someone a present and he doesn't want it, you will have to return it. Of the two possible referents, only the choice of 'it' = 'the top Janet wants to buy' will fit with these inferences.

Since these inferences are so specific, a natural language system will have to store many thousands of them in order to analyze a variety of texts. How should these inferences be organized? Charniak notes that the inferences mentioned in the last paragraph are relevant to the giving of presents, and suggests that they should be grouped together with *presents* as their topic. More generally, we would form groups of inferences associated with particular situations or classes of objects. Thus we might have groups of theorems about birthday parties, about buying groceries, and about kitchens, for example. A single theorem might apply to several topics and hence be in several groups.

At any given moment, most of these myriad theorems would be inactive (ignored by the theorem-prover). When a particular topic, such as *presents*, is mentioned in the text, the theorems associated with this topic will be activated. Presumably when the text moves on to another topic they will be deactivated. In this way the system avoids having to sort through all its world knowledge each time a new sentence must be processed; only the facts relevant to the topic of discussion are considered.

These efforts at information structuring were very preliminary and have since been substantially developed both by Charniak and others, as we shall discuss in the next few sections. Charniak has also discussed further the problems of selecting and activating chunks of knowledge (Charniak 1982).

4.3 Frames

Much of the recent work on organizing knowledge in order to process new data is based on the following observation: people generally assimilate new information by identifying it as an instance of a pattern with which they are already familiar. For example, when people see a room for the first time, they try to classify it as a bedroom, kitchen, dining room, etc. They may do this by a partial pattern match (for example, guessing that a room is a kitchen by peeking in and seeing an oven). The remainder of the pattern, and information associated with the pattern, can be used to generate inferences and expectations (for example, that the room probably also contains a sink and a refrigerator). Even if a situation or object doesn't match any pattern exactly, it will be remembered as an instance of a pattern with some exceptions (for example, a kitchen without a refrigerator). If we take this observation as guidance for the mechanical processing of discourse, we should make this process of classifying new information in terms of known patterns central to the analysis of texts. Accordingly, the groups of facts into which our knowledge is divided should be organized to facilitate and make use of such pattern matching.

The best known paper on this theme is Minsky's 'A framework for representing knowledge' (Minsky 1975). Minsky called these patterns *frames*, and systems using this approach have therefore become known as *frame-based systems*. Minsky described a general strategy for knowledge organization, and did not offer details of a knowledge representation formalism or how it might be applied to language analysis. However, since this paper was written, quite a few frame-based knowledge representation languages have been developed (such as FRL (Goldstein and Roberts 1977) and KRL (Bobrow and Winograd 1977)), so it is possible for us now to describe a 'typical' frames formalism.

The basic 'chunk' of knowledge is the frame. There are *prototype frames*, which describe classes of objects or situations (for example, kitchens, buying groceries), and *instance frames*, which describe individual objects or situations (for example, Escoffier's kitchen, Sam Spade's trip to the supermarket last Friday). Each instance frame must be an instance (instantiation) of some prototype frame. In addition to this two-level class–instance hierarchy, there will usually be a multi-level 'generalization hierarchy' in which some prototypes (such as 'kitchen') are viewed as instances of a more general prototype (such as 'room').

Each frame contains a set of labeled *slots*. These specify the properties, constituents, and/or participants in the object or situation represented by the frame. The value of a slot may be an integer, a character string, or another frame (thus, a frame for an individual shopping trip may have a date slot, whose value is a character string, and a shopper slot, whose value is a frame representing the shopper – an instance of the person frame). The slots of a frame need not all be filled with values; this may be the case, for example, if a particular property is unknown or if an individual doesn't possess a particular constituent.

A variety of information may be associated with each slot of a prototype frame. *Constraints* indicate what type of value (for example, instances of what prototype frame) can be assigned to a slot. *Default values* determine the value to be assigned to a slot if no value is specified by the input data. Procedures of several types may be associated with a slot: 'TO-FILL' procedures compute a value for an empty slot when it is needed; 'WHEN-FILLED' procedures are executed when a value is assigned to a slot. Much of the detailed world knowledge is embedded in such procedures. This is, however, no longer one big bag of facts – the frame–slot structure gives organization to the procedures and guidance in their application.

This situation is analogous to that of augmented context-free grammars. In both cases there is a specification of constituent structure (in one case, the frame–slot structures, in the other the context-free grammar), to which are attached a set of procedures. Most of the detailed (world/grammatical) knowledge is embedded in the procedures. The constituent structure specifications provide a framework and a degree of modularity to the system, since the procedures interact only with constituent structure, not directly with each other.

The frame–slot structures form an alternative semantic representation; each prototype frame is in effect a predicate, with each of its slots an argument position. An input text may first be translated into logical forms based on more traditional predicates, closely corresponding to the vocabulary of the text.

These logical forms can then be mapped into frames, with each argument of a traditional predicate typically filling one frame slot. The complexity of this mapping depends greatly on the richness of the set of frames, and hence on the semantic richness of the texts being processed. In the simple domains characteristic of today's systems, one can determine from each individual predicate, or possibly from the predicate with its immediate context within the sentence, which frame it fits into. In more complex domains, a predicate may correspond to slots in several different frames, so pattern matching over a larger context will be required to select the appropriate frame.

4.4 Analyzing narrative: scripts and plans

Texts may be classified both according to the subject domain involved and according to the type of discourse, such as narrative, argument, or instruction. As we have noted above, a language analyzer must have a model of the objects and relationships in the subject domain. In addition, the analyzer must understand the organizing principles for the particular type of discourse. These organizing principles enable us to understand, for example, why an instruction manual 'What to do when an earthquake strikes' is organized quite differently from a narrative 'How I survived the great 1989 earthquake'.

Narrative has been the most intensively studied form of discourse. Narrative is an appealing object of study because its primary organizing principle – at least for simple stories – is straightforward: events are related in the order in which they occur. The task of understanding a narrative is therefore largely one of reconstructing a sequence of events and their interrelationship from 'highlights' which appear explicitly in the narrative.

4.4.1 Scripts

Schank and his co-workers at Yale have been at the forefront of the effort to understand narrative. Their studies have led them to define large semantic patterns similar to the frames we have been considering. Their first effort at defining such chunks of knowledge was the *script* (Schank and Abelson 1975, 1977). The script is intended to capture a person's knowledge about a stereotyped sequence of events.

Their 'classic' example is the restaurant script. From many visits to many kinds of restaurants, people build up detailed expectations – a script – of what will happen in a restaurant. The usual sequence of events includes (among other things) entering, being seated, ordering, receiving one's food, eating, receiving the check, paying, and leaving. Because people share such a detailed script, they can assemble coherent descriptions of such experiences from fragmentary information. In particular, the script contains actors and objects (the food, the check, etc.) which can be referred to in a text without having been previously introduced. The restaurant script would thus enable us to solve the reference problem for 'the check' in the paragraph at the beginning of our discussion of anaphora resolution. It would also allow us to figure out who 'he' is in

> The customer carefully gave his order to the waiter.
> Thirty minutes later he returned with the wrong entrée.

(since the script indicates that the waiter brings the food). Because the script supplies default information which is assumed in the absence of explicit information, we could also infer from a sentence like 'The food arrived cold.' that the food was probably brought by the waiter.

There are different kinds of restaurants, ranging from haute cuisine to fast-food, and our expectations of what will happen are different for different restaurants. In a fancy restaurant, we wait for the maître d' to seat us; in a fast-food place, we go up to a counter and order. This variety is reflected in different *tracks* in the script. Each track is a sequence of *scenes*, such as entering, ordering, eating, and leaving. Each scene is described in turn as a sequence of primitive actions, using conceptual dependency notation (section 3.1.6). The actions in the script involve a set of *roles* – the people in the script, such as the customer and waiter – and a set of *props* – the objects acted on, such as the menu and the food. We show in figure 4.1 the coffee shop track of Schank's restaurant script. Note that even within this single track there are several alternate paths, such as one for the situation where the food ordered by the customer is not available.

Scripts were used by a program called SAM (Script Applier Mechanism) for analyzing simple paragraphs of narrative text (Schank and Abelson 1975, 1977; Cullingford 1981). To determine when a script is applicable, various *headers* are associated with a script. For the restaurant script these include precondition headers ('the customer is hungry') and locale headers (something happened 'at a restaurant'). If a text matches one of the headers of a script and in addition mentions some action within the script, the script will be activated. SAM then fills in the script with information from the text. Using the script, it makes the inferences necessary to complete a causal chain connecting the events in the text.

4.4.2 Plans

Scripts are only effective for analyzing texts which describe stereotyped situations. To analyze descriptions of novel sequences of events, Schank and Abelson proposed another type of knowledge, *plans* (Schank and Abelson 1977). To construct a causal chain for a novel sequence, a means–ends analysis must be performed; that is, we must try to understand how later events in a text act to further previously stated goals. Often the connection will be indirect – an action will further an implicit subgoal which is a precondition of some previously mentioned goal. A plan consists of a goal, alternative sequences of actions for achieving that goal, and preconditions for applying the various sequences.

As an example of a direct connection involving a single plan, consider

> John wanted Bill's bicycle. He walked over to Bill and asked him if he would give it to him.

(from Wilensky 1978). The asking in the second sentence can be identified as part of an 'asking plan' corresponding to the goal of getting something. This goal can be identified with the goal of John wanting to get Bill's bicycle, as mentioned in the first sentence. A more complex chain is required to analyze

> Willa was hungry. She grabbed the Michelin guide. She got in her car.

(from Wilensky 1981, p. 182). To understand the connections between these sentences, we must recognize that Willa can satisfy her hunger by dining at a restaurant (the 'eating-at-restaurant plan'), that to dine there she must find out where the restaurant is (which she can do using the Michelin guide) and must get to the restaurant (which she can do using her car).

The analysis of brief stories in terms of plans was implemented in PAM, the Plan Applier Module (Wilensky 1978, 1981). For didactic purposes, Wilensky developed a version called MCPAM (micro-PAM) with a simpler control structure (Wilensky 1981). We shall use this simpler structure in explaining the principles of plan recognition. In MCPAM, a plan is represented using rules of four different types. These rules will form the links of a causal chain. The four types are:

(1) *initiate* rules link a property of the current state (what Schank calls a 'theme') to a plausible goal:

theme → goal

for example,

theme (x is hungry) → goal (x is not hungry)

(2) *plans-for* rules link a goal to a plan which achieves that goal:

goal → plan

for example,

goal (x is not hungry) → plan (x eat at restaurant)

(3) *subgoal* rules link a plan to a precondition of that plan, which will be itself a goal:

plan → precondition of plan

for example,

plan (x eat at restaurant) → goal (x be at restaurant)

(4) *instantiation* rules link a plan to a conceptual dependency action which is a part of that plan:

plan → action

for example,

plan (walk to x) → PTRANS to x

Script: RESTAURANT
Track: Coffee Shop   Roles: S-Customer
Props: Tables   W-Waiter
       Menu   C-Cook
       F-Food   M-Cashier
       Check   O-Owner
       Money

Entry conditions: S is hungry   Results: S has less money
                  S has money   O has more money
                                              S is not hungry
                                              S is pleased (optional)

Scene 1: Entering

S **PTRANS** S into restaurant
S **ATTEND** eyes to tables
S **MBUILD** where to sit
S **PTRANS** S to table
S **MOVE** S to sitting position

Scene 2: Ordering

(menu on table)   (W brings menu)   (S asks for menu)
S **PTRANS** menu to S   S **MTRANS** signal to W
                                     W **PTRANS** W to table
                                     S **MTRANS** 'need menu' to W
                                     W **PTRANS** W to menu

        W **PTRANS** W to table
        W **ATRANS** menu to S

        S **MTRANS** food list to CP(S)
      *S **MBUILD** choice of F
        S **MTRANS** signal to W
        W **PTRANS** W to table
        S **MTRANS** 'I want F' to W

            W **PTRANS** W to C
            W **MTRANS** (ATRANS F) to C

C **MTRANS** 'no F' to W   C **DO** (prepare F script)
W **PTRANS** W to S   to Scene 3
W **MTRANS** 'no F' to S
(go back to *) or
(go to Scene 4 at no pay path)

Scene 3: Eating

C **ATRANS** F to W
W **ATRANS** F to S
S **INGEST** F

(Optionally return to Scene 2 to order more;
otherwise go to Scene 4)

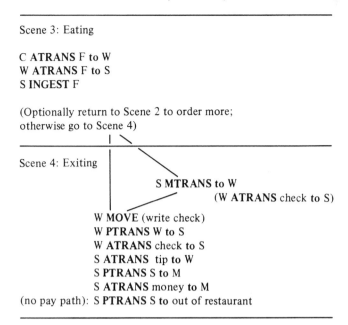

Scene 4: Exiting

S **MTRANS** to W

(W **ATRANS** check to S)

W **MOVE** (write check)
W **PTRANS** W to S
W **ATRANS** check to S
S **ATRANS** tip to W
S **PTRANS** S to M
S **ATRANS** money to M
(no pay path): S **PTRANS** S to out of restaurant

Figure 4.1 (from Schank and Abelson 1977)

A text analysis system for any realistic domain must have a large number of such rules, corresponding to many different plans.

PAM operates by building causal chains using these rules. PAM has a 'data base' (collection) of active plans and goals; initially, this data base is empty. When PAM reads a new input clause it adds it to the data base. It then tries to find a chain of items C_i (plans or goals)

$$C_0 \rightarrow C_1 \rightarrow ... \rightarrow C_{n-1} \rightarrow C_n$$

such that every link $C_i \rightarrow C_{i+1}$ corresponds to a rule, C_0 is in the data base, and C_n is (the conceptual dependency representation of) the clause just read. If PAM finds such a chain, the input is 'justified' by this chain and all the C_i are added to the data base.

Getting back to Willa, the first sentence ('Willa was hungry.') will simply be put in the data base, since there is initially nothing else for it to link up to. When the next clause ('She grabbed the Michelin guide.') is read, PAM will construct a causal chain as follows:

theme (Willa was hungry)
    → goal (Willa be not hungry)
    → plan (Willa do eat-at-restaurant plan)
    → goal (Willa be at restaurant)

> → goal (Willa know where restaurant is)
> → plan (Willa read restaurant guide)
> → goal (Willa possess restaurant guide)
> → plan (Willa take restaurant guide)
> → Willa GRASP restaurant guide

All of these plans and goals will be added to the data base. Then, to justify 'she got in her car.', PAM will construct the chain:

> goal (Willa be at restaurant)
> → plan (Willa use car)
> → goal (Willa be in car)
> → plan (Willa walk to car)
> → Willa PTRANS to car

Note that, as the starting point for this chain, PAM can use one of the intermediate goals created in justifying the previous input.

4.4.3 *MOPS, story points, and plot units*

Scripts and plans represented initial explorations in the analysis of narrative structure by Schank and his colleagues. More recently, Schank has focused on more modular and hierarchical memory structures, while others have developed higher-level narrative patterns capable, for example, of representing multiple interacting goals.

Scripts were designed as self-contained chunks of knowledge. The representation could not take advantage of the similarities between tasks, such as visiting a doctor's office, a dentist's office, and a lawyer's office. The result was a need for many scripts, each with a large amount of detail and many 'tracks'. To remedy this and other shortcomings of the earlier theory, Schank has proposed a memory scheme based on smaller units called MOPS ('memory organization packets') (Schank 1980, 1982). These MOPS can be combined as they are needed to form scripts corresponding to those of the earlier theory. For example, there would be a MOP of dentist-specific information to generate the expectations regarding a visit to the dentist. In this way, MOP-based systems have become more similar to frame-based systems, which typically use hierarchies of more general and more specific frames in order to represent world knowledge efficiently.

If a narrative follows a single script or relates actions in pursuit of a single goal, we may judge it coherent, but it is not likely to be very interesting. Why would anyone want to hear that

> Fred entered the restaurant at 7:30. He sat down and ordered a large steak. After twenty minutes the waiter brought it. Fred ate the steak, paid his bill and left.

Interesting stories must have some extra ingredient beyond coherence. As a natural outgrowth of the initial study of scripts and plans, several researchers examined this issue. Wilensky, in his work on story points (Wilensky 1982), examined situations where multiple goals led to problems. He identified some problem-causing goal relationships (such as 'goal conflict', where one person has two conflicting goals) and the typical ways in which these problematic relationships are resolved. Individual stories could then be classified in terms of these shifting goal relationships. Lenhert, in her work on plot units (Lenhert 1982), focused on how events in a story pleased or displeased the individuals involved. By classifying events as pleasing or displeasing, and also classifying the different causal relationships between events, she built up an inventory of basic event patterns (the 'primitive plot units') and larger patterns with names like 'honored promise' and 'double-cross'.

The significance of the specific patterns developed by these researchers may be debated, but a more general lesson is evident: by looking at these narratives at a more abstract level we may observe common patterns which are obscured when we focus on the specific sequences of events.

4.5 Information formats

In an earlier section on semantic constraints (section 3.3), we considered how linguistic patterns reflected underlying semantic structures. Within the texts of a sublanguage, the set of meaningful predicate–argument relations takes linguistic form as a set of constraints on the classes of subjects and objects which appear with any particular verb. The patterns involved are very local ones – basically subject–verb–object and host–adjunct relations. We could, however, imagine inferring larger semantic structures, akin to frames, by observing more global linguistic patterns, sometimes covering an entire sentence or even several sentences. This approach has been adopted by Sager and her group at New York University; the resulting structures are called *information formats* (Sager 1972).

An information format is a labeled set of columns, analogous to the slots of a frame. A text is mapped into a table with these columns and with one or more rows (called *format entries*) for each sentence. Each column can be filled with words from a sublanguage word class (or classes) which play a particular informational role in the texts. The format represents a maximal or complete sublanguage sentence pattern; in any single format entry normally only a small subset of the format columns will be filled.

To clarify these concepts, let us consider the information format developed for radiology reports (Hirschman, Grishman, and Sager 1976). These reports contain sentences such as

(1) X-rays taken 3-22-65 reveal no evidence of metastases.
(2) Chest X-ray on 8-12-66 showed no metastatic disease.

Table 4.1

			TEST		
	TESTN	TESTLOC	VERB-DONE	P	TESTDATE
(1)	X-rays		taken		3-22-65
(2)	X-ray	chest		on	8-12-66
(3a)	film	chest			3-2-68
(3b)	film	chest			3-2-68

				FINDING			
	NEG	BE-SHOW	INDIC	MED-FIND	REGION		
					POS	PT-BODY	
(1)	no	reveal	evidence	metastatic disease			
(2)	no	showed		metastatic disease			
(3a)		shows		clouding	along	(left) thorax	
(3b)		shows		thickening		pleural	

(3) 3-2-68 chest film shows clouding along left thorax and pleural thickening.

This is a relatively simple type of text, so it was possible to develop a single information format encompassing all the types of information in these texts (for more complex domains which have been studied, such as a subfield of pharmacology, a number of formats were required (Sager 1972)). The format columns divide into two groups, those describing the test itself and those describing the findings of the test. For simplicity, we show here only those columns required by the three sentences given above (we have split the test columns from the format columns in table 4.1 above, so that it will fit on the page; two lines with the same number constitute a single format entry). Sentences (1) and (2) each create a single format entry; because of the conjunction, sentence (3) leads to two format entries, labeled (3a) and (3b).

We have noted already the value of mapping text into a regular structure such as a frame or format in order to establish text coherence and, in particular, identify co-reference. The New York University Linguistic String Project has emphasized in addition the direct value of the formats for information retrieval. Because words playing a particular informational role get placed in specific columns, it is often possible to answer a question regarding the text by examining only a few format columns. Using formatted medical records and existing data base systems, retrieval requests have been programmed to obtain statistics and apply medical screening criteria. The formatted text has also been used as the data base for a natural language question-answering system (Grishman and Hirschman 1978).

The procedure for converting text into a formatted data base involves four steps (Sager 1978). The first two we have already discussed: parsing and transformational decomposition using the Linguistic String Parser. The third step is the mapping into the format. In cases where a sublanguage word class appears in only a single format column, the mapping can be based entirely on the word class. For word classes which can appear in several format columns (such as negatives and time modifiers), syntactic information must be used as well. In the final stage, normalization, implicit information is filled in from previous format entries or from default values; the normalization procedures are thus analogous to the attached procedures in the frame formalism.

A significant difference between information formats and the other knowledge structures we have discussed is that the formats are linguistically based. This offers two advantages. First, since the formats are developed from linguistic patterns, it provides some assurance that we can create a systematic procedure for mapping decomposition trees into format entries. Second, it raises the possibility of a discovery procedure. A format for a new domain can be developed by taking a sample set of sentences, analyzing them syntactically, replacing words by their word classes, and then aligning and merging the resulting structures. Although considerable judgement is still required (to decide when to merge and how large a pattern to make into a single format), it does provide a methodology not available with the other approaches.

On the other hand, the formats are not directly comparable to high-level structures such as scripts or plot units. Any non-trivial text will have several levels of structure, ranging from individual predicates to structures covering the entire text (such as story points). The formats provide the next level of structure above the basic predicates. By mapping the text into a limited number of structures at this level, formatting facilitates the tasks of discourse analysis. It does not, however, provide the top-level structures which tie the format entries of a discourse together. It remains to be seen whether the same distributional linguistic techniques which have been used to develop the formats can be extended to these higher-level structures.

4.6   Analyzing dialog

Dialog is the exchange of natural language messages between two people or between man and machine.[1] The study of dialog is of both theoretical and practical interest to the computational linguist. It is of theoretical interest because the study of dialog forces us to confront issues regarding the *goals* of speakers in making natural language statements and the effect of natural language statements on others – in short, the pragmatics of natural language utterances. We shall touch on these issues very briefly at the end of this section.

---

[1] Or perhaps, some day, between two machines.

The study of dialog is of practical interest because most current applications of natural language processing involve man–machine interaction: question-answering systems and natural language command systems, for example. These systems will be most effective only if we are able to understand and use in our programs the techniques which people employ in conversation.

Most currently implemented systems use only the simplest dialog structure, with unilateral initiative. In such a system, one party completely controls the conversation, giving commands or asking questions; the other party simply responds to the last command or question. In a computerized interviewing system (for collecting patient histories, for example) the computer would ask questions and the user would respond to them one-by-one. In a question-answering system, the user would pose the questions and the system would respond to each in turn.[2] Such systems are relatively simple to implement, since they need not analyze the structure of the preceding dialog (although they may have to consult the preceding dialog to resolve anaphora and ellipsis). On the other hand, such systems are very constraining for the user – far from our ideal of 'natural dialog'.

4.6.1   A mixed initiative system

To see how these constraints can be relaxed in relatively simple ways, we shall look at GUS (the 'Genial Understanding System'), which was developed at Xerox Palo Alto. GUS acted as a travel agent who was only able to arrange for plane trips to the west coast (Bobrow *et al.* 1977). A portion of a typical dialog handled by GUS follows:

GUS:	Hello. My name is GUS. I can help you plan a simple trip by air. Where do you want to go?
CLIENT:	I want to go to San Diego on May 28.
GUS:	What time do you want to leave?
CLIENT:	I must be in San Diego before 10 a.m.
GUS:	Would you like PSA flight 102 that arrives at 9:15 a.m.?
CLIENT:	When is the next flight?
GUS:	Air California flight 310 that leaves at 8:30 a.m. and arrives at 10:00 a.m.
CLIENT:	I'll take the first one.

As this example shows, GUS is a *mixed initiative* system – either GUS or the 'client' may control the dialog. GUS will start by asking questions, but will allow the user to respond with a question of his own instead of a direct answer.

---

[2] The system might initiate queries to resolve ambiguities in the user's input, but these queries would be very restricted in nature (e.g., multiple choice) and handled separately from the main dialog.

Table 4.2

Slot	Type of value	Procedures
HOMEPORT	city (default: Palo Alto)	
FOREIGNPORT	city	
OUTWARDLEG	trip leg	TO-FILL: create frame
AWAYSTAY	place stay	
INWARDLEG	trip leg	TO-FILL: create frame

Table 4.3

Slot	Type of value	Procedures
FROMPLACE	city	TO-FILL: find from HOMEPORT
TOPLACE	city	TO-FILL: Ask-client
TRAVELDATE	date	TO-FILL: Ask-client
DEPARTURESPEC	timerange	TO-FILL: Ask-client
		WHEN-FILLED: propose flight by departure
ARRIVALSPEC	timerange	WHEN-FILLED: propose flight by arrival
PROPOSEDFLIGHTS	(set of flight)	
FLIGHTCHOSEN	flight	TO-FILL: Ask-client
TRAVELER	person	TO-FILL: Ask client

GUS is also of interest to us in this chapter because of its use of frames. The information gathered in the dialog is stored in a set of frames. The frame structure is quite simple; the chief frame is a *trip specification*, which has the slots shown in table 4.2. Two of the slots are to be filled with instances of *trip leg*, another frame (table 4.3).

GUS is a *frame-driven* system; its 'goal' is to complete a trip specification frame.[3] When GUS has the initiative, it looks for the first unfilled slot and executes the TO-FILL procedure associated with that slot. For many slots this procedure is Ask-client, which generates a question pertinent to that slot. GUS tries to parse the client's response as either a direct answer to the question or a full-sentence assertion or question (an ATN parser is used). If it is a direct answer or assertion, the output of the parse is mapped into an intermediate semantic representation and then into a set of operations for entering data into frame slots. If it is a question, GUS tries to answer the question. In the sample dialog given above, GUS begins by creating an instance of *trip specification* and then an instance of *trip leg* to fill the OUTWARDLEG slot. In trying to fill in *trip leg*, it encounters an Ask-client procedure attached to TOPLACE and generates

---

[3] GUS actually has a 'dialog' frame at the very top, but we have omitted this here for simplicity.

the question 'Where do you want to go?' The response, 'I want to go to San Diego on May 28.', causes the TOPLACE and TRAVELDATE slots to be filled. Continuing in this way, GUS eventually fills all the slots. Although the frame structure here is obviously very simple, it does indicate how the frames serve to integrate the information from separate sentences and guide the dialog.

A simple mixed initiative system like GUS implicitly recognizes the existence of more than one goal in the conversation. GUS has its permanent goal of filling all the slots in the TRIP frame and its descendents. The user may express his own goal (for getting a particular piece of information) by asking a direct question. This goal takes precedence temporarily over GUS's permanent goal.

The idea of maintaining multiple goals in a conversation was extended and made explicit by Bruce (1975). His 'demand model' incorporated a queue holding both user goals (as evidenced by direct questions to the system, for example) and system goals (arising from the need for clarification or the desire to give a warning).

More recently there has been a growing body of literature which formally analyzes each utterance in a conversation in terms of the goals and beliefs of each participant. We shall close this chapter with a brief discussion of this work.

4.6.2 *Planning to say something*

In trying to understand the actions of rational agents, or make a computer act like a rational agent, artificial intelligence makes extensive use of *planning*. A task is defined in terms of a starting point, a set of goals to be achieved, and a set of possible actions, with each action defined in terms of its effect on the world. A plan is a sequence of such actions which brings us from the initial state to the goal. We saw earlier in this chapter how PAM (the Plan Applier Mechanism) analyzed narratives by constructing plans which related a person's actions and goals.

This general approach can be extended to the analysis of natural language utterances. Uttering a sentence is a particular type of communicative act. Its effect is to alter the beliefs of the hearer.

For example, if I say to you 'Please pass the salt.' then (assuming you believe that I do not intend to deceive) you will believe that I want you to pass the salt. If you are cooperative, you will adopt this goal as your own (you will want to pass the salt). Then, since you are a volitional agent, providing there are no impediments to passing the salt, you will pass it. Thus I will have achieved my goal of getting the salt.

Similarly, if I say 'What time is it?' then (under similar assumptions) you will believe that I want you to inform me what the time is.

The linguistic groundwork – the identification of the speech acts and the basic assumptions underlying their use – was developed by philosophers of language, such as Austin (1962) and Searle (1969, 1975). The development of a formal, plan-based theory of speech acts has been the work primarily of Perrault, Allen, and Cohen (Cohen and Perrault 1979; Allen and Perrault 1980; Perrault and Allen 1980; Cohen, Perrault and Allen 1982). Some of these planning mechanisms have been implemented in a small dialog system which acts as a railroad information agent. The formalism is somewhat complex, in as much as it involves the representation of beliefs and beliefs about beliefs, so we shall not present it here. One of the early papers by Allen and Perrault (1980) provides a good introduction and several examples.

Without delving into the formalism, however, it is possible for us to consider why such a detailed analysis of the dialog process is worthwhile. If we examine any natural conversation, we will see that often a direct answer to a question is not the appropriate or most helpful response. We can develop a catalog of techniques for identifying different cases and providing helpful responses, and many good systems incorporate some such techniques. The virtue of a plan-based theory of dialog is that it provides a coherent formalism for explaining many of these techniques.

The use of a plan-based theory assumes that we have some idea of what the 'plausible goals' of the speaker are. In analyzing the speaker's question, we try to identify one of these plausible goals as the current goal of the speaker, and then key our response to this inferred goal rather than to the speaker's direct request.

For example, consider the question:

Do you know when the train to Boston leaves?

A literal response (assuming the system is well informed) would be

Yes.

The traveler, slightly irate, then tries

I want to know when the train to Boston leaves.

Our literal-minded system would record this desire in its record of the traveler's beliefs and wants, and then respond

I understand.

At this point we are lucky that our system is behind bulletproof glass.

How could a system employing a plan-based analysis handle a question such as 'Do you know when the train to Boston leaves?' It would have to recognize that the explicitly stated goal (that the system inform the user whether the system knows when the train leaves) is probably not the traveler's true goal. It would have to know what the plausible goals for the traveler are, such as knowing when a particular train leaves. Then, to identify the 'true goal' implicit in a question, it would have to create a plan linking the explicitly stated goal to one of the plausible goals of the traveler.

For the question at hand, the system would start with the explicitly stated goal of the traveler: that the system inform the traveler whether the system knows when the train to Boston leaves. The system would then reason as follows:

(1) If the traveler desires this action (that the system inform the traveler whether . . .), he must want the effect of this action: that the traveler know whether the system knows when the train leaves.

(2) Next the system applies what Allen and Perrault call the 'Know-Positive' rule: 'if A wants to know whether a proposition P is true, then it is possible that A wants to achieve a goal that requires P to be true' (Allen and Perrault 1980, p. 155). In our example, $A =$ the traveler and $P =$ 'the system knows when the train leaves'. So we're looking for some goal (or action) which can only be realized if the system knows when the train leaves. One such goal is that the system tell the traveler when the train leaves (it couldn't do that unless it knew the time itself).

(3) Again (as in step (1)), if the traveler desires this action, he must want the effect of this action: that the traveler know when the train leaves. This is a plausible 'true goal' for the traveler, so the system can stop its chain of inference here.

This rather involved chain of reasoning has led the system to identify the traveler's probable true goal: to know when the train to Boston leaves. It then can construct a response which will satisfy this goal: 'It leaves at 5.'

A similar approach works for other types of questions. If the traveler asks 'Does the train for Boston leave at 4?' the system could again infer that the traveler's goal is to know when the train leaves (not just whether it leaves at 4 or not). Thus it would respond not just 'No.' but rather 'No, it leaves at 5.'

This approach to the design of a question-answering system requires that we model not just the subject domain but also the user's expected interaction with the system. At present, when the modeling of subject domains still raises many difficulties, this may be too ambitious for operational systems. In the long term, however, we may expect that such techniques will produce systems with more natural and more helpful responses.

5 Language generation

5.1 The poor cousin

As we noted in the first chapter, language generation has generally taken second place to language analysis in computational linguistics research. This imbalance reflects a basic property of language, namely, that there are many ways of saying the same thing. In order for a natural language interface to be fluent, it should be able to accept most possible paraphrases of the information or commands the user wishes to transmit. On the other hand, it will suffice to generate one form of each message the system wishes to convey to the user.

As a result, many systems have combined sophisticated language analysis procedures with rudimentary generation components. Often generation involves nothing more than 'filling in the blanks' in a set of predefined message formats. This has been adequate for the simple messages many systems need to express: values retrieved from a data base, error messages, instructions to the user.

More sophisticated systems, however, have more complex messages to convey. People querying a data base in natural language often begin by asking about the structure or general content of the data base rather than asking for specific data values (Malhotra 1975); we would like to extend natural language data base interfaces so that they can answer such questions. For systems employing lengthy sequences of inferences, such as those for medical diagnosis (e.g., Shortliffe 1976), user acceptance and system improvement depend critically on the ability of the system to explain its reasoning. Applications such as these will require the generation of complex sentences and multi-sentence texts; fixed format messages will no longer be adequate. These needs and challenges have prompted a considerable increase of interest in natural language generation in the 1980s. In reading this chapter keep in mind, however, that most of this research is more preliminary than the work on language analysis.

Just as discourse analysis is more than the analysis of individual sentences, text generation is more than the generation in sequence of isolated sentences. If the text is to be easily understood, it must be well organized and flow smoothly from one sentence to the next (using such devices as anaphora and sentence connectives). Therefore, in parallel with our study of language analysis, we shall consider generation in two parts: first the generation of individual sentences and then the generation of texts.

5.2   Sentence generation

We have viewed language analysis as the task of translating from natural language into a meaning representation such as predicate calculus. So, as you may expect, we will view language generation as the reverse translation, from a meaning representation into natural language. We will try to take advantage of the parallels between the two tasks by using the same intermediate representations and rule systems when possible. In particular, we shall use transformational deep structure as an intermediate representation and so divide our task into mapping logical form into deep structure and then deep structure into sentences. However, as we shall see, the problems which arise in generation are often different from those in the corresponding analysis components.

5.2.1   *From logical form to deep structure*

The analysis component which translates deep structures into logical forms has two principal functions: mapping words into predicate and set names, and building explicitly scoped logical quantifiers. This component, as described in section 3.2, is organized as two mutually recursive functions: one function which analyzes noun phrases and builds restricted quantifiers, the other which analyzes sentential structures and builds predicates with arguments bound by quantifiers. We shall adopt an analogous structure for the generation component which takes logical forms into deep structures: two mutually recursive functions, one for building noun phrases (from restricted quantifiers), the other for building sentential structures (from predicates with arguments bound by quantifiers). We shall limit ourselves to the structures processed by our analysis component, avoiding the more difficult issues of verbs with sentential objects,[1] coordinating and subordinating conjunctions, and so forth.

5.2.1.1   *Building noun phrases*
The quantifiers produced by our analysis component have the form

$$(k\, x \in \{y \in G \mid P(y)\})$$

where k is one of the quantifiers $\forall, \exists$, or ι, G is derived from the head noun of the noun phrase, $P(y)$ from the adjuncts, and k from the determiner. If the quantifiers in the logical form received by the generation component have the same structure, we can build noun phrases by more-or-less reversing the analysis process: converting G to a noun, converting $P(y)$ to a series of adjuncts

---

[1] That is, objects which are themselves sentences, such as 'I believe *John is a Republican.*'

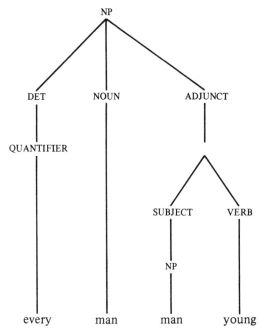

Figure 5.1

(by invoking the procedure for building sentential structures), and choosing a determiner based on k. For example,

$$(\forall x \in \{y \in men \mid \text{young}(y)\})$$

would be converted to figure 5.1, which will eventually become 'every young man' (we could also have generated 'all the young men').

The input to generation, however, may not have the form appropriate for such direct translation to linguistic structure. This may be the case if the input did not arise from natural language analysis, or if the logical forms produced by language analysis were substantially transformed by an inference component. The predicate calculus expressions, may, for example, use only unrestricted quantification. We then must restructure the expressions so that the quantifiers have the required form. This involves, in effect, deciding which portion of the information is to be conveyed at the noun phrase level and which at the sentence level (by verbs and sentence connectives). For example, if given the expression

$$(\forall x)((\text{artist}(x) \land \text{young}(x)) \to \text{poor}(x))$$

we first convert this to a restricted quantifier

$$(\forall x \in \{y \mid \text{artist}(y) \land \text{young}(y)\}) \text{poor}(x)$$

We then try to find some predicate in the set-former which corresponds to a named set (i.e., which can be expressed as a noun) and use it as the base set of the set-former:

$$(\forall x \in \{y \in artists \mid \text{young}(y)\}) \, \text{poor}(x)$$

We now have the expression in a form which can be converted to a linguistic structure (ultimately, 'All young artists are poor.'). As you may expect, most predicate calculus expressions do not work out so nicely; a number of different cases are discussed in Chester (1976).

A quite different problem in noun phrase construction arises from the use of *internal identifiers*. Most objects in the real world do not have names of their own. For example, Mary Smith's car, her eyeglasses, or her personal computer are not likely to have their own name (they may have a name for the model, such as Citation or Apple III, but not a name for her particular unit). In order to record information or make inferences about such objects, however, it is usually convenient to associate a unique internal identifier with each object. These identifiers are meaningless to the user, so when we are generating text we must replace these identifiers by appropriate descriptive phrases.

What should such a phrase consist of? The head of the phrase will be a noun corresponding to the most specific named set of which this object is a member. Attached to this noun will be adjuncts corresponding to predicates in which this object participates; the difficult task is choosing the appropriate set of adjuncts. Presumably not all the predicates involving the object should be included – if we knew a lot about Mary's car, we would get an essay instead of a noun phrase. We want to include just enough adjuncts to characterize the object uniquely. Furthermore – since there may be several such adjuncts – we must select the adjunct(s) which would be meaningful to the reader. For example, to someone who knows Mary, one might describe the vehicle as 'Mary's car' whereas to someone standing in a parking lot one might describe it as 'the car with the dented left fender'. In addition, we should suppress adjuncts which are implied by the context of the noun phrase (McDonald 1981). For instance (to adapt an example of McDonald's), an arc in an ATN network might be described as

> the jump arc from state 1 to state 3

However, in response to the question 'What arcs go to state 3?' we should trim the description of this arc to

> the jump arc from state 1

Context may even affect the type of description desired: in response to the question

> Which car did Mary buy?

a description of the vehicle as 'Mary's car' would clearly be inappropriate; a response such as 'the white Rolls-Royce' is called for.

5.2.1.2 Building sentential structures

Simple sentences will be represented in logical form by expressions such as

$$Q_1 Q_2 \ldots Q_n P(x_1, x_2, \ldots, x_n)$$

where the Q_i are restricted quantifiers binding the variables x_i of the predicate P.[2] We have considered some of the problems of translating the Q_i into noun phrases. We shall now turn our attention to putting these noun phrases together to form a sentence.

One basic problem here is choosing an appropriate 'operator' (verb, adjective, or preposition) from our natural language vocabulary to represent the predicate P. If we have defined our predicates in close correspondence with actual words, selecting a suitable word won't be difficult. On the other hand, if we have used a small set of more 'elementary' predicates, or if we want to make more subtle distinctions between verbs or incorporate several predicates into a single verb, our task of choosing an operator becomes more difficult.

Goldman has discussed a number of these problems in the context of a program called BABEL for translating conceptual dependency structures (see section 3.1.6) into English (Goldman 1975). BABEL could recognize a pattern consisting of several predicates and combine it into one – an important ability because of the very elementary nature of conceptual dependency predicates. For example, a conceptual dependency structure which might be described as 'X prevented Y from breathing by grabbing Y's neck' could be reduced to 'X choked Y'. BABEL can select among alternative realizations of a conceptual dependency expression by testing properties of the expression. For instance, conceptual dependency representation has a single predicate, PTRANS (a,o,s,d), to represent the physical transfer of object o by agent a from source s to destination d. If $a = s$, this can be realized by 'give'; if $a = d$, by 'take'. BABEL can also make choices based on information about the current context which is not part of the message itself. For example, if d previously possessed o, it will generate 'a returned o to d' instead of 'a gave o to d'. In a similar vein, Goldman considers the message 'John told Mary that he was going to kill her husband'. If BABEL is supplied with the fact that the telling will make Mary much less happy, it will generate 'John threatened to kill Mary's husband'; if it would make her much happier, it will generate 'John promised to kill Mary's

---

[2] The order of the quantifiers is not necessarily the same as the order of the variables – Q_i does not necessarily bind x_i.

husband'. These isolated examples illustrate how difficult the task is of selecting the 'right word' for a given situation.

The procedure for generating sentential structures must also decide on syntactic features such as tense, aspect, and voice, since all of these features have semantic implications. The choice between active and passive voice, for example, plays a role in focusing (which we shall consider in the section on text generation) and quantifier scoping. Quantifier scope becomes important when we have a predicate whose arguments are bound by different quantifiers – one by $\forall$, one by $\exists$. Recall our examples from section 3.2.3:

(1) Everyone in the room speaks two languages.
(2) Two languages are spoken by everyone in the room.

As we noted in that section, sentences are usually interpreted with a quantifier order in logical form corresponding to quantifier order in surface structure. So, to insure that the generated sentence will be interpreted properly, we must choose between active and passive voice in order to put the quantifier of broader scope first.

5.2.2   From deep structure to sentence

Syntax analysis – the mapping from sentences into deep structures – has been dominated by the use of augmented context-free grammars. As we described in section 2.6, there have been two primary approaches to the use of such grammars: ATNs, which build deep structures in registers during the scan of the input, and Restriction Language grammars, which transform the parse tree incrementally to a deep structure. This dichotomy has its parallel in the approaches used for sentence generation – in going from deep structure to sentence.

The approach used by Simmons and Slocum (1972) was modeled on the ATNs used for sentence analysis. Their procedure generated a sentence in a single traversal of the deep structure tree. The generation process was directed by an ATN, i.e., by a recursive transition network augmented with procedures associated with the arcs of the network. The recursive transition network specified the order in which the deep structure tree is traversed; the procedures associated with the arcs actually assembled the sentence. Just as analytic ATNs use registers to hold portions of the deep structure being built, the generative ATN used registers to hold segments of the sentence being assembled.

The input to Simmons and Slocum's procedure was a semantic network in which the arc labels are case relations such as AGENT, OBJECT, DATIVE (indirect object), and LOCATION, and features such as TENSE (past / present / future), VOICE (active / passive), ASPECT (imperfect: 'John eats' / perfect: 'John has eaten'), and FORM (which distinguishes simple tenses from progressive tenses like 'is eating'). In presenting the procedure here, we shall modify it slightly to

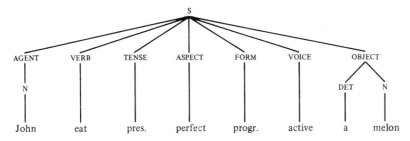

Figure 5.2

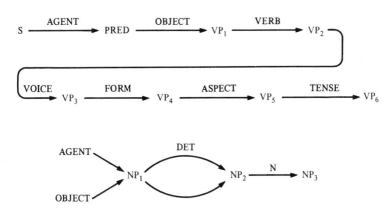

Figure 5.3

accept input closer in form to the deep structure trees we have been using; this should not obscure the basic ideas of their approach. We shall represent the sentence

John has been eating a melon.

by the deep structure tree of figure 5.2. We consider the word categories (N, DET, VERB) and feature names (TENSE, ASPECT, FORM, VOICE) to be terminal symbols. For each non-terminal symbol (S, AGENT, and OBJECT in this tree) there is a node with the same label in the generating ATN (figure 5.3) – the labels on the other nodes are not significant, and are included only for convenience in describing the network. The arcs are labeled with non-terminal and terminal grammar symbols. The arc labels on a path through the network indicate the order in which the children of a non-terminal node are to be visited. We begin at the S (root) node of the deep structure tree and at the S node of the ATN. The network directs us to 'visit' the AGENT, OBJECT, VERB, VOICE, FORM, ASPECT, and TENSE nodes below S in that order, returning to the S node after each visit.

If the node visited is a non-terminal, this process is recursive. Thus, the first node to be visited under s is AGENT. We save our current position (node s in the tree and node s in the ATN) and turn our attention to the AGENT node in the tree and the AGENT node in the network. The AGENT node in the network has an unlabeled arc to NP₁. Unlabeled arcs are followed unconditionally, without visiting any node in the tree, so this arc brings us to NP₁ (while still at node AGENT in the tree). If there were a DET node below AGENT, we would visit it and then follow the upper arc in the ATN to NP₂; there isn't any DET below AGENT in this tree, so we follow the lower, unlabeled arc to NP₂. Next, we visit node N in the deep structure and move on to node NP₃ in the ATN. This is a terminal node, so we pop back up to our previously saved positions: node s in the tree and node PRED in the ATN. We now continue visiting the children of node s.

So far we've had a good time touring the deep structure tree, but we haven't *done* anything about building the sentence. The actual work of constructing the sentence is performed by procedures associated with the arcs of the ATN. Based on the value of the node currently being visited, these procedures build up word sequences in registers and eventually emit them as parts of the sentence. For example, the procedures associated with the arcs VERB, VOICE, FORM, ASPECT, and TENSE assemble in register VSTRING the verb and its auxiliaries. We suppose that by the time these procedures are executed the word sequences for the agent and object have been placed in registers SUBJECT and OBJECT respectively. The VERB procedure will put the verb (in our example, 'eat') into register VSTRING. If the value of VOICE is 'passive', the VOICE procedure will replace VSTRING by 'be' + the past participle of the old value of VSTRING; it will also place the value of OBJECT in SUBJECT and 'by' + the value of SUBJECT in OBJECT. Next, if the value of FORM is 'progressive', the FORM procedure will replace the first word in VSTRING by 'be' + its present participle (in our example, changing 'eat' to 'be eating'). If the value of ASPECT is 'perfect', the ASPECT procedure will replace the first word in VSTRING by 'have' + its past participle (in our example, changing 'be eating' to 'have been eating'). Finally, the TENSE procedure will change the first word of VSTRING to its tensed form (giving us 'has been eating').

Simmons and Slocum's approach has clear analogs in the ATNs used for parsing, but there are also substantial differences in the way the networks are interpreted. A greater commonality of mechanism between analysis and generation is achieved in Restriction Language grammars. Recall that in this approach to syntax analysis a sentence is first parsed by an augmented context-free grammar and the parse tree is then incrementally transformed to a deep structure. For sentence generation, we can prepare inverse transformations and apply them to the deep structure in the reverse order from that used for analysis. The frontier of the resulting surface structure tree is the generated sentence (we may view the extraction of the frontier in generation as being the inverse of the parsing step in analysis). The same extended Restriction Language is used for both classes of transformations, and there is an approximate one-to-one correspondence between transformations in the analysis and generation grammars, thus facilitating their parallel development. The inverses of individual transformations of the analysis component must be prepared manually, but this is not too difficult a task because most transformations make small changes to the tree.

Consider for example the T-TOVO transformation presented towards the end of section 2.6.1. This transformation operates on sentences with TOVO ('to' + verb + object) objects, such as 'John wants to eat a melon.' It duplicates the subject, transforming the object into a full ASSERTION: 'John wants (John eat a melon).'. When we generate deep structures from logical form, we will presumably create full ASSERTIONs in positions such as the object of 'want'. We will therefore want a generative transformation which converts an ASSERTION in object position into a TOVO under appropriate circumstances. What are the 'appropriate circumstances'? First, we must verify that the verb can take a TOVO object (so that we don't transform 'John taught John [i.e., himself] to read.' into 'John taught to read.'); this can be tested by examining the OBJLIST attribute of the verb. Second, we must check that the subjects of the embedded and upper ASSERTIONS are identical (so that we don't transform 'John wanted Mary to cook cabbage.' into 'John wanted to cook cabbage.'). In Restriction Language, a transformation to check these conditions and then change the ASSERTION into a TOVO is[3]

> G-TOVO = IN OBJECT:
>   IF BOTH VALUE OF OBJECT IS ASSERTION
>   AND BOTH CORE OF COELEMENT VERB HAS ATTRIBUTE OBJLIST: TOVO
>   AND $SAME-SUBJECT
>   THEN REPLACE ASSERTION
>   BY < TOVO > (LVR OF VERB OF ASSERTION
>   + THIRD SA OF ASSERTION
>   + OBJECT OF ASSERTION
>   + FOURTH SA OF ASSERTION)

$SAME-SUBJECT is a procedure (not shown here) which tests whether COELEMENT SUBJECT and SUBJECT OF ASSERTION are identical; the precise predicate to be used depends on how the deep structure is generated from logical form (one possibility is to associate a numeric index with each noun phrase, with the same index being assigned to noun phrases arising from the same variable in logical form; $SAME-SUBJECT would then test for the identity of these indices).

A matched set of such analysis and generation transformations has been developed for question analysis and answer generation as part of a small question-answering system (Grishman 1979).

In order to reduce the overall labor of developing a natural language system,

---

[3] To simplify the transformation, we have omitted the code which would be required if either of the first two SAs of the ASSERTION may be filled.

it would surely be desirable to have a *single* rule system which can be automatically adapted for use in both analysis and generation. In principle, the grammars developed by theoretical linguists have this property – they specify languages and not analysis or generation procedures. In actuality, however, transformational generative grammars are described in terms of a generative mechanism and, as we saw in section 2.5, cannot be easily adapted to an analysis procedure.

One approach which has been relatively successful at unifying generative and analytic grammars has been that based on PROLOG. As we noted in section 2.6.5, PROLOG is well suited for implementing augmented context-free grammars because it incorporates the search mechanism which is at the core of context-free analysis. The productions, written as PROLOG statements, can readily be augmented by calls on PROLOG procedures to enforce grammatical constraints and map the analysis into a deep structure or logical form. The property of PROLOG procedures which is of interest to us here is that they do not distinguish between input and output parameters. As a simple example of this, suppose we have a multiplication procedure

(PROD *a b c*)

which, if invoked with constants for *a*, *b*, and *c*, will be true if and only if $a*b = c$. We can use this in PROLOG to compute a product: if X is a variable,

(PROD 3 4 *X*)

will 'bind' the value 12 to X. We can also use it to divide:

(PROD *X* 4 12)

will bind the value 3 to X. In similar fashion, functions which are written to map sentence constituents into a deep or semantic structure will also work in the other direction, assembling sentence constituents from an internal structure (see, for example, Simmons and Chester 1982). It is not clear, however, whether both processes can be made to operate *efficiently* using a single set of PROLOG rules – whether rules structured for efficient analysis can generate sentences at an acceptable cost.

5.3   Text generation

As we noted at the beginning of this chapter, text generation is a lot more than generating individual sentences correctly and then printing them out one after another. If the text lacks good organization or continuity, it may be semantically 'correct' but seem bizarre or unintelligible. Suppose King Henry VIII went to a restaurant for dinner; what would happen? Well, we know from our restaurant script (section 4.5) that the basic facts would be

(1) Henry entered the restaurant.
(2) Henry ordered a cold pheasant.
(3) A cold pheasant arrived.
(4) Henry ate the cold pheasant.
(5) Henry paid the bill.
(6) Henry left the restaurant.

These six sentences, strung together, would convey the essential facts, although not in the sort of style that we would want to read for page after page. To make it read more smoothly, we could try to introduce some subordinating conjunctions ('before', 'after'), some passives, and some pronouns:

> Before Henry ordered a cold pheasant, he entered the restaurant. After it arrived, Henry ate the cold pheasant. The bill was paid by Henry and he left the restaurant.

A little syntactic variety can be a dangerous thing unless guided by principles of text *organization* and *continuity*. In the next subsection we shall describe some preliminary experiments at providing such guidance.

5.3.1   Organizing the text

In order to generate text, we have to impose a *linear ordering* on the information to be presented (which may be a collection of predicate calculus formulas). In addition, we have to impose one or more levels of *grouping*: to group clauses into sentences and sentences into paragraphs. Sometimes the information itself provides strong guidance for ordering or grouping. A simple narrative with no parallel activities, for example, offers a natural linear order. In a formal proof, the graph connecting premises and conclusions of individual deductions provides a partial ordering and may be used to create groupings (Chester 1976). More often, however, the structure of the information is more complex, and the ordering and grouping must be provided by the language generator.

A straightforward way of providing this ordering and grouping is to traverse the incoming information structure in a standard order (e.g., depth first) and have some criterion for starting a new sentence (e.g., a limit on the amount of information per sentence). This is termed by Mann and Moore (1981) the *partitioning* paradigm. This paradigm is workable for some small texts but is not very flexible. It assumes that the best items to join in a sentence are items which are contiguous in the semantic structure, and that decisions about sentence and paragraph breaks can be made on a local, incremental basis.

To provide greater flexibility, Mann and Moore have suggested the *fragment-and-compose* paradigm (Mann and Moore 1981). In this approach the message is initially divided into its atomic constituents (elementary propositions). These propositions are segmented and ordered using a few rather general rules, such as that time-dependent propositions are ordered according to their time-values. The propositions are then combined to form sentences using rules of aggregation; where alternative aggregations are possible, preference rules are used to evaluate the different resulting sentences, and the alternative with the highest score is selected. This procedure has been used to generate a text about what to do in case of a fire alarm, given in effect a flowchart with a number of different decisions and possible responses (so that the semantic structure is far from linear).

Mann and Moore's procedure can be described as a predominantly bottom-up approach to text organization: the main work is performed by aggregation rules which build larger and larger structures. In contrast, the approach taken by McKeown in a quite different domain (McKeown 1982, 1985a, 1985b) is basically top-down. McKeown was concerned with answering questions about the structure of a data base. Using information from the data base model, her 'TEXT' system generates answers to questions about the definition of a data base entity, the information available about an entity, or the difference between two entities. Depending on the question and the information available in the model, TEXT selects a rhetorical technique for answering the question. These rhetorical techniques are associated in turn with schemas, which are loose outlines of text structure. For example, the identification schema, which can be used in response to requests for definitions, consists in essence of

* an identifying proposition (e.g., describing an entity in terms of the class to which it belongs and its distinguishing attribute)
* zero or more descriptive predicates (mentioning constituents or attributes of the entity)
* one or more examples of the entity
* optionally, a further descriptive predicate
* optionally, a further example

The schema is used to guide the text generator in selecting information from the model to form sentences (thus, McKeown's generator differs from those mentioned earlier in selecting as well as organizing the information).

Since these schemas provide only a loose, high-level structure, McKeown has looked to other mechanisms to provide low-level coherence. Specifically, she has used *focusing* criteria to insure continuity in the text. Following Sidner (1979), she requires that the focus of the next sentence in the text be (1) the focus of the current sentence (the 'immediate focus'), (2) a 'potential focus' mentioned in the current sentence, or (3) a past immediate focus. Furthermore, she observes that the reintroduction of topics can be minimized by preferring potential foci to the immediate focus, and the immediate focus to past foci. The schemas used by TEXT allow for many alternative continuations at any point in the text; the preference rules are used to select from among these alternatives.

5.3.2 What's best left unsaid

One basic point of the chapter on text analysis was that much of what is conveyed by the text, and particularly the relationship between sentences, is implicit. Making this information explicit was one of the basic jobs of text analysis. Conversely, we would expect a sophisticated text generator, if presented with an explicit, fully detailed semantic representation, to be able to omit some of the details which the reader would be able to figure out anyway. Although, as with the other aspects of text generation, we have not achieved such sophistication, some systems (e.g., Mann and Moore 1981) do at least maintain a simple user 'model' listing the assertions which the user is assumed to know and suppress such assertions during text generation.

Exercises

Section 1.1

(1) Cite an additional possible or actual application of natural language processing.

Section 2.4.1

(2) Give an example of a sentence (not necessarily covered by the tiny sample grammar) with an ambiguity which would be resolved by one of the four constraints mentioned.

(3) Cite an additional grammatical constraint (beyond the four mentioned) and give an example of an ambiguity which is resolved by this constraint.

(4) Draw the two syntactic analyses (parse trees) which would be produced for the sentence

    The fair features live music.

using the tiny grammar given in the text. Which grammatical constraint would resolve this ambiguity?

Section 2.4.2

(5) Using the grammar

    <SENTENCE> ::= <SUBJECT> <*TV> |
                   <SUBJECT> <*TV> <OBJECT>
    <SUBJECT> ::= <NSTG>
    <OBJECT>   ::= <NSTG>
    <NSTG>   ::= <*N> | <*T> <*N>

and the sentence
    The program answers questions.
trace through the operation of the top-down and bottom-up parsing algorithms described in this section; follow the top-down parser through to the point where it has determined that no more parses are possible. For each production (i.e., for each option in the case of BNF rules with more than one option), state in the case of the top-down algorithm how often an expansion using that production is tried, and in the case of the bottom-up algorithm how many partial analyses using that production are created. Caution: several of the words in this sentence are both nouns and tensed verbs. (Note: the detailed bottom-up algorithm is given in the text

only for grammars with one or two symbols on the right side of a production, but it can be naturally extended to grammars with longer productions, such as the sample grammar in this exercise.)

Section 2.5.2

(6) Using the tiny transformational grammar given in the text, display (as a series of trees or labeled bracketings) the derivation of the sentence 'Was Mary shot by John?'. What does this derivation tell you about the relative ordering of the passive and question transformations in our grammar? (Note: a small extension is needed to the passive transformation as given in the text in order to handle question sentences.)

(7) The embedding transformation in the tiny transformational grammar handles only relative clauses with subject deletion, such as 'the crocodile which ate Peter'. Write an embedding transformation to handle relative clauses with object deletion, such as 'the crocodile which Peter ate', and give an example of its application (draw the tree before and after the transformation).

Section 2.5.4

(8) (a) Using the procedure developed by Petrick, create reverse (string) transformations corresponding to the passive, question, and do deletion transformations of the tiny transformational grammar.
(b) For these same transformations, see if you can also create true reverse transformations – transformations which recreate the tree structure which the forward transformations accept.

(9) A covering grammar can be built up by considering the transformations in sequence and determining what structures they add to or delete from the base component. Perform this task for the passive, question, do deletion, and do replacement transformations of the tiny transformational grammar.

Section 2.6.2

(10) Using the ATN given, trace the register assignments and determine the final structure generated for the sentence 'Albert has asked Sam to shoot Peter.'

(11) Specify all the additions which are needed to the ATN to accept TOVO objects (TOVO = 'to' + verb + object, as in 'Albert wanted to shoot Peter.') and generate an embedded structure similar to that produced for 'N-to-V-object' objects (and similar to that produced by the Restriction Language transformation).

(12) Specify all the additions which are needed to the ATN to accept the progressive tense (such as 'Marie is eating cake.').

Section 2.8

(13) (a) Using the tiny grammar of section 2.4.1, draw all the parse trees for the sentence

I saw the man in the park with a telescope.

(to reduce the writing involved, you may introduce abbreviations for common subtrees).

(b) One shortcoming of this grammar is that it does not allow more than one adjunct to fill an adjunct position. For example, it could not analyze

I eat pretzels frequently in Philadelphia.

because there are two SAS (sentence adjuncts) after the object, 'frequently' and 'in Philadelphia'. Modify the grammar so that an SA node can subsume any number (zero or more) of DS (adverbs) and PNS (prepositional phrases). Reanswer part (a) using this modified grammar.

Section 2.9

(14) In analogy with the definitions given for conjoined SENTENCE strings, create a series of productions to express the possible conjoinings of LNR (from the grammar of section 2.4.1), and give an example using each production.

(15) Consider the following sentence (from the *New York Times*, March 13, 1982):

Women should carry credit cards in the bottom of purses and men where they are inaccessible to pickpockets.

The structure of the intended reading could be described as subject – tense – verb – object – sentence-adjunct – and – subject – sentence-adjunct. There are several other parses besides the intended reading. Characterize these alternative parses in terms of the word to which 'men' is conjoined.

Section 3.1

(16) For at least some speakers, the sentence

Everyone saw a cat.

is ambiguous. Formalize this ambiguity by expressing its two readings in predicate calculus.

(17) Formalize the difference between the following two sentences

John read a book and Mary read it too.
John read a book and Mary read one too.

by expressing their meanings in predicate calculus.

(18) Express the following in idiomatic English

(a) $(\forall x)$ loves(Arthur,x)
(b) loves(Fred,Fred)
(c) $(\forall x)$ (rich(x) $\rightarrow$ loves(Ronald,x))
(d) $\sim (\exists x)(\forall y)$ loves(x,y)

(19) A *factive* verb (such as 'regret', mentioned in section 3.1.5.2) presupposes the truth of the sentence which appears as the object of the verb. Give two other examples of factive verbs.

Section 3.2

(20) Following the rules given in section 3.2.1, indicate how the sentence

Every farmer who bought a sheep sold a deer.

would be translated into predicate calculus.

(21) The translation procedure of section 3.2.1 includes several cases where a quantifier must be generated even though no noun phrase is present.
(a) One of these cases (noted at the end of the section) arises when a predicate has a time argument but there is no corresponding time adjunct in the sentence. Suppose, for example, that *kiss* is a predicate of three arguments: the kisser, the kissee, and the year in which the kissing took place. Translate into predicate calculus the sentence

Everyone kissed Nancy.

(b) Another case involves passives without a 'by' phrase ('agentless passives'). How would you translate into predicate calculus the sentence

Nancy has been kissed every year since 1975.

(c) Based on these examples (and similar ones you may care to construct), venture a hypothesis regarding the scope of quantifiers which do *not* arise from explicit noun phrases, relative to the scope of quantifiers which do.

(22) We noted in section 3.1.5.2 that 'the' + singular noun phrase gives rise to the presupposition that there is exactly one of the item described; we captured this notion in logical form using the definite quantifier ι. Do other noun phrases, such as those with 'some' or 'every', carry a presupposition? If so, how might we modify the meaning of the standard quantifiers of logic to capture this presupposition? (Consider, for example, the sentence 'Every woman on Mars wants to be an astronaut.')

Section 3.3

(23) Suppose we add to the microworld described in section 3.3.3 the domain objects

seltzer
gin

and the two-place predicates

serve(x,y) = x is serving y
drink(x,y) = x is drinking y

with the domains as follows:

serve (1st arg):   Jack, Jill
     (2nd arg):   berries, nuts, seltzer, gin
drink (1st arg):   Jack, Jill, Fuzzy, Snoopy
     (2nd arg):   seltzer, gin

'seltzer' and 'gin' are added to the domain of 'disappear'; all other domains remain the same.

(a) Modify the hierarchical taxonomy of the microworld to accommodate these changes, and list the predicate domain names for the new predicates.

(b) Extend the semantic grammar (given in section 3.3.4) to accommodate these changes.

Section 3.5

(24) For the pair of sentences

Mary bought a lion on Monday.
It ate her on Tuesday.

give the logical form of the first sentence, the discourse entities arising from this sentence, and the logical form of the second sentence after anaphora resolution.

(25) Do the same for the sentence pair

Elaine brought every student an alligator on Friday.
They returned to Elaine on Saturday.

for the interpretation where 'they' are the alligators. You may use a predicate 'return to' (return-to(x,y) = x returned to y), in order to avoid the complications of encoding the prepositional phrase 'to Elaine'.

(26) State the rule for number agreement between a definite pronoun and its antecedent. (This is a bit tricky – consider for example the sentences in the previous exercise.)

(27) Is the resolution of the pronoun 'them' in the following sentence pair (an input to the BBN LUNAR – the 'moon rocks' system):

Give me all the analyses of sample 10046 for hydrogen.
Give me *them* for oxygen.

handled by the rules given in the text? Explain.

Section 3.6

(28) Many newspaper headlines are sentence fragments rather than full sentences. Select ten such headlines from your favorite newspaper, and characterize the fragments either in terms of the words or constituents omitted from a full sentence structure or in terms of the sequence of constituents which forms the fragment.

Section 4.4

(29) Modify the restaurant script as shown in figure 4.1 (the 'coffee shop track') to provide a track for fast-food restaurants, where food is ordered at a counter and carried by the customer to a table.

(30) Develop a detailed script for some activity you have participated in frequently. Identify the roles and props involved. Review in your mind several instances of this activity, and verify that your script includes tracks for all these instances. As possibly suitable activities we suggest:

(a) a visit to the library (returning a book, looking for a book, borrowing a book);
(b) a plane or train trip;
(c) registering for courses at a university.

Section 4.5

(31) Section 4.5 indicates how sentences from radiology reports can be mapped into a tabular structure called an information format. The format contains a column for each type of information which can appear in a sentence. You are to construct an information format adequate for the three soup recipes shown below, which are adapted from the *Fanny Farmer Cookbook*. Write out in full the format entries for the cheese soup recipe.

   To develop the format, first expand all sentences containing conjunctions into conjoined full assertions. Then try to match up words in different sentences which have the same informational function (for example, the verbs of cooking, numbers, measures, foods, cooking utensils, etc.). Line these words up one below the other in a table, and give an appropriate label to the column. As you examine new sentences, you will occasionally have to add columns to the table. You should treat compound nominals ('peanut butter') and idioms ('double boiler') as single units, and can ignore articles.

   If you have designed your format properly, it should be easy to answer questions such as 'What ingredients are required? In what order are they added? How much butter do I need? How long does each cooking step last (in absolute time or in terms of a stopping condition)? How should the onion be prepared?' by simple retrieval operations on the table.

   Peanut butter soup
   Put in a pan 1 tablespoon butter, 3 tablespoons peanut butter, and 1 teaspoon minced onion. Cook 5 minutes. Add 2 tablespoons flour. Stir until smooth. Add slowly 3 cups milk. Cook 20 minutes in a double boiler.

   French onion soup
   Melt in a large pan 1 tablespoon butter. Add $\frac{3}{4}$ cup sliced onion. Cook until soft. Add $\frac{1}{2}$ teaspoon sugar and 1 tablespoon flour. Stir and cook 1 minute. Add 4 cups consomme. Simmer 30 minutes.

   Cheese soup
   Melt in a large saucepan 1 tablespoon butter. Add 1 tablespoon chopped onion. Cook slowly until onion is yellow. Stir in 1 tablespoon flour. Slowly

add 1 cup consomme. Boil. Strain. Add $\frac{3}{4}$ cup grated cheese. Stir until cheese melts.

Section 4.6

(32) Complete the analysis of the GUS script given in the text, indicating for each exchange the slots which get filled in and the slot whose attached procedure generates the next output from GUS.

(33) The basic strategy of GUS for frame-driven dialog is potentially applicable to other situations where 'interviewing' is appropriate. One such situation is the purchase of a complex piece of equipment with lots of options, such as a component stereo, a car, or a computer system. Develop a set of frames to represent the structure and parameters of one such type of equipment. Following GUS's 'fill-in-the-slots' strategy, create a possible dialog for ordering a piece of equipment.

Section 5.2

(34) In section 5.2.1.1, we showed how a quantificational expression could be restructured into a form (with restricted quantifiers and base sets) suitable for translation into English. Often several different restructurings are possible, depending, for example, on which predicate is selected to form the base set. Each restructured logical form can then be rendered in English in several ways, through different choices of words and syntactic structures.

Consider

$$(\forall x)[(\text{male}(x) \wedge \text{unmarried}(x) \wedge \text{lives-in}(x,\text{Texas}) \wedge \text{raises}(x,\text{cattle}))$$
$$\rightarrow \text{smokes}(x,\text{Marlboro})]$$

This could be restructured as

$$(\forall x \in \{y \in cattlemen | \text{unmarried}(y) \wedge \text{lives-in}(y,\text{Texas})\})$$
$$\text{smokes}(x,\text{Marlboro})$$

by combining the constraints male(x) and raises (x,cattle) to form the base set *cattlemen*. This could then be translated into English as

Every unmarried Texas cattleman smokes Marlboros.

or

Every unmarried cattleman living in Texas smokes Marlboros.

Generate several more alternative translations by using different restructurings and syntactic forms.

Bibliography

(Note: *ACM = Assn. for Computing Machinery.*)

Aho, A. V., and Ullman, J. D. (1972) *The Theory of Parsing, Translation, and Compiling, Vol. 1: Parsing.* Prentice-Hall, Englewood Cliffs, NJ

Allen, J. F., and Perrault, C. R. (1980) Analyzing intention in utterances. *Artificial Intelligence 15*, 143–78

Allwood, J., Andersson, L., and Dahl, O. (1977) *Logic in Linguistics.* Cambridge Univ. Press, Cambridge, England

Anderson, B., Bross, I., and Sager, N. (1975) Grammatical compression in notes and records: Analysis and computation. *Am. J. Comp. Ling. 12*, 4 (Sept. 1975), 34

Austin, J. L. (1962) *How To Do Things With Words.* Oxford Univ. Press, New York

Bates, M. (1978) The theory and practice of augmented transition network grammars. In *Natural Language Communication with Computers*, L. Bolc, ed. Springer, Berlin

Bellert, S. (1973) On various solutions of the problem of presupposition. In *Studies in Text Grammar*, J. S. Petof and H. Reiser, eds., Reidel, New York

Birnbaum, L., and Selfridge, M. (1981) Conceptual analysis of natural language. In *Inside Computer Understanding*, R. Schank and C. Riesbeck, eds. Lawrence Erlbaum Assoc., Hillsdale, NJ, 318–53

Bobrow, D., and Fraser, B. (1969) An augmented state transition network analysis procedure. *Proc. Int. Joint Conf. on Artificial Intelligence*, Washington DC

Bobrow, R. J., and Webber, B. L. (1980) Knowledge representation for syntactic/semantic processing. *First Annl. Natl. Conf. on Artificial Intelligence*, AAAI, Stanford, CA, 316–23.

Bobrow, D., and Winograd, T. (1977) An overview of KRL, a Knowledge Representation Language. *Cognitive Science 1*, 1 (Jan. 1977), 3–46

Bobrow, D., Kaplan, R., Kay, M., Norman, D., Thompson, H., and Winograd, T. (1977) GUS, a frame-driven dialog system. *Artificial Intelligence 8*, 2 (Apr. 1977), 155–73

Borgida, A. (1975) Topics in the understanding of English sentences by computer. Tech. Rep. 78, Dept. of Comp. Sci., Univ. of Toronto

Brown, G. and Yule, G. (1983) *Discourse Analysis.* Cambridge Univ. Press, Cambridge, England

Bruce, B. C. (1975) Discourse models and language comprehension. *Am. J. Computational Linguistics 35*, 19–35

Burton, R. (1976) Semantic grammar: An engineering technique for constructing natural language understanding systems. BBN Report No. 3453, Bolt, Beranek, and Newman, Cambridge, MA

Cautin, H. (1969) Real English: A translator to enable natural language man-machine conversation. Thesis, Moore School of Electrical Engineering, Univ. of Penn.

Charniak, E. (1972) Towards a model of children's story comprehension. MIT AI Report TR-266

Charniak, E. (1982) Context recognition in language comprehension. In *Strategies for Natural Language Processing*, W. Lenhert and M. Ringle, eds., Lawrence Erlbaum Assoc., Hillsdale, NJ

Chester, D. (1976) The translation of formal proofs into English. *Artificial Intelligence 7*, 3 (Fall 1976), 261–78

Chomsky, N. (1957) *Syntactic structures*. Mouton and Co., The Hague

Chomsky, N. (1959) On certain formal properties of grammars. *Information and Control 2*, 137–67

Chomsky, N. (1965) *Aspects of the Theory of Syntax*. MIT Press, Cambridge, MA

Clocksin, W. F., and Mellish, C. S. (1981) *Programming in Prolog*. Springer-Verlag, Berlin

Cocke, J., and Schwartz, J. T. (1970) Programming languages and their compilers. Lecture Note Series, Courant Inst. of Math. Sci., New York Univ.

Cohen, P. R., and Perrault, C. R. (1979) Elements of a plan-based theory of speech acts. *Cognitive Science 3*, 3 (1979), 177–212

Cohen, P. R., Perrault, C. R., and Allen, J. F. (1982) Beyond question answering. In *Strategies for Natural Language Processing*, W. Lenhert and M. Ringle, eds. Lawrence Erlbaum Assoc., Hillsdale, NJ

Colmerauer, A. (1970) Les Systems-Q ou un formalisme pour analyser et synthetiser des phrases sur ordinateur. Publ. interne no. 43, Faculté des sciences, Université de Montreal

Colmerauer, A. (1978) Metamorphosis grammars. In *Natural Language Communication with Computers*, L. Bolc, ed., Springer-Verlag, Berlin, 133–89

Craig, J. A., Berenzer, S. C., Carney, H. C., and Longyear, C. R. (1966) DEACON: Direct English access and control. *Proc. 1966 Fall Joint Computer Conf.*, Thompson Books, Washington, DC

Culicover, P. W. (1976) *Syntax*. Academic Press

Culicover, P., Kimball, J., Lewis, C., Loveman, D., and Moyne, J. (1969) An automated recognition grammar for English. IBM Tech. Rep. FSC 69–5007

Cullingford, R. (1981) SAM and Micro-SAM. In *Inside Computer Understanding*, R. Schank and C. Riesbeck, eds. Lawrence Erlbaum Assoc., Hillsdale, NJ, 75–135

De Chastellier, G., and Colmerauer, A. (1969) W-grammar. *Proc. 24 Nat. Conf. ACM*

Damerau, F. (1981) Operating statistics for the transformational question answering system. *Am. J. Computational Linguistics 7*, 1 (Jan.–Mar. 1981), 32–40

Davis, M., and Weyuker, E. (1983) *Computability, Complexity, and Languages: Fundamentals of Theoretical Computer Science*. Academic Press, New York

Dewar, H., Bratley, P., and Thorne, J. P. (1969) A program for the syntactic analysis of English sentences. *Comm. ACM 12*, 8 (Aug. 1969), 476–9

Dostert, B., and Thompson, F. (1971) How features resolve syntactic ambiguity. *Proc. Symposium on Info. Storage and Retrieval*

Earley, J. (1970) An efficient context-free parsing algorithm. *Comm. ACM 13*, 2 (Feb. 1970), 94–102

Evens, M., and Karttunen, L. (1983) Directory of Graduate Programs in Computational Linguistics. *Am. J. Computational Linguistics 9*, special supplement (Dec. 1983)

Findler, N. V., Ed. (1979) *Associative Networks.* Academic Press, New York

Friedman, J. (1971) *A Computer Model of Transformational Grammar.* American Elsevier, New York

Gawron, J. M., King, J., Lamping, J., Loebner, E., Paulson, E. A., Pullum, G., Sag, I., and Wasow, T. (1982) Processing English with a generalized phrase structure grammar. *Proc. 20th Annl. Meeting Assn. Computational Linguistics, 74–81*

Gazdar, G. (1981) Unbounded dependencies and coordinate structure. *Linguistic Inquiry 12, 2* (Spring 1981), 155–84

Gazdar, G., Pullum, G., and Sag, I. (1982) Auxiliaries and related phenomena in a restrictive theory of grammar. *Language 58, 3* (Sept. 1982), 591–638

Goldman, N. (1975) Sentence paraphrasing from a conceptual base. *Comm. Assn. Computing Machinery 18, 2* (Feb. 1975), 96–106

Goldstein, I. P., and Roberts, R. B. (1977) NUDGE: a knowledge-based scheduling program. *Proc. Fifth Int. Joint Conf. Artificial Intelligence, 257–63*

Green, C. C. (1969) Theorem-proving by resolution as a basis for question-answering systems. In *Machine Intelligence 4,* B. Meltzer and D. Michie, eds., American Elsevier, New York, 183–205

Griffiths, T. V., and Petrick, S. R. (1965) On the relative efficiencies of context-free grammar recognizers. *Comm. ACM 8, 5* (May 1965), 289–300

Grishman, R. (1973) Implementation of the string parser of English. In *Natural Language Processing,* R. Rustin, ed., Algorithmics Press, New York

Grishman, R. (1976) A survey of syntactic analysis procedures for natural language. *American J. Computational Linguistics,* microfiche 47

Grishman, R. (1979) Response generation in question-answering systems. *Proc. 17th Annl. Meeting Assn. Computational Linguistics, 99–101*

Grishman, R. (1980) Conjunctions and modularity in language analysis procedures. *Proc. 8th Int. Conf. Computational Linguistics, 500–3*

Grishman, R., and Hirschman, L. (1978) Question answering from natural language medical data bases. *Artificial Intelligence 11, 25–43*

Grishman, R., and Kittredge, R., eds. (1986) *Analyzing Language in Restricted Domains: Sublanguage Description and Processing.* Lawrence Erlbaum Assoc., Hillsdale, NJ

Grishman, R., Sager, N., Raze, C., and Bookchin, B. (1973) The Linguistic string parser. *Proc. 1973 Natl. Computer Conf.,* AFIPS Press, Montvale NJ

Harris, L. (1977) User oriented data base query with the ROBOT natural language query system. *Int. J. Man-Machine Studies 9, 6* (Nov. 1977), 697–713

Harris, Z. (1957) Co-occurrence and transformation in linguistic structure. *Language 33, 3,* 283–340

Harris, Z. (1958) Linguistic transformations for information retrieval. *Proc. Int. Conf. on Scientific Info., vol. 2,* 158

Harris, Z. (1962) *String Analysis of Sentence Structure.* Mouton and Co., The Hague

Harris, Z. (1968) *Mathematical Structures of Language.* Wiley Interscience, New York

Hays, D. (1967) *Introduction to Computational Linguistics.* American Elsevier, New York

Hendrix, G. (1977) Human engineering for applied natural language processing. *Proc. 5th Intl. Joint Conf. Artificial Intelligence,* Cambridge, MA

Hendrix, G. (1978) Semantic knowledge. In *Understanding Spoken Language*, D. E. Walker, ed., North-Holland, New York, 121–226

Hendrix, G., Sacerdoti, E., Sagalowicz, D., and Slocum, J. (1978) Developing a natural language interface to complex data. *ACM TODS 3*, 2 (June 1978), 105–47

Hirschman, L., and Puder, K. (1982) Restriction grammar in PROLOG. *Proc. First Int. Conf. Logic Programming*, Marseilles, 85–90

Hirschman, L., and Sager, N. (1982) Automatic information formatting of a medical sublanguage. In *Sublanguage: Studies of Language in Restricted Semantic Domains*, R. Kittredge and J. Lehrberger, eds., de Gruyter, Berlin

Hirschman, L., Grishman, R., and Sager, N. (1976) From text to structured information: automatic processing of medical reports. *Proc. 1976 National Computer Conf.*, AFIPS Press, Montvale, NJ, 267–75

Hirst, G. (1981) *Anaphora in Natural Language Understanding: A Survey*. Springer, Berlin

Hiz, D. and Joshi, A. (1967) Transformational decomposition: A simple description of an algorithm for transformational analysis of English sentences. *2ème Conf. Internationale sur le Traitement Automatique des Langues*, Grenoble

Hobbs, J. (1974) A metalanguage for expressing grammatical restrictions in nodal spans parsing of natural language. Courant Comp. Sci. Rep. 2, Courant Inst. of Math. Sci., New York Univ.

Hobbs, J. (1976) Pronoun resolution. Research report 76–1, City College, City Univ. of New York

Hobbs, J. (1982) Towards an understanding of coherence in discourse. In *Strategies for Natural Language Processing*, W. Lenhert and M. Ringle, eds., Lawrence Erlbaum Assoc., Hillsdale, NJ

Hobbs, J., and Grishman, R. (1976) The automatic transformational analysis of English sentences: An implementation. *Intern. J. Computer Math., Section A, 5* (1976), 267–83

Hopcroft, J., and Ullman, J. (1979) *Introduction to automata theory, languages, and computation*. Addison-Wesley

Irons, N. (1963) Error-correcting parse algorithm. *Comm. ACM 6*, 11 (Nov. 1963), 669–73

Jackendoff, R. (1972) *Semantic Interpretation in Generative Grammar*. MIT Press, Cambridge, MA

Joshi, A. (1962) A procedure for transformational decomposition. Transformations and Discourse Analysis Papers 42, Univ. of Penn.

Joshi, A. (1973) A class of transformational grammars. In *The Formal Analysis of Natural Languages*, M. Gross, M. Halle, and M. P. Schutzenberger, eds., Mouton, The Hague

Kaplan, R. (1973) A general syntactic processor. In *Natural Language Processing*, R. Rustin, ed., Algorithmics Press, New York

Kaplan, S. J., ed., (1982) Special section – natural language. *SIGART Newsletter 79* (Jan. 1982), 27–109

Kaplan, J. (1983) Cooperative responses from a portable natural language query system. In *Computational Models of Discourse*, M. Brody and R. Berwick, eds., MIT Press, Cambridge, MA

Kay, M. (1967) Experiments with a powerful parser. In *2ème Conf. Internationale sur le Traitement Automatique des Langues*, Grenoble

Keyser, S. J., and Petrick, S. R. (1967) Syntactic analysis. Report AFCRL-67-0305, Air Force Cambridge Research Laboratories

Kittredge, R., *et al.* (1973) TAUM 73. Report of the Projet de Traduction Automatique de l'Université de Montreal

Kittredge, R., and Lehrberger, J., eds. (1981) *Sublanguage: Studies of Language in Restricted Semantic Domains.* de Gruyter, Berlin

Kittredge, R. (1983) Sublanguage. *Am. J. Computational Linguistics 8,* 2 (Apr.-June 1982), 79–82

Kuno, S., and Oettinger, A. G. (1962) Multiple-path syntactic analyzer. In *Information Processing 1962,* North-Holland, Amsterdam

Kuno, S. (1963) The multiple-path syntactic analyzer for English. Report no. NSF-9 in Mathematical Linguistics and Automatic Translation of the Computation Lab., Harvard Univ.

Kuno, S. (1965) The predictive analyzer and a path elimination technique. *Comm. ACM 8,* 7 (July 1965), 453–62

Langacker, R. (1969) Pronominalization and the chain of command. In *Modern Studies in English,* D. Reibel, and S. Schane, eds., Prentice-Hall, Englewood Cliffs, NJ

LaLonde, W. (1977) Regular right part grammars and their parsers. *Comm. ACM 20,* 10 (Oct. 1977), 731–41

Lees, R., and Klima, E. (1963) Rules for English pronominalization. *Language 39,* 1 (Jan.-Mar. 1963), 17–28

Lenhert, W. (1982) Plot units: a narrative summarization strategy. In *Strategies for Natural Language Processing,* W. Lenhert and M. Ringle, eds., Lawrence Erlbaum Assoc., Hillsdale, NJ

Loveman, D., Moyne, J., and Tobey, R. (1971) CUE: A preprocessor system for restricted, natural English. In *Proc. Symposium on Info. Storage and Retrieval, 1971*

Malhotra, A. (1975) Design criteria for a knowledge-based English language system for management: an experimental analysis. MAC TR-146, MIT, Cambridge, MA

Mann, W., and Moore, J. (1981) Computer generation of multiparagraph English text. *Am. J. Computational Linguistics 7,* 1 (Jan. 1981), 17–29

Marcus, M. (1980) *Theory of Syntactic Recognition for Natural Language,* MIT Press, Cambridge, MA

Marcus, M., Hindle, D., and Fleck, M. (1983) D-theory: talking about talking about trees. *Proc. 21st Meeting Assn. Computational Linguistics,* 129–36

Marsh, E. (1983) Utilizing domain-specific information for processing compact text. *Proc. Conf. Applied Natural Language Processing, 1983,* Santa Monica, CA, 99–103

McDonald, D. (1981) Language production: the source of the dictionary. *Proc. 19th Annl. Meeting Assn. Computational Linguistics,* 57–62

McKeown, K. (1982) The TEXT System for natural language generation: an overview. *Proc. 20th Annl. Meeting Assn. Computational Linguistics,* 113–20

McKeown, K. (1985a) *Text Generation.* Cambridge Univ. Press, Cambridge, England

McKeown, K. (1985b) Discourse strategies for generating natural-language text. *Artificial Intelligence 27,* 1 (Sept. 1985), 1–41

Minsky, M. (1975) A framework for representing knowledge. In *The Psychology of Computer Vision,* P. Winston, ed., McGraw-Hill, New York

Montague, R. (1974) *Formal Philosophy: Selected Papers of Richard Montague,* R. Thomason, ed., Yale Univ. Press, New Haven, Conn.

Montgomery, C. (1983) Distinguishing fact from opinion and events from meta-events. *Proc. Conf. Applied Natural Language Processing, 1983*, Santa Monica, CA, 55–61

Owens, P. (1975) A comprehensive survey of parsing algorithms for programming languages. Courant Comp. Sci. Rep. 4, Courant Inst. of Math. Sci., New York Univ.

Paxton, W. H., and Robinson, A. E. (1973) A parser for a speech understanding system. *Advance Papers of the Third Int. Joint Conf. on Artificial Intelligence*, Stanford Research Institute, CA

Pereira, F., and Warren, D. (1980) Definite clause grammars for language analysis – a survey of the formalism and a comparison with augmented transition networks. *Artificial Intelligence 13*, 3 (May 1980), 231–78

Perrault, C. R., and Allen, J. F. (1980) A plan-based analysis of indirect speech acts. *Am. J. Computational Linguistics 6*, 3–4 (July–Dec. 1980), 167–82

Petrick, S. R. (1965) A recognition procedure for transformational grammars. MIT Doctoral Dissertation

Petrick, S. R. (1966) A program for transformational syntactic analysis. Report *AFCRL*-66-698, Air Force Cambridge Research Labs

Petrick, S. R. (1972) Mapping of linguistic structures with computer interpretable form. Report AFCRL-TR-73-0055, Air Force Cambridge Research Labs

Petrick, S. R. (1973) Transformational analysis. In *Natural Language Processing*, R. Rustin, ed., Algorithmics Press, New York

Petrick, S. R. (1975) Design of the underlying structure for a data base retrieval system. In *Directions in Artificial Intelligence: Natural Language Processing*, R. Grishman, ed., Courant Computer Science Report 7, Courant Inst. of Math. Sci., New York Univ.

Plath, W. J. (1974a) Transformational grammar and transformational parsing in the REQUEST system. In *Computational and Mathematical Linguistics*, A. Zampolli, ed., Proc. Int. Conf. on Computational Linguistics

Plath, W. J. (1974b) String transformations in the REQUEST system. Rep. RC 4947 (21963), IBM T. J. Watson Research Center

Plath, W. J. (1976) REQUEST: A natural language question-answering system. *IBM J. Res. Devel. 20*, 4 (July 1976), 326–35

Postal, P. (1967) *Constituent Structure: A study of contemporary models of syntactic description*. Indiana Univ.

Pratt, V. (1975) Lingol, a progress report. *Advance Papers 4th Intl. Joint Conf. Artificial Intelligence*, 422–8

Quillian, M. R. (1969) The teachable language comprehender: a simulation program and theory of language. *Comm. ACM 12*, 8 (Aug. 1969), 459–76

Raze, C. (1976) A computational treatment of coordinate conjunctions. *AM. J. Computational Linguistics*, microfiche 52

Robinson, J. (1982) DIAGRAM: a grammar for dialogue. *Comm. Assn. Computing Machinery 25*, 1 (Jan. 1982), 27–47

Sager, N. (1967) Syntactic analysis of natural language. In *Advances in Computers, No. 8*, F. Alt and M. Rubinoff, eds., Academic Press, New York

Sager, N. (1972) Syntactic formatting of scientific information. *Proc. 1972 Fall Joint Computer Conf.*, AFIPS Press, Montvale, NJ, 791–800

Sager, N. (1973) The string parser for scientific literature. In *Natural Language Processing*, R. Rustin, ed., Algorithmics Press, New York

Sager, N. (1975) Sublanguage grammars in science information processing. *J. Am. Soc. Info. Science 26*, 1 (Jan.–Feb. 1975), 10–16

Sager, N. (1978) Natural language information formatting: the automatic conversion of texts to a structured data base. In *Advances in Computers 17*, M. C. Yovits, ed., Academic Press, New York

Sager, N. (1981) *Natural Language Information Processing*. Addison-Wesley Reading, MA

Sager, N., and Grishman, R. (1975) The restriction language for computer grammars of natural language. *Comm. ACM 18*, 7 (July 1975), 390–400

Salkoff, M., and Sager, N. (1967) The elimination of grammatical restrictions in a string grammar of English. *2eme Conf. Internationale sur le Traitement Automatique des Langues*. Grenoble, Aug. 1967

Schank, R. (1973) Identification of conceptualizations underlying natural language. In *Computer Models of Thought and Language*, R. Schank and K. Colby, eds., W. H. Freeman and Co., San Francisco, CA

Schank, R. (1975) *Conceptual Information Processing*. North-Holland, Amsterdam

Schank, R. (1980) Language and memory. *Cognitive Science 4*, 3, 243–84

Schank, R. (1982) Reminding and memory organization: an introduction to MOPs. In *Strategies for Natural Language Processing*, W. Lenhert and M. Ringle, eds., Lawrence Erlbaum Assoc., Hillsdale, NJ

Schank, R., and Abelson, R. (1975) Scripts, plans and knowledge. *Advance papers 4th Intl. Joint Conf. Artificial Intelligence*

Schank, R., and Abelson, R. (1977) *Scripts, Plans, Goals, and Understanding*. Lawrence Erlbaum Assoc., Hillsdale, NJ

Schank, R., and Riesbeck, C., eds. (1981) *Inside Computer Understanding: Five Programs Plus Miniatures*. Lawrence Erlbaum Assoc., Hillsdale, NJ

Schwarcz, R., Burger, J., and Simmons, R. (1970) A deductive question-answer for natural language inference. *Comm. ACM 13*, 3 (March 1970), 167–83

Searle, J. R. (1969) *Speech Acts*. Cambridge Univ. Press, Cambridge, England

Searle, J. R. (1975) Indirect speech acts. In *Syntax and Semantics, Vol. 3: Speech Acts*, P. Cole and J. L. Morgan, eds., Academic Press, New York

Shortliffe, E. (1976) *Computer-based Medical Consultations: MYCIN*. Elsevier

Sidner, C. (1979) The role of focusing in interpretation of pronouns. *Proc. 17th Annual Meeting of the Assn. Computational Linguistics*, La Jolla, CA, 77–8

Sidner, C. (1983) Focusing in the comprehension of definite anaphora. In *Computational Models of Discourse*, M. Brody and R. Berwick, eds., MIT Press, Cambridge, MA

Simmons, R., and Bennett-Novak, G. (1975) Semantically analyzing an English subset for the CLOWNs microworld. Tech. Rep. NL-24, Dept. of Comp. Sci., Univ. of Texas at Austin

Simmons, R., and Chester, D. (1982) Relating sentences and semantic networks with procedural logic. *Comm. Assn. Computing Machinery 25*, 8 (Aug. 1982), 527–47

Simmons, R., and Slocum, J. (1972) Generating English discourse from semantic networks. *Comm. Assn. Computing Machinery 15*, 10 (Oct. 1972), 891–905

Slocum, J. (1981) A practical comparison of parsing strategies. *Proc. 19th Annl. Meeting Assn. Computational Linguistics*, Stanford, CA, 1–6

Slocum, J. (1984) Machine Translation: its history, current status, and future prospects. *Proc. Coling 84 (Tenth Int'l Conf. Computational Linguistics)*, Stanford, CA, 546-61

Slocum, J. (1985) A survey of machine translation: its history, current status, and future prospects. *Computational Linguistics 11*, 1 (Jan.–Mar. 1985), 1–17

Stockwell, R., Schacter, P., and Partree, B. H. (1973) *The Major Syntactic Structures of English.* Holt, Rinehart, and Winston, New York

Tennant, H. (1981) *Natural Language Processing.* Petrocelli, New York

Thompson, F. B., Lockeman, P. C., Dostert, B., and Deverill, R. S. (1969) REL: A rapidly extensible language system. *Proc. 24th Nat. Conf. ACM*

Thompson, H. (1981) Chart parsing and rule schemata in phrase structure grammar. *Proc. 19th Annl. Meeting Assn. Computational Linguistics*, Stanford, CA, 167–72.

Thompson, H. and Ritchie, G. (1984) Implementing natural language parsers. In *Artificial Intelligence Tools, Techniques and Applications*, T. O'Shea and M. Eisenstadt, eds., Harper and Row, New York

Thorne, J. P., Bratley, P., and Dewar, H. (1968) The syntactic analysis of English by machine. In *Machine Intelligence 3*, D. Michie, ed., American Elsevier, New York

Tucker, A. (1984) A perspective on machine translation: theory and practice. *Comm. Assn. Computing Machinery 27*, 4 (Apr. 1984), 322–9

Van Dijk, T. (1973) Text grammar and text logic. In *Studies in Text Grammar*, J. S. Petrofi and H. Reiser, eds., Reidel, New York

Walker, D. (1973) Automated language processing. In *Annual Review of Information Science and Technology, vol 8*, C. Cuadra, ed., Amer. Soc. for Info. Sci., Wash., DC

Walker, D., ed. (1978) *Understanding Spoken Language.* North-Holland, New York

Walker, D., Chapin, P., Geis, M., and Gross, L. (1966) Recent developments in the MITRE syntactic analysis procedure. MITRE report MTP-11

Waltz, D. (1978) An English language question answering system for a large relational data base. *Comm. ACM 21*, 7 (July 1978), 526–39

Webber, B. (1979) *A Formal Approach to Discourse Anaphora.* Garland, New York

Weiner, J. (1980) BLAH, A system which explains its reasoning. *Artificial Intelligence 15*, 1 (Nov. 1980), 19–48

Weischedel, R., Voge, W., and James, M. (1978) An artificial intelligence approach to language instruction. *Artificial Intelligence 10*, 3 (Nov. 1978), 225–40

Wilensky, R. (1978) Why John married Mary: Understanding stories involving recurring goals. *Cognitive Science 2*, 3 (July–Sept. 1978), 235–66

Wilensky, R. (1981) PAM and Micro-PAM. In *Inside Computer Understanding*, R. Schank and C. Riesbeck, eds. Lawrence Erlbaum Assoc., Hillsdale, NJ, 136–96

Wilks, Y. (1975) An intelligent analyzer and understander of English. *Comm. ACM 18*, 5 (May 1975), 264–74

Winograd, T. (1971) Procedures as a representation of data in a computer program for understanding natural language. MIT Report MAC TR-48

Winograd, T. (1972) *Understanding Natural Language.* Academic Press, New York

Winograd, T. (1983) *Language as a Cognitive Process, Volume I: Syntax.* Addison-Wesley, Reading, MA

Woods, W. A. (1968) Procedural semantics for a question-answering machine. *Proc. 1968 Fall Joint Computer Conf.*, 457–71.

Woods, W. A. (1970a) Context-sensitive parsing. *Comm. ACM 13*, 7 (July 1970), 437–45

Woods, W. A. (1970b) Transition network grammars for natural language analysis. *Comm. ACM 13*, 10 (Oct. 1970), 591–606

Woods, W. A. (1973) An experimental parsing system for transition network grammars. In *Natural Language Processing*, R. Rustin, ed., Algorithmics Press, New York

Woods, W. A. (1975) What's in a link: Foundations for semantic networks. In *Representation and Understanding*, D. Bobrow and A. Collins, eds., Academic Press, New York

Woods, W. A. (1978) Semantics and quantification in natural language question-answering. In *Advances in Computers, vol 17*, M. C. Yovits, ed., Academic Press, New York

Woods, W. A. (1980) Cascaded ATN grammars. *Am. J. Computational Linguistics 6*, 1 (Jan. 1980), 1–12

Woods, W. A., Kaplan, R. M., and Nash-Webber, B. The lunar sciences natural language information system: Final report. Report 2378, Bolt, Beranek, and Newman, Cambridge, MA

Zadeh, L. (1978) PRUF – A meaning representation language for natural languages. *Int. J. Man-Machine Studies 10*, 4 (July 1978), 395–460

Zwicky, A., Friedman, J., Hall, B., and Walker, D. (1965) The MITRE syntactic analysis procedure for transformational grammars. *Proc. 1965 Fall Joint Computer Conf.*, Thompson Books, Washington, DC

Name index

Abelson, R., 145, 146
Aho, A., 28, 31, 36
Allen, J., 157
Allwood, J., 91, 113
Anderson, B., 135
Andersson, L., 91, 113
Austin, J., 156

Bates, M., 68
Bellert, S., 141
Bennett-Novak, G., 85
Birnbaum, L., 122
Bobrow, D., 71, 144
Bobrow, R., 71, 118
Bookchin, B., 70
Borgida, A., 85
Bratley, P., 71
Bross, I., 135
Brown, G., 141
Bruce, B., 156
Burger, J., 95
Burton, R., 119

Cautin, H., 71
Chapin, P., 49
Charniak, E., 142–3
Chester, D., 162, 168, 169
Chomsky, N., 16, 18, 35, 36, 46, 47
Clocksin, W., 73
Cocke, J., 34
Cohen, P., 157
Colmerauer, A., 76, 79, 80, 81, 82
Craig, J., 80, 108
Culicover, P., 41, 71
Cullingford, R., 146

Dahl, O., 91, 113
Damerau, F., 50
Davis, M., 12
DeChastellier, G., 82
Dewar, H., 71
Dostert, B., 81

Evens, M., 1

Findler, N., 118
Fleck, M., 85
Fraser, B., 71
Friedman, C.; see Raze, C.
Friedman, J., 5, 48

Gawron, M., 84, 108
Gazdar, G., 83
Geis, M., 49
Goldman, N., 163
Goldstein, I., 144
Green, C., 138
Griffiths, T., 33
Grishman, R., 7, 50–1, 58, 60, 70, 71, 85, 113, 119, 135, 151, 152, 167
Gross, L., 49

Hall, B., 48; see also Partee, B.
Halliday, M., 72
Harris, L., 111
Harris, Z., 22, 34, 35, 70, 114
Hays, D., 30, 34
Hendrix, G., 96, 136
Hindle, D., 85
Hirschman, L., 4, 71, 80, 135, 151, 152
Hirst, G., 124
Hiz, D., 70
Hobbs, J., 60, 85, 88, 131, 141
Hopcroft, J., 12

Jackendoff, R., 129
James, M., 99
Joshi, A., 70

Kaplan, R., 33, 71
Kaplan, S.J., 1, 99
Kartunnen, L., 1
Kay, M., 81
Keyser, S., 41, 49
Kittredge, R., 81, 113
Klima, E., 130
Kuno, S., 33, 34

LaLonde, W., 65
Langacker, R., 129

Subject index

adjunct string, 22
adjuncts, analyzing, 84–5
ambiguity
    due to conjunction, 87
    of adjunct placement, 84–5
anaphora, 124
anaphora resolution, 124–34, 142
antecedent, 124
ASSERTION, 24
ATN, 64–8, 71, 72–3
    cascaded, 73, 118
    for generation, 164–166
atom (in predicate logic), 93
attribute (of word), 58
    see also features
augmented context-free grammar, 57–80
    in PROLOG, 79–80
augmented context-free parsers, 56–80
augmented transition network
    see ATN

BABEL, 163
backtracking, 27, 75
Backus-Naur Form, 19
base component, 36, 41–2, 45–7
belief, 97
best-first parser, 88–9
binary transformation, 39, 40
BNF, 19
bottom-up parser, 27, 30–3
bound variable, 94

CA, 122–4
cascaded ATN, 73, 118
categorial presupposition, 113
causal chain, 149–50
center string, 22
chart parser, 33
Chomsky hierarchy, 16
Chomsky normal form, 34
classes
    object, 116–17
    predicate, 116
    see also word classes
coelement relation, 58

cognitive science, 6
coherence relation, 141
command-and-precede constraint, 129–30
complex symbol, 47
concept case frame, 137
conceptual analyzer, 12, 121–4
conceptual dependency representation, 101,
    121, 163
conjunct string, 22
conjunction, 85–7
constituent sentence, 38–9
context register, 137
context-free grammar, 18–20, 65
    in PROLOG, 76–80
context-sensitive grammar, 20–1, 45–7, 80
contextual reference, 124
CO-OP, 99
coordinate conjunction, 85–87
CORE routine (in Restriction Language), 58
count noun constraint, 26, 59
covering grammar, 48, 51
cut (of a tree), 36

data base retrieval, 5
    see also question-answering system
DEACON, 80, 108
deep structure, 36
definite clause, 74
definite clause grammar, 76–80
definite description, 98
definite noun phrase
    anaphora resolution for, 132–3
definite pronoun
    anaphora resolution for, 126–9
definite quantifier, 98
derivation, 19–20
description anaphora, 133
DIAGRAM, 71
dialog analysis, 153–8
discourse, 141
discourse analysis, 140–58
discourse description, 133–4
discourse entity, 126–9
discourse generation, 168–71

5514